THE NOMADIC DEVELOPER

THE NOMADIC DEVELOPER

Surviving and Thriving in the World of Technology Consulting

Aaron Erickson

✦✦ Addison-Wesley

Upper Saddle River, NJ • Boston • Indianapolis • San Francisco
New York • Toronto • Montreal • London • Munich • Paris • Madrid
Cape Town • Sydney • Tokyo • Singapore • Mexico City

The publisher offers excellent discounts on this book when ordered in quantity for bulk purchases or special sales, which may include electronic versions and/or custom covers and content particular to your business, training goals, marketing focus, and branding interests. For more information, please contact:

U.S. Corporate and Government Sales
(800) 382-3419
corpsales@pearsontechgroup.com

For sales outside the United States please contact:

International Sales
international@pearson.com

Visit us on the Web: informit.com/aw.

Library of Congress Cataloging-in-Publication Data

Erickson, Aaron, 1972-
  The nomadic developer : surviving and thriving in the world of technology consulting / Aaron Erickson.
      p. cm.
  Includes index.
  ISBN 978-0-321-60639-6 (pbk. : alk. paper)

  1. Technology consultants. 2. Computer industry—Vocational guidance. 3. Computer science—Vocational guidance. I. Title.
  QA76.25.E75 2009
  609.2—dc22

                          2009009837

Pearson Education, Inc.
Rights and Contracts Department
501 Boylston Street, Suite 900
Boston, MA 02116
Fax (617) 671-3447

ISBN-13: 978-0-321-60639-6
ISBN-10: 0-321-60639-6

Text printed in the United States on recycled paper at RR Donnelley in Crawfordsville, Indiana.
First printing May 2009

To Dad, who always told me (paraphrasing)
"Go big or go home."

CONTENTS

About the Author   xiii

About the Annotators   xv

Acknowledgments   xix

Foreword   xxi

Preface   xxv

CHAPTER ONE
Why Consulting?

Job Security Through Networking   2

Expanding Your Horizons   7

Why Companies Hire Consultants   9

Consulting Firm Economics 101   13

The Profession of Technology Consultant   24

Summary   25

CHAPTER TWO

The Seven Deadly Firms

Brief Descriptions of theSeven Deadly Firms	28
BOZO Consulting	30
FEAR Consulting	34
The Body Shop	40
CHEAP Consulting	44
Personality Cult Consulting	47
Smelzer and Melzer Accounting	51
Push the SKU Consulting	54
Summary	57
Works Cited	58

CHAPTER THREE

How Technology Consulting Firms Work

Technology Consulting: Two Pipelines	59
The Players	73
Challenges You Will Face as a Consultant	91
Summary	95

CHAPTER FOUR

Getting In: Ten Unstated Traits That Technology Consulting Firms Look For

Tip #1: Appearance	99
Tip #2: Be Really Good at Being Interviewed for Jobs	101
Tip #3: Always Be Learning	107
Tip #4: Be a Scarce Commodity	112
Tip #5: Be Active in Your Technical Community	114
Tip #6: Be Easy to Work With	115

Tip #7: Energy, ENERGY, Energy *$&%!   117
Tip #8: Demonstrate Great Writing Skills   119
Tip #9: Develop Your Network   121
Tip #10: Live a Balanced Life   123
Summary   124

CHAPTER FIVE

What You Need to Ask Before You Join a Technology Consulting Firm

Interviews Are Not Just for the Employer   126
Basic Business Questions   127
Sales-Related Questions   136
Delivery-Related Questions   144
Community Involvement Questions   153
Summary   156

CHAPTER SIX

Surviving

Reality Check: Avoid Fear and Greed   157
People Who Create Profit Don't Get Fired   160
Rainmakers Are Always Welcome   162
One-Trick Pony? Better Be Good at Your Trick!   164
Leave the Drama at the Theater   166
Being Overpaid Is a Curse   168
Early to Bed, Early to Rise   170
Billing Work = Good Work (with Few Exceptions)   172
The Three Words You Want to Hear: You've Been Extended   174
Don't Live "Three Steps Ahead"   175
Summary: What's The Worst That Can Happen?   178

CHAPTER SEVEN

Thriving

In a Position to Thrive	182
Enjoying What You Do	186
How to Do Work That Matters	191
Keep Moving: Constantly Learning	195
Learning to Think "Win-Win"	199
Building Your Brand	202
Summary	206

CHAPTER EIGHT

Your Career Path

Path #1: Rise to Management	208
Path #2: Rise to Sales	218
Path #3: Rise to Evangelist/Guru	223
Path #4: Rise to Entrepreneur	226
Summary: Paths and Direction	229

CHAPTER NINE

Avoiding Career-Limiting Moves

Career-Limiting Move Category #1: Gluttony	232
Career-Limiting Move Category #2: Lust	235
Career-Limiting Move Category #3: Greed	238
Career-Limiting Move Category #4: Sloth	243
Career-Limiting Move Category #5: Wrath	248
Career-Limiting Move Category #6: Envy	251
Career-Limiting Move Category #7: Pride	254
Summary	257

CHAPTER TEN
Is Consulting Right for You?

Sign #1: Lack of Risk Tolerance	260
Sign #2: Incompatible Personality	263
Sign #3: Incompatible Lifestyle and/or Responsibilities	265
Sign #4: Desire for Single Product Focus	269
Sign #5: Doing It for the Money	269
Summary	270

CHAPTER ELEVEN
An Anthology of Sage Advice

Adaptation and Resistance: By Jason Bock	274
On Being Independent: By David Chappell	277
Becoming an Independent Consultant: By Bruce Eckel	281
It's Been Fun So Far: By Michael Hugos	290
15 Bytes of Consulting Wisdom: By Deborah Kurata	293
Learning from Your Mistakes: By Ted Neward	297
The Many Ways to Fail: By Derik Whittaker	301
Lessons from the Trenches: By Chris G. Williams	306

APPENDIX A
Consultopia: The Ideal Consulting Firm

Foundations	312
Financial Transparency	314
Community of True Professionals	317
A Mission with Purpose	320
Does "Consultopia" Exist?	323
Works Cited	323

APPENDIX B
A Consulting Lexicon

Index	343

About the Author

Aaron Erickson is a veteran technology consultant, writer, and technical evangelist with Magenic Technologies, based out of Chicago. He has spent the majority of his career catering to the individual needs of companies of all sizes. His strategic consulting focus has been centered around delivering high-value solutions that break new technological ground and bringing added value to both up-and-coming clients, as well as those who are already established.

For the past 16 years, Aaron has worked with leading-edge companies, providing prescriptive guidance to both the knowledge workers—those who actually produce the software—as well as the management side of the business, including CEOs, CTOs, and other executive staff. His experience has led him to do business with a variety of clients across financial services, supply chain, and insurance, vertical industries. His consulting mantra in recent years has been *technology matters, but business results matter more.*

Aaron is frequently invited to speak at events such as TechEd, VSLive, and .NET user groups on topics ranging from the highly technical (F#, C#, LINQ, and Functional Programming), to more business-focused topics that open the floor to an exchange of ideas, best practices, and observations about the specialized world of technology consulting.

Aaron has been a Microsoft MVP since 2007. He has written for .NET Developers Journal and InformIT. He blogs at both nomadic-developer.com as well as for Magenic at blog.magenic.com/blogs/aarone. Readers can follow him on Twitter at twitter.com/AaronErickson.

About the Annotators

Jason Bock is a principal consultant for Magenic (www.magenic.com), a Microsoft MVP (C#), and an INETA (www.ineta.org) speaker. He has worked on a number of business applications using a diverse set of substrates and languages, such as C#, .NET, and Java. He is the author of *Applied .NET Attributes*, *CIL Programming: Under the Hood of .NET*, *.NET Security*, and *Visual Basic 6 Win32 API Tutorial*. He has written numerous articles on software development issues and has presented at a number of conferences and user groups. He also runs the Twin Cities Code Camp (www.twincitiescodecamp.com) and the Twin Cities Languages User Group (www.twincitieslanguagesusergroup.com). Jason holds a master's degree in electrical engineering from Marquette University. Visit his Web site at www.jasonbock.net.

Michael Hugos, principal with Center for Systems Innovation [c4si], mentors companies in business and IT agility and supply chain management. Previously, he spent six years as Chief Information Officer of a multibillion dollar distribution organization where he built the suite of supply chain and business systems that transformed the company's business model from old-line distributor to value-added provider of products, information, and supply chain services.

He won the CIO 100 Award in 2003 and 2005 and the Information Week 500 Award in 2005, and in 2006, he was selected for the Computerworld Premier 100 Award for career achievement. Michael earned his MBA from Northwestern University's Kellogg School of Management. He writes a blog titled "Doing Business in Real Time" for *CIO* magazine, and he has authored several books, including *Building the Real Time Enterprise* and *CIO Best Practices*; his newest book is *Business Agility: Sustainable Prosperity in a Relentlessly Competitive World.*

Derik Whittaker is a software developer currently working with AllscriptsMisys Healthcare. Derik has nine years of experience developing, mentoring, and leading Microsoft-based products for a wide variety of different professional fields.

Derik is a C# MVP and is a member of the ASPInsiders group. He has been working exclusively with .NET since its inception and has professional experience in both VB.NET and C#. He is also a follower and believer in the Agile methodologies and has a wide array of experience using various Agile techniques in the real world. You can catch Derik online as a member of the blogging group Devlicio.us (http://devlicio.us/blogs/derik_whittaker/) or at www.DimeCasts.Net.

Outside of his day job, you can find Derik hanging out with his wife and two sons. He also enjoys all things sports (go Braves) and can be found at the local climbing gym on most weekends.

Chris G. Williams is a senior consultant and technology evangelist for Magenic. He is the founder of several .NET user groups on the East coast, and most recently the Twin Cities XNA User Group and Twin Cities Developers Guild, both in Minneapolis, Minnesota. He is a frequent blogger at BlogusMaximus.net, author of the very popular NINE Questions series and owner of the VB Community site www.ILoveVB.net. His most recent project is the Charity Fragathon, a fundraiser event for Children's Hospitals and Clinics of Minnesota.

He's also a Microsoft MVP, MCT, MCSD (.NET) Early Adopter, MCAD, member of the INETA Speakers Bureau, freelance game developer, occasional author, tech editor, conference speaker, vintage arcade game collector, and INETA Community Champion. And he plays a pretty mean guitar in Rock Band/Guitar Hero.

Lastly, yes, the rumors are true. He loves Visual Basic so much, he even named his dog VB.

ACKNOWLEDGMENTS

IT IS A SHAME I have only a couple pages to write acknowledgments; there are so many people who deserve praise for helping me, formally in some cases, informally in others. I want to start with my reviewers, Dan Sullivan, Martin Heller, and Michael S. Hugos, who all provided me with great feedback throughout this journey.

The editorial team at Pearson is due a huge debt of gratitude for having the courage to publish a book like this—something that is a little edgier than the technology book that I was initially going to write. Joan Murray, Olivia Basegio, Sheri Cain, and Jovana San Nicolas-Shirley all worked very hard to help make this book a reality!

I also want to thank Michael Lester and Greg Frankenfield, the COO and CEO of Magenic, respectively, who provided me with both formal and informal advice, especially around the chapter on how senior management of a larger consulting firm operates its business. Although this is not a book about how Magenic specifically runs its business, having Michael and Greg as sounding boards from time to time has been incredibly helpful. Carole Cuthbertson, Recruiting Director, was also very helpful in this regard.

I want to thank Thomas Cole, my colleague and friend who works with me at the Chicago branch at Magenic, who also very much served as a sounding board, especially in some of the term definitions in Appendix B. (He is specifically responsible for the term *resource romance*.) I also want to thank my many other colleagues in Chicago, especially Keith and Tami Franklin, all of whom help make Magenic the great workplace that inspired me to write a book in the first place!

Of course, this book would not be possible without the contributions of Ted Neward, David Chappell, Deborah Kurata, Jason Bock, Chris Williams, Bruce Eckel, Michael Hugos, and Derik Whittaker, all of whom were kind enough to write essays for Chapter 11, "An Anthology of Sage Advice," as well as the various real-life stories interspersed throughout the book. And it goes without saying that I thank Rockford Lhotka, who as a friend, mentor, and writer of the Foreword for this book, has been very much an inspiration to me.

Lastly, I want to thank my wonderful wife, Erin (yes, we share a name too), who in her role as both spouse and font of wisdom about publishing (being an award-winning editor in her own right), has demonstrated immense patience, understanding, and support as I have spent most evenings and weekends over the past six months writing this book. I thank my children, Adriana and Matthew, as well, for continually giving me joy and a broader perspective in which to view the world.

A Word About Opinion

The opinions in this book are my own or, in the cases of the essays written by others in this book, the writer of the particular essay. They are not, and in some cases, most certainly not, the opinions of my employer, clients, coworkers, or anyone other than the writer of the material.

FOREWORD

THIS IS THE type of book I wish I'd had in 1995. That was the year I left a comfortable, though frustrating, IT role and started work for a consulting company with no idea what I was getting into. Looking back on it, I made the right decision, but there were days when I really wondered what I'd done!

I became a consultant in the seventh year of my career. By that time, I'd worked as a programmer for a small ISV, and I'd worked in IT for a biomedical manufacturing company. But I was really quite naïve. I had no idea about all the different types of consulting companies. And having worked for only two companies, I had relatively little experience with different corporate cultures, various management styles, or what the real possibilities were within the computer industry.

In some ways, times were different then. The Internet as we know it would start to come into being two to three years later, and I still believed in quaint concepts like "if you do a great job, your employer will take care of you." So I didn't directly subscribe to trade magazines or other sources of industry information, and my employer carefully ensured that such magazines weren't lying around for the IT staff to read. I now know the reason was to minimize the chance of the staff (including me) seeing the salary survey issues and the articles about how the industry was changing and opportunities were rising.

But in many ways, times aren't all that different. In my current role, I get to interact with many developers from around the world.

I left the biomedical manufacturing company because I'd worked my way into a leadership role. I was the manager of application development, and that meant I did a lot of managing and virtually no development. The lesson I learned from this role, above all others, is that I love development a lot more than I love managing people. So I looked for another job and considered several options.

I interviewed at a couple of other traditional companies, looking for IT programmer roles. It became pretty clear to me that I'd end up doing much the same thing I was already doing, just for some other type of company. Or I'd take a pay cut to go back to being a developer (instead of a manager of developers), and I had a hard time getting excited about that! Of course, doing the same thing under a different roof seemed kind of silly, so I couldn't get too excited about any of these possibilities.

Based on those experiences, I branched out and talked to a "recruiter" from a consulting company. Today I know that it is a body shop and that the "recruiter" was actually one of the salespeople. He was one of those people who come across as being oily, to the point that you want to wash your hand after shaking his. Trying to get a straight answer out of the guy was a serious challenge.

My wife and I had a new baby, so stability and benefits were quite important to us. As I pried information out of this guy, I found that the company's business model offered no security and nearly no benefits. Really, it offered the same kind of arrangement as any clerical or manufacturing temp agency, but for IT professionals. The guy was motivated by getting people hired and sold as efficiently as possible. I don't think he really had much concern for me and my worries, and he wanted me to just say "yes" and get billing so he could make his commission.

I'm not saying that the body shop approach is a universally bad business model, but it isn't a good fit for someone new to consulting, someone who has a new baby and really needs a level of guaranteed income, health insurance, and other benefits. To this day, I'm glad I passed on that opportunity.

I also talked to recruiters for a couple other consulting firms. Both offered full-time employment, benefits, and what seemed like stability. One of them came across as warm and welcoming, the other cold and perhaps overly professional. You can probably guess which one I chose.

My point thus far is that the content of this book would have been invaluable to me. By spelling out the types of consulting organizations out there, the way their business models work, and how they interact with consultants and clients, the book would have saved me from learning all this the hard way.

Now back to my story. Before I even started working for my new employer, a warm and welcoming salesperson bought me breakfast and introduced me to my first gig: a development project using technologies I vaguely knew at a client that was more than 90 miles from my home.

Remember, I hadn't even started. No meeting with HR, no training, no orientation, just a sales guy telling me I was going to spend three to five hours a day in my car. I really started to wonder whether I'd made a horribly bad decision in leaving my previous job!

The gig turned out to involve building a VB 3.0 application to run on OS/2, using a DB2 database. I spent most of my time learning that the IBM "red book" documentation was nowhere near as nice or complete as the DEC VAX "Orange Wall" or Microsoft's new MSDN idea. Just trying to get these technologies to interact at all was a far bigger challenge than any of the actual development work. But it was interesting, and I learned a lot (about the value of decent documentation, if nothing else).

Fortunately, that gig lasted only about three months. Between working nine- and ten-hour days and driving four hours on a typical day, I was starting to see that this type of work would have a high cost on my family life. My next gig was just a 20-minute drive each way, which was the shortest commute I've ever had as a consultant.

I worked at several other clients over the next few years, each one offering something interesting and new. Sometimes it was interesting technology; other times the work was interesting because of the business itself. I worked in many industries, including medical, financial, manufacturing, and agricultural.

This is the kind of breadth that's virtually impossible to achieve outside consulting. The ability to see so many industries, so many management styles, so many corporate cultures—that's invaluable.

Years ago, when I was working in IT, my boss said he thought it was nearly impossible for IT leaders to be really good unless they had spent some time in consulting. I think he was probably right.

I've consulted for companies where I would never be an employee, due to their corrosive culture or management styles. I've consulted for companies I would absolutely work for because they are well run, respectful of their employees, and all-around very impressive organizations.

This, to me, is the primary upside of being a consultant. It is a nomadic lifestyle and is not for someone who likes consistency, predictability, or stability. Nor is it good for anyone who can't handle long hours, long commutes, and sometimes unpleasant clients.

But being a consultant is a great life for people who want varied experiences, especially around business, industry, and culture. And it is a way to stay highly technical and still make a reasonable income doing what you love.

—Rocky Lhotka
Eden Prairie, Minnesota
February 2009

PREFACE

Sorry, I beg to differ—Information Technology does matter!
—My response to Nicholas G. Carr's seminal Harvard Business Review *article,*
"IT Doesn't Matter"

Technology work—making companies, governments, and other organizations leverage information to work more effectively and reach more markets—is one of the most exciting places in which to scratch out a living. In one day, a really good practicing doctor might deliver a couple dozen babies. A technology practitioner, on the other hand, might write an algorithm that matches advertisements to searches that leads to billions of dollars of profits (and with these profits, jobs for tens of thousands of people) for not only the company that employed the developer who wrote the algorithm, but thousands of other companies that are smart enough to leverage the service of the company that employs the developer who wrote the algorithm. Although certainly not an accomplishment on the scale of delivering life, creating that much economic value and productivity—enough to feed an entire small nation—is certainly a significant contribution to society!

To put it another way, there is nothing more powerful or potentially game changing (and sometimes, more *disruptive*) than information technology in the hands of smart, innovative, and disciplined people. There are examples we are familiar with as consumers—everything from email to calendars to tools to manage budgets like MS Money and Quicken. They are just the tip of the iceberg, though; most large companies use some sort of technology to do everything from understanding their customers, trading securities, balancing the books, performing medical diagnoses, underwriting insurance, controlling spacecraft, controlling your car, designing energy-efficient power grids, and doing dozens upon dozens of other things that companies—not to mention, society at large—literally depend on every single day.

In other words, technology touches, in some way, shape, or form, almost every decision, every action, and every strategy a modern enterprise might undertake. A good friend of mine, technology strategy consultant Michael Hugos, has an expression: "Technology, by automating the routine, allows knowledge workers to concentrate on the exceptional conditions, leading to a more responsive, more capable enterprise." From that standpoint, it is hard to see any company on the face of the earth that could not be made better and more efficient through the use of technology. The only limiting factor becomes the limits of creativity (finding solutions), the limits of our expertise, and the limits of our discipline (developing solutions).

Of course, with respect to Mr. Carr and his assertion regarding information technology in the May 2003 issue of *Harvard Business Review*, he is almost right: Information technology devoid of people doesn't matter. What does matter is innovative *application* of information technology by people, which is the entire point of the business of technology consulting.

~

Creativity, Expertise, and Discipline

The three elements that really need to be mixed to create useful technology solutions are, ironically enough, hardly about technology at all. Technology is just a mechanism by which these three primary elements—creativity, expertise, and discipline, which exist in *people*—can be transformed into business results.

Of course, these three elements are really the keys to being successful anywhere. The issue really is that, in the context of a company, being good at all three is hard because they apply to all things. A car company can typically have creativity and expertise as it relates to building cars because that is where the company's investment and passion are. The same is true for most other areas of expertise, including technology. The reason we have technology consulting companies is so that we can create a community of technology professionals dedicated to using their creativity, expertise, and discipline to produce great technology solutions for clients. Having such a community of professionals, where success of the community is not dependent on success of something they don't directly control (as it would be in a car company because a car company sells cars, not technology), is the chief reason why technology consulting companies exist.

⤠

What This Book Is About

This book is about technology consulting companies and how a technology professional might be successful working for one. It is the collected wisdom drawn from not just my own mistakes (which are legion), but mistakes of others who have been kind enough to share their experiences in this book as well (their insights appear as shaded sidebars embedded in the text). Of course, you can't have a careers book without a happy ending, so we talk about and celebrate successes alongside our failures. But as everyone knows after a few years, failure is frequently a much better teacher than success!

Consider this book something of a career guide that maps out how most firms work, covers the kinds of employers to avoid, and provides some sample career paths beyond the career paths you would normally think about in a technology company. I have aimed to provide a good mixture of advice and realism, mixed with a bit of inspiration and unconventional advice, so you don't confuse this book with something that might be written by one of those folks you watch during 3 a.m. infomercials when you have job-worry insomnia and someone is telling you "Rah, rah, power of positive thinking."

Why I Wrote This Book

Technology consulting is a business that globally employs well over three million people. To put it in perspective, more than 1 in every 2,000 humans alive today work in technology consulting. If all the world's technology consultants lived in one city, it would have a population roughly on par with the city where I live and work, Chicago, Illinois. I would add that such a mystical city would be a great place indeed—if you could get past all the pizza and Mountain Dew consumed there. (Hey, let's admit it, some stereotypes are true!)

To put it another way, although definitive numbers are hard to find, the quantity of technology consultants and technology service professionals is comparable with that of many major professions such as accounting or law. However, although there are many books on how to run a law practice, how to advance in a law practice, not to mention television dramas and movies about the practice of law, and so forth, there are not many books on how a technology services practice is run.

The evidence of this, of course, is that because there is such a dearth of information, many people come into this business unprepared. To the budding technologist who finds himself or herself in the technology consulting business by accident, not understanding how a firm works can lead him or her to not only being taken advantage of, but to making scary career-limiting moves. For example, a firm might say, "We think consultants should rotate to new clients every nine months." A consultant who is unaware of the real pitfalls of the business might request to be moved off a less-than-perfect client nine months into a project during a recession. This might lead to the request being granted but also leads to a layoff a few weeks later, when that person is sitting on the bench.

I know this because I, as a consultant, have made that mistake and many others. And I have friends and colleagues who have done the same.

Of course, the other main reason I wrote this book was, to be blunt, that as this book goes to press in 2009, there is a certain urgency and need for relevant career advice. Although economics is called "the dismal science" for a reason—one of which is the difficulty in predicting what will happen even with the best information—it's important to have a conversation about the skills necessary to survive a downturn in the economy.

Who This Book Is For

This book is designed for

- Currently practicing technology consultants
- Students entering the field of technology who are considering consulting as an option
- People who work in technology for a "brick-and-mortar" (that is, nontechnology) company, who are considering switching to technology
- Spouses of people in technology consulting, so they know what is driving their spouse nuts
- Managers or owners of technology consulting firms who want to improve their companies
- People with idle curiosity on the topic

Note that I am a software developer by trade, and some of the advice will seem suited toward that particular sector of the technology consulting business. That said, most of the advice can be translated easily to other areas of technology consulting, whether it is interaction design, infrastructure consulting, database consulting, product implementation, or the dozens of areas adjacent to software development consulting—the area where I live and breathe on a day-to-day basis as a practicing consultant myself.

How to Read This Book

You can be thankful that this book is not like a novel, a la *Lord of the Rings*, where you will have no clue about what is going on if you don't read Chapter 6. You can read most of the chapters in this book independently.

Chapter 1, "Why Consulting?," provides you with a deeper understanding of why this industry exists and why you might consider working as a consultant. It is oriented toward those who might be considering technology consulting: people who have recently entered consulting and suddenly are having some sort of identity crisis or who otherwise want to understand the ontology of "why do I exist?" (in the occupational sense, not the "I think; therefore I am" sense).

Chapter 2, "The Seven Deadly Firms," helps you understand some of the traps, pitfalls, and other problems you might encounter when looking at some of the more unscrupulous players in the technology consulting marketplace. The chapter defines a set of consulting "anti-patterns"; that is, common types of firms that, frankly, you should either avoid entirely or at least join with an understanding of exactly what you are getting yourself into. It is important to understand that although this chapter demonstrates a good number of these anti-patterns, the percentage of consulting firms that represent one or more of these patterns is less than 10 percent—a significant number to be sure, but not so high that it would bring the entire business model into question.

Chapter 3, "How Technology Consulting Firms Work," gets to much more practical matters, explaining the details on how consulting firms work. Although independent consultants, consultants at small consulting firms, and consultants at large consulting firms may have slightly different nuances on these concepts, the general principles of utilization, backlog, revenue, and margin tend to hold, regardless of size. The purpose of this chapter is to explain these mechanics so that everyone who wants to know can understand how these concepts work.

Chapter 4, "Getting In: Ten Unstated Traits That Technology Consulting Firms Look For," helps you understand what kinds of people consulting firms look for and, thus, how to break into this business. The chapter is all about practical tips for how to not only break into technology, but to specifically break into consulting. If you are looking for interview tips, this is probably the chapter to turn to.

Chapter 5, "What You Need to Ask Before You Join a Technology Consulting Firm," is also about preparation for consulting, but with a different twist: It specifically prepares you to ask the questions you need to ask before you join. Yes, you are in charge of your own destiny! You need to prepare not only for interviews but, because this is a two-way street, actually working there! You need to always interview your employer, and the goal of Chapter 5 is to help in that endeavor.

Chapter 6, "Surviving," is a timely piece for those who will work in consulting through a recession, which ironically, at the time of publication (2009), happens to be right now. The point of consulting is not just to survive, but to thrive. However, getting to that thriving part depends on surviving, and therefore, Chapter 6 presents a set of principles that helps you accomplish survival, even during challenging economic times.

Chapter 7, "Thriving," is about specific strategies for advancing your career. It puts forth a foundation for understanding what separates mere survival ("I managed to get food for *this* winter") from thriving ("I built a machine that makes me never have to worry about food again"). The goal of this chapter is to put forth the mindset of most of the consultants who achieve high levels of success.

Chapter 8, "Your Career Path," describes the specific career paths that many consultants tend to take. Nobody starts out as an independent, CEO, or guru, but there are paths that various people have taken; and who knows, maybe the trails they blazed will work for you, too. (Yes, we know Bill Gates and perhaps a few others were exceptions here, but chances are they won't read this book!)

Chapter 9, "Avoiding Career-Limiting Moves," defines various career-limiting moves that, I hope, you will avoid after reading this chapter, whether you choose to work in consulting or any other field. This chapter describes a mix of well-known issues (such as "don't date coworkers") with more technology-oriented advice (such as "no gold-plating").

After spending nine chapters talking about the mostly good points of consulting as a career, I owed you one that tries to talk you out of it. That is the point of Chapter 10, "Is Consulting Right for You?" It explains why you might want to *not* consider consulting as a career. I am the first to admit that this lifestyle isn't for everyone, and this chapter explains various reasons why you would *not* want to be a technology consultant.

Chapter 11, "An Anthology of Sage Advice," is an anthology of essays from experienced technology consultants who work in a variety of settings, in companies with a staff of one to a staff of several thousand. If you get bored reading my material, I encourage you to turn to the stories in Chapter 11, which easily provide as much wisdom on any single page as I could ever provide.

Last, I provide two appendixes: Appendix A, "Consultopia: The Ideal Consulting Firm," is a work in the broader tradition of utopian writing—my own vision of the perfect consulting company. Note that this essay explains my own views on matters related to consulting and economics, so you should take it for what it is worth: the opinions of a humble technologist about matters that are probably beyond his normal area of expertise. That said, I think what I have accomplished in the appendix is thought-provoking as one of many possible goals we could try to reach as an industry. If you have goals in your own career that stretch beyond simply making money, I encourage you to take a careful look at some of the ideas in this appendix.

Appendix B, "A Consulting Lexicon," is more about fun—a somewhat snarky guide to jargon you might hear as a consultant. Again note that, like a lot of things in this book, it is informed by my own experiences and prejudice (much like most writing is, for the record). It is inspired by the work of Eric S. Raymond and his work with the Jargon file, a work I read during my own formative years as a software professional. For years as a consultant, I dreamed about writing such a thing specific to consulting—a feat that Appendix B represents. I hope I have accomplished even a tiny fraction of what Mr. Raymond did.

Authenticity

If anything, I have worked to write a book that provides good advice to consultants. As you read this book from start-to-finish, I fully expect you might find yourself with at least mixed feelings about consulting.

That, of course, is by design. I am a big fan of critical thinking. As a consultant, I want my colleagues to understand what they are getting into, what they should expect, and what they should not expect. I want you to know the good, the bad, and the ugly. This book gives you all three. Make no mistake; this is a great way to make a living. But it is no picnic, either. Frankly, neither is any other occupation. Ask an editor, teacher, firefighter, nurse, or CEO on Wall Street (okay, scratch the last one)—no job is really a pure path of bliss and happiness.

In other words, in the spirit of transparency (a big value of mine) when you read this book, expect to have mixed feelings from time to time. Some chapters spend more time talking you out of consulting than talking you into it. Indeed, my goal is to help you *learn* about consulting so that you can make good decisions about it. I happen to believe that, after the evidence is in, there is a good case for being a consultant, but ultimately, I would tell anyone that the decision to consult or not is a decision you need to make on your own, based on your own circumstances, goals, and aspirations.

Whether or not consulting is the path you choose, I hope you enjoy this book.

CHAPTER ONE

WHY CONSULTING?

Want job security? Be a consultant!

It took me years, as someone who is a technology professional first and business person only to the degree that I need to be to do what I love in the first place—namely, working on technology—to realize one of the most important things I have ever learned. Namely, I realized that technology skill would not really control my destiny, but rather skills in relating to people, building a network, and learning to be a politician. In fact, even today, I am amazed at how much the day-to-day world of technology is much more of a people business than a technology business. I've been consulting for more than 15 years, and even now, I screw this up all the time!

It's true: You can have a high IQ, great work ethic, fabulous personality, and deep knowledge of eight different computer languages; however, if nobody knows what you're capable of, your job security is at risk. In this chapter, you learn why technology consulting exists, why you should consider being a technology consultant, and how technology consulting firms actually work.

Aspiring software developers seldom wake up on the first day of their junior year of college and think to themselves, "Man, it would be really cool to work as a hired gun consultant." Work on a cutting-edge product at Google? Perhaps. Work at a startup and make $50 million two years out of school?

Sure. Work for clients in companies of all shapes and sizes writing code to integrate systems? Well, probably not. Okay, some might, but doing so isn't a mainstream choice of budding software engineers, especially those who see themselves as the next Bill Gates (founder of Microsoft) or Larry Page (cofounder of Google).

So why do it? There is a sad truth out there. Not all of us are going to work for Google or Microsoft or even Fog Creek Software (where Joel Spolsky of joelonsoftware.com fame operates his software-developer-friendly Independent Software Vendor, or ISV). It's a matter of mathematics and economics. There are perhaps 100,000 software development jobs at those three companies, yet there is a need for software that is not yet available from software vendors. Someone *is* going to do that work, and if circumstances dictate you are not going to work in the fun part of Microsoft where people are inventing new computer languages or at Blizzard building the next dungeon in World of Warcraft, you can still very much enjoy your profession in areas that perhaps are less glamorous. You might not be the one writing the next Napster, yet you may be doing something much more rewarding and sustainable in the long term.

⤳

Job Security Through Networking

Employer loyalty is an illusion. If we have learned anything from the dot-com crash of 2000–03 and the housing crash/credit crunch of 2007, it is that when the going gets tough, no one knows when the employers will start making large, savage cuts in the workforce. Ask anyone who worked for Enron, Arthur Andersen, Pets.com, Webvan, or more recently, folks in the mortgage business who worked for one of the investment banks that either no longer exist or have drastically changed the way and structure under which they operate. Corporations are interested in your well-being and future only to the extent that you can do something for them in return. When that stops being the case, as it often does for reasons beyond your control, corporations will, almost without fail, sever your relationship with them.

Michael Hugos   I finally came to understand that we are always working for ourselves; unless you have an employment contract, you are an employee at will and you will be let go at any time. That is not good or bad; it's just the way things are.

Unlike the apathetic corporation, people can and often do look out for your best interests. Supervisors (see the sidebar "On the Word Supervisor" later in this chapter) and other coworkers, whether former or present, tend to be more prone to develop a personal relationship with you. Trust is a powerful force in human relationships; the concept of trust in human relationships goes back to the hunter-gatherer times when we learned that survival depends on finding those we can count on time and time again and depending on them over people whom we have never met (that is, other tribes).

The corporate manifestation of this phenomenon is simple: When the going gets tough, those in your network—the people with whom you have built trust relationships over time—are more likely to hire you and provide you with job security.

Good Consultants Build Large Networks

Having a strong network of people you trust and who trust you is a critical employment strategy. Working as a technical consultant, an occupation in which you tend to move around multiple companies helping them solve problems, is a good way to build this network.

For a technology consultant, the network of colleagues and clients that would recommend him or her is the equity upon which a career is built. Seniority isn't measured in years at the company, but in the number and quality of relationships developed over time.

Now, of course, not all consulting projects are network builders. There are people in this business you will not want to work with again. The good news is that one of the first truisms in consulting is if you don't like your job, wait a few months. Consulting engagements, by their nature, are short- to medium-term gigs; of course, there are always a few exceptions. If a company wanted to retain someone for a longer time period, hiring an employee makes more sense than hiring a consultant.

Corporate Network Diversity

When you have a personal network that extends into sufficiently varied companies, upon a major layoff, there is a lower chance you and all your friends will be chasing the same jobs.

Derik Whittaker   With the recent rise in popularity of the various social networking tools such as Twitter, Facebook, and LinkedIn, networking has never been easier. Using these various tools, I have increased my network more than tenfold in the past 18 months. In fact, it was because of this network that when I found my last position (full-time, not consulting), I really did not have to even interview for the position; it was simply offered to me.

Stunted Growth: Networks Inside a Single Corporation

The result of being a software developer for a single company is that you get to know a group of people—your coworkers—very well. This could be good if you like your coworkers or bad if you dislike them. In either case, in most companies, getting to know these people stunts the growth of your network.

Let's say you work for XYZ Corp, which is a large company that employs 100,000 people, has a great benefits package, and offers enough opportunity inside its walls that you should never need to leave the building. XYZ Corp has been very successful in the financial services industry in the past few years, and the opportunities there have been great indeed.

In fact, you have built a network of almost 200 of your closest colleagues, and 98 percent of them work at XYZ. The good camaraderie has translated into very little turnover, which means almost everyone you know works with you at XYZ. Unfortunately, one of XYZ Corp's largest funds just failed, and it needs to find $30 billion in new capital. Positions that are not directly related to selling financial services will be drastically cut to make up part of the shortfall. The corner office decides to cut 60 percent of XYZ Corp's IT staff based on assumptions that the technology systems will run well enough for the next three years. You're out on the street along with most of your network.

This example is, of course, a very painful way to realize your network lacks the sort of healthy corporate network diversity that you need. Almost all the people you might turn to in order to scout out new opportunities for work are, simultaneously, looking for work themselves. Adding fuel to the fire, those few people outside your company probably also work in your *vertical*, that is, financial services. In other words, your network lacks sector diversity too, making you worse off because those still employed are probably getting more requests for help than they can possibly handle, assuming they have opportunities in the first place!

The Über-Networked Consultant

Good technology consultants deliver great results for clients and thus get a variety of assignments early in their careers and build a diverse corporate network. It is especially important to make extra effort to invest in your network when times are good. When times turn, people tend to remember those who help them when there wasn't obvious self-interest. Starting your network when you suddenly need a new position is not the best time.

The network you build should have folks who are not only fellow geeks, but also

- Account executives in your company who see you as someone who delivers consistently (making their commissions safer)
- Purchasers of consulting services who see you as someone who delivers consistently (making their jobs safer)
- Owners of the current and former firms you have worked for or with who see you as someone who delivers consistently (making their profits or bonuses safer)

- Recruiters in the current and former firms that have recruited you who see you as someone who delivers consistently (making their recruiting commission safer)

- ...you get the idea

You need to build a good network base that spreads across different companies and industries and also contains all the aforementioned elements. You also need to be a consistent player for all these contacts. Doing so gains you a loyal following of people who trust you to deliver the goods.

> **Michael Hugos** It's important to be selective about how you build your network. Just having 500+ connections in LinkedIn does not mean you have a good network because most of those people don't know you and you don't know them. Better to add people only when you have worked with them, and they really know you and vice versa.

On the Word Supervisor

It is time to stop using the word *supervisor*. The word alone makes people feel watched, as if there is a limit to their trust. In the context of a tech worker, this word brings up an image of someone who supervises your code. The idea of a software manager supervising code is considered meddlesome to most tech workers. The person writing the code is better suited to know what good code looks like than his or her MBA-attaining supervisor.

Personally, I prefer the term *leader* to *supervisor*, or the slightly less irritating *manager*. Leader means someone who "leads by example," inspires those he or she leads, and serves the people he or she leads, which puts the responsibility in the right place. People want leaders, they almost never want supervisors, and they generally don't like having managers very much either.

Chris Williams   This is so true. I'll take a leader over a manager any day.

⌒

Expanding Your Horizons

When you work for a single company, there is a tendency toward specialization based on your interactions within that company. You could be hired to come in and work on a certain system, at which point you have a clean slate within the new company. However, as the years pass, you will attain certain knowledge of systems that you have worked on. That you have that knowledge usually does not go unnoticed as you become the default maintainer of certain systems the longer you stay in a company.

Some companies do a good job of making sure you move around to different divisions and work on different projects. Some places make sure they clean your slate such that you can concentrate on new projects. However, like companies that purchase free backrubs for their employees, such places are hard to find and, more to the point, tend to engage in those activities only when everything else is going well.

In fact, one of the unstated reasons there is a lot of turnover in the technology business is that changing jobs is frequently the only way to escape a lifetime of maintenance of old applications that, while needed, are no longer interesting to the original author. People move because at some point, even the idea of working on someone else's old problem becomes interesting to them; it is a way to learn a new language and work on different technology, a sort of "one man's garbage is another man's treasure" effect in the world of software development.

Consulting provides a mechanism for making sure that you get to work on different solutions over time. In fact, unless you go through a lot of effort to work only on certain types of problems, being a technology consultant is a great way to gain expertise in many types of industries without having to explain on your resume why you changed jobs every 15 months. Now, of course, some folks choose to specialize in certain types of solutions in certain types of industries because they truly love that kind of work and have become noted experts in a manner that commands more money and prestige. Even in those cases, that expertise was attained *after* said consultants worked in a variety of different industries earlier in their career and hit it off with the right one.

> **Jason Bock**   Another benefit of expanding your horizons is developing the ability to work effectively with different people and their personalities. Not everyone you work with is someone you'd really *want* to work with if you had the choice, but learning how to succeed with difficult relationships is a skill that becomes very valuable as a consultant's career lengthens.

How Frequently Are You Changing Jobs?

"How frequently are you changing jobs?" is, of course, a loaded question. Software developers tend to change jobs every 18 to 24 months. It might surprise more than a few nonconsulting software folks that the typical consultant tends to change clients about every 9 to 18 months. Amazingly, in some cases, it is not uncommon for consultants to have been in an organization longer than most of the salaried employees.

> **Derik Whittaker**   I was once at a client for almost three years. When I left, most of the staff did not even realize I was not an actual employee of the company. To be honest, it felt nice because that told me I was treated the same as everyone else there.

Corporate IT software developers are slightly different animals. These developers might discover that they really are consultants with a corporate IT salary. That corporate salary seems just, considering the job security attached to a corporate position, but corporate IT software developers often change positions as frequently as consultants change clients. Corporate developers, in many cases, would be much better served working in consulting, where changing clients is expected and planned.

In other words, you might already be a consultant and not even realize it!

〜

Why Companies Hire Consultants

It is common to wonder why people hire consultants at all. If you have not been in the business of consulting, it's not always apparent why a company would hire, at what can appear to be obscenely high rates, outside help to solve problems when it could just hire such a staff person. To understand this, we need to go back to basics and understand why a company might decide to utilize technology and, in so doing, hire technology consultants to implement that technology.

Let's say you are the owner of a company that manufactures cups—those devices that frequently contain the coffee that allows geeks to write code. Your business works by taking raw materials, in this case, various forms of paper from a paper mill and converts said raw materials into finished cups. From here, you put a design on the paper that is going to be converted into cups. You then convert that paper into a form usable for drinking. You do this by using a machine that converts paper into cup form. Then, through another series of steps, you end up with a finished product you send to various consumers of cups, be it Starbucks, McDonald's, or other purveyors of coffee. Not too complicated, right?

As an owner of this enterprise, you have a lot to worry about! You are worried about the cost of raw materials, such as paper and ink for the cups. You are worried about the cost of capital equipment, such as cup-making machines, which convert the paper into cups. You are worried about the cost of a barrel of oil, because when that cost rises, the shippers who bring you raw materials and ship your product to customers start to charge fuel surcharges to cover their increasing costs. And, of course, you are worried about the cost of labor, which goes into the people who operate the machinery that processes those inputs into the outputs that make you money.

Building a Human-Replacement Machine

Over time, you realize humans are the most expensive part of your business. Unlike a machine, for which you pay the substantial costs up front, people have to be paid continuously. And sometimes they complain and demand raises. And even worse, sometimes they quit and make you go find more people! What a hassle! Life would be much easier if you could get a "thinking machine" that could, say, process all these orders.

The economics of human replacement can work wonders for your business. A human can take, at best, maybe 10 complex orders per hour. Assuming you let your human perform typical human maintenance functions such as powering itself (usually through a substance called food), you may get 7.5 hours of useful life for such a human over the course of each day, which results in a maximum capacity of 75 complex orders per day.

For a simple data entry task in a typical city in the United States after the cost of benefits and taxes, you pay $16 per hour, or around $200 per day. This is roughly the cost of one hour of consulting from one high-end technology consultant from a top-tier firm in 2009. Such a person will be charged with development of a software solution that automates this order-taking process, which takes into account the specific options that the cup manufacturer allows its customers to take advantage of.

Let's assume that such a solution, customized as it is, takes a high-end technology consultancy six person-months to deliver. Six months, at 160 hours per month (40 per week, roughly), is 960 overall hours, or about $192,000 at $200 per hour. A large sum to be sure, but let's compare this to the manual cost. Remember, you are paying $16 per hour, or around $32,000 per year, to be able to process 15,000 orders in a year. This amounts to, roughly, $2.13 *per order*.

Now, let's say the system was built in a highly scalable fashion, and let's face it, at $200 per hour, it had better be scalable. A million orders in a year would not be unreasonable for such a system. If you hire someone to operate the system at the going rate of around $75K per year plus benefits, or $100,000 total, and use the system for five years before it is obsolete, you get a cost per order, shown in Table 1-1.

TABLE 1-1

Hypothetical Cost per Order with Technology

Software cost, $192,000, amortized over 5 years	$38,400 per year
System operator/maintenance	$100,000 per year
Total	**$138,400 per year**
Orders Processed	1,000,000 per year
Cost per order	$0.14 per order

At that rate, you are at $0.14 per order, roughly a 93 percent cost savings over the $2.13 you were paying before. Clearly, technology has an economic benefit. And although not all companies will immediately see this, all it takes is one company experiencing this huge economic benefit and cost savings over its competitors. When one firm is offering the same cups for 30 percent less than another firm (and pocketing the rest of the savings as profit), all similarly situated companies that want to stay in business will have to offer the same price break, causing all the competitors to invest in the same kind of technology. This cycle of one firm investing in technology, reaping an economic benefit, and causing competitors to spend money to catch up and remain competitive is the virtuous cycle that brings down costs and keeps the modern software engineer employed.

> **Jason Bock**   Of course, the downside is if the high-paid consultant is woefully underqualified to do the expected work. I've seen cases in my life where someone was creating terrible software at a high hourly rate. While one can argue that the company should monitor the consultant's production continuously (which should be the story for *any* employee), sometimes "high prices" equate to "immediate trust" and the consultant is left alone for months, spinning his or her wheels.

Why Not Just Hire the Geeks?

Now, of course, the preceding section explains "why technology?" but does not explain "why hire consultants?" Consultants exist because many companies have what are often called "lumpy" demand for technology. Your hypothetical firm might need a very high-end developer for six months but in subsequent years will need much less skill for maintenance of the system. It may not be cost effective or desirable to keep around that $200 per hour consultant continuously, and even if it were, that consultant usually is not interested in working for the same company for the rest of his or her life because he or she wants to build up a diverse corporate network, as we have previously discussed. For the same reason that most people do not continuously pay a plumber a salary to keep the household toilet working, it is more effective for most companies to utilize technology professionals when needed rather than forming a permanent employment relationship.

Adding to this is the fact that technologists are in such high demand that most companies have problems retaining technology professionals for long periods of time. In particular for those at the top of their field, most companies lack the flexibility to pay truly good software developers the superstar salaries that they can make on the open consulting market. For many organizations that are limited in what they can pay in salary, access to these professionals is available only through the consulting marketplace.

Looking from the perspective of the high-performing software professional, what is more alluring, working in a company where the superstars are technologists because they bring in the revenue through their fees? Or standard "brick-and-mortar" companies where the superstars are usually not the software developers?

Michael Hugos   It took me a while to finally figure out that I have the greatest opportunities for raises and promotions when I work for companies that make money by doing the things that I do. Companies value the activities and people that generate revenue for them.

Chris Williams   Another trend I've seen at some really large companies is for a geek to work there for a few years and then leave (or retire, in some cases) and immediately form his or her own "consulting company" with a single client: the previous employer. Of course, this is usually less about building a better network and more about filling a fatter wallet.

⤳

Consulting Firm Economics 101

Now that we know why consulting firms exist, the next step is gaining a high-level understanding of how the firms themselves work. Understanding the economics of consulting is critical to understanding why sometimes the firm leadership may be happy and generous and why at other times, the leadership may be grumpy, worried, or out of sorts. It is also critical because, like in marriage, choice in your firm can determine whether your own life feels miserable, making every day a chore to wake up in the morning, or fabulous, making your work barely seem like work at all!

To understand the basics of how a consulting firm works, you must understand how owners of a consulting firm tend to measure its performance. This section helps you understand how these metrics work (see Table 1-2).

TABLE 1-2

Key Metrics of Consulting Firms

Performance Metric	What It Is	Why It's Important
Revenue	The money that the company makes, mostly through exchanging a technology consultant's time for money.	No business survives long without money.
Margin	The money left over after paying for consultant salaries, laptops, training, taxes, management, sodas in the office, foosball tables, and XBoxes in the conference rooms.	Owners don't invest money in a consultancy if they are not going to get a return on their investment. Not to mention, it isn't a bad idea to have money in case business slows and you don't want to lay off everyone.
Utilization	The number of hours you bill to a client divided by the number of hours for which you are paid a salary.	When you have a low utilization, you are not making the firm money. This is typically bad for your career as a consultant. The reverse, all other things being equal, is typically good.

(continues)

TABLE 1-2

Key Metrics of Consulting Firms (continued)

Performance Metric	What It Is	Why It's Important
Hourly Rate	The amount of money you are able to charge for one hour of time working for a client.	The higher your skills, the higher your hourly rate will be. Generally speaking, this also causes your margin to be higher, unless you are taking salary and benefits that are high compared to your hourly rate.
Backlog	The amount of work currently sold, but not yet done, by a given consulting firm or division.	If the backlog is zero, the company ceases to have a reason to exist. A high backlog is generally indicative of job security for consultants.
Overhead	The amount of money spent on nonconsulting operations in a technology consulting firm.	Although many consulting firms have different nuances, one common thread is that all seek to minimize overhead costs that are not seen as directly contributing to revenue.

Revenue: The Reason Any Business Exists

Every business, regardless of its intention, must at some point generate revenue to allow people who work in it to do simple things like eat and have a place to live. Although some companies survived for a while during the dot-com boom using venture capital as their sole support, times like that are very much the exception and not the rule.

Revenue for a technology consulting business comes almost exclusively from consultants working on technology projects, either under the direction of the company that is purchasing the services (often called *staff augmentation*) or under the direction of the consulting company itself (often called *project work*). Although some companies may sell software or have other revenue streams, such as referral revenue from software companies or license revenue for in-house software developed and marketed (what is often called, somewhat derisively, *consultingware*), most consulting companies make money strictly by selling the professional services of people, a.k.a. consultants, to clients who need said services.

In Chapter 4, "Getting In: Ten Unstated Traits That Technology Consulting Firms Look For," you learn that there are a lot of players, beyond yourself, who help in the generation of revenue. That said, it is safe to say that nearly every job in any organization somehow ultimately relates to either generation of revenue directly, or at least the facilitation of an environment that allows others to generate revenue effectively.

Profit Margin: How Much Are We Making After All These Expenses?

Profit margin is what you have left over after you reduce your expenses from your revenue. Accountants like to talk about lots of different types of profit, such as before taxes and amortization, net profit, gross profit, and so forth, but unless you are an accountant or an investor, those distinctions are mostly academic. What ultimately matters is that, from the standpoint of a consultant, you are responsible not only for bringing in revenue, through completing projects or billing hours to clients, but also for bringing in profit; that is, after paying you, there should be money left over.

You may ask why money should be left over at all. Why should the investors, who do nothing, get money based on your work? Understanding this point is critical because the truth is, margin plays several important functions in the overall functioning of the firm.

Chiefly, without some sort of margin, the investors—that is, the people who risk their life savings, their capital, to start a firm—have little incentive to make any sort of investment. You have to ask yourself if you would be interested in making an investment—one that is fairly risky to make, say, 5 percent, a rate of return that is commonly available through low-risk investments like Certificates of Deposit.

The following risks are inherent in consulting:

- Clients decide to stop investing in technology.
- Consultants fail to deliver to expectations.

- An account executive leaves and clients leave as a result.
- A client goes bankrupt.

All these are risks to the owners of the company; the entire value they have built up can, literally, go away in a few very unlucky months. Because these risks are substantial, a reasonable rate of return is expected to compensate for those risks. In most cases, this "expected" rate of return is somewhere in the 10–15 percent of revenue range.

Within this 10–15 percent margin typical for consulting firms, many owners reinvest at least some of this money back into the business. Often this means money for expansion into new regions, building up some unique intellectual capital, or other strategic investments that help the company grow. Regardless of how this money is spent, clearly, having your firm being a superior investment to bonds is probably a good idea.

Backlog: The Inventory of Work to Do

The best way to think of backlog is as a number that allows you to figure out how long the company would survive if the entire sales force quit tomorrow. Backlog is defined as the amount of work that is sold but not yet billed. Every time you bill an hour, you reduce backlog. Every time the company sells work, it increases backlog. When backlog hits zero, it means the firm is effectively out of business.

The job of the technical consultant is to convert backlog into actual revenue. By contrast, typically the job of the sales force—regardless of the particular form that may take in a company (such as account executives, partners, engagement managers, and various other titles)—is to add to the backlog. Nearly every important job in technical consulting is involved in either increasing the backlog by selling work or converting the backlog into revenue by executing work.

One of the most efficient ways to make the managers of your technology consulting firm angry is to take action that reduces the backlog. Getting fired from a client or resigning from the consultancy at the start of an engagement, particularly if there is no way to replace you on the engagement, reduces the backlog and makes everyone, including your fellow consultants, very nervous. Sometimes, particularly when getting a bad project canceled or getting out of a hostile work environment, it is necessary to prematurely end an engagement. If, however, you want to maintain a relationship with your current firm, it is imperative that you work out the problem with your company management first prior to taking any action that would cause work that has already been "sold" to become "unsold."

Of course, a client can always cause backlog to decrease by exiting a relationship early. Almost all consulting contracts contain cancellation clauses that allow for a project to end with some level of notice, typically two to four weeks. And often, there is a high likelihood that contracts will be extended as well. Backlog does not mean "we are guaranteed to get this revenue if we deliver well," but generally it is a reasonably good indication of what is likely to be produced over the period of the contract.

Hourly Rate

The metric of hourly rate is what the market considers one hour of your time to be worth. Generally speaking, a company that has the following traits is able to ask for a higher hourly rate:

- Good relationships with clients, frequently at the "C" level (CEO, COO, CTO...) of the organization
- Consultants who are considered very specialized and in demand
- A brand that is recognized in the marketplace, which implies value beyond a typical skill set would be valued independently

On the other hand, smaller companies that lack good brand, lack relationships with high-level executives, or employ consultants that the market considers easier to find have lower hourly rates.

The goal of an individual consultant is to be employable on a regular basis at the highest possible hourly rate in the market. This increases a number of factors important to you:

- The amount of money you can be paid. Generally speaking, your upward salary potential is driven by the potential revenue that you can personally bring to the firm when you are a consultant.

- The amount of margin you contribute. Even if you are not paid more right away, if you are seen as a person who is highly profitable to the firm when billing at a client, your job security is likely to be substantially higher.

Of course, the key is being employable at that rate on a regular basis. Other factors that have much less to do with your skills individually also affect hourly rate. If you are in a position that is in demand, but only for short bursts of time, you might have a high hourly rate when you are working, but your *utilization* is lower, which balances things out.

Why Is My Hourly Rate So High?

Some people are shocked that a company might hire an entry-level consultant at $75 per hour when that same company might hire that same consultant as an employee for only $75,000 per year. A naïve examination of the math may look like what's shown in Table 1-3.

TABLE 1-3
Naïve Comparison of Consultant and Employee Rates: Where Is the Missing $72,000?

Consultant	Employee
$75 per hour	
× 1,960 work hours/ year	
(vacation and holidays excluded)	
$147,000	$75,000

However, to understand the economics of why consultants exist, we need to look a little deeper. First, the costs for an employee—after considering factors such as health insurance, taxes, provision of equipment, and other fringe benefits—typically add around 30 percent to the base salary. Second, it is atypical for a consultant to bill—that is, work hours that are paid for by a client—for 1,960 working hours in a year. A much more typical number is 1,650 expected billing hours in a year, although this number can be higher or lower depending on the particular company. Taking these two factors into account, the comparison looks more like what's shown in Table 1-4.

TABLE 1-4

Comparison of Consultant and Employee Rates after Vacation and Benefits: $26,250 Is Still Missing!

Consultant	Employee
$75 per hour	
× 1,650 working hours in a year	$75,000
(vacation and holidays excluded)	× 1.3 (add 30% of salary for benefits and taxes)
$123,750	$97,500

At this point, things get a little more interesting (see Table 1-5). A consulting company usually invests in training its people, hires account executives and marketers to make sure that the next project is lined up for the consultant, provides specialized equipment, and provides an office and facilities that are available to the client if required. On top of all this, the consultancy provides a backstop to the company it works for by making sure that in the event such an employee leaves, it has the capability to add a new person with similar skills to the project. All of that and of course the consulting business, just like any other business, needs to make money so that its investors have motivation to take the risks involved in starting a consultancy in the first place!

TABLE 1-5

Comparison of Consultant and Employee Rates after All Factors Are Considered
(Prices Roughly Equivalent after All Factors)

Consultant	Employee
$75 per hour	
× 1650 working hours in a year	
(vacation and holidays excluded)	
$123,750	
– $3,000 Sales Commission	
– $10,000 Office and Admin Expenses	
– $250 Lunches and Greens Fees for Closing Deal	$75,000
– $13,000 Profit (~12%)	× 1.3 (add 30% of salary for benefits and taxes)
$97,500	$97,500

You can look at the situation this way: Pretend you are an independent consultant and are looking to sell your services. That is a perfectly good option in certain circumstances. One of the biggest mistakes that new "independents" make, however, is assuming that the revenue they make when they are billing 40 hours per week will continue indefinitely and they can treat it as salary. Many new independent consultants start out "living large" (for example, leasing a 7-series Beamer); discover that consulting, like almost all other businesses, has sales, marketing, and administrative expenses; and after the initial gig is up, learn the hard way that there is no way to hide from the economic realities of running a practice. In fact, most independent consultants are served well by the general rule of "$1 per hour per $1,000 you would make in salary."

A Technology Consultant's Mantra: "You Are What You Bill."

Derik Whittaker During my time as an independent, my rule of thumb was as follows: If my "projected" salary was not 15–20 percent higher working 40 billable weeks a year [52 weeks – 4 weeks vacation – 2 weeks holiday (Christmas, etc.) – 6 weeks down time (bench time, training, etc.)] then it would be as a full-time employee and it was not worth my time/effort.

Utilization

In consulting, the term *utilization* means the number of hours you bill to a client relative to the number of hours you are paid to work in a year, typically some number divided by 2,000 (40 hours per week, 52 weeks per year, minus some holidays). The more working hours that are billable to a client you work in a year, the better your own utilization number is.

When you work as a technology consultant, you are almost always expected to achieve a certain amount of utilization. Some firms measure this number more day-to-day and quarter-to-quarter than others, but by and large, all consulting firms, as a matter of survival, use this metric, if not on each individual, on an overall basis (for example, the Chicago office achieved 95 percent utilization for the year).

A high utilization number, depending on the company, can be anywhere from above 90 percent to, in some extreme cases, above 110 percent (that is, cases where everyone on average is pulling more than 40 hours per week). Generally, this means the money is rolling in. A low utilization number, especially a utilization number below 60 percent, means trouble, especially if that number is maintained at that level for any length of time.

Overhead

The last major piece of the picture in understanding the economics of a consulting organization is knowing what *overhead* means. Broadly speaking, overhead is money spent on everything other than sales (bringing in clients), recruiting (bringing in consultants), and the consultants themselves. Some organizations even consider the former two roles (sales and recruiting) overhead because, technically, those roles are not part of the utilization equation that is the main direct driver that determines the profit margin of the company.

In many consulting organizations, overhead is viewed as something to be minimized to the extent possible. Although everyone would agree that a certain amount of overhead is needed—because somehow we have to be able to report time to bill the customers the correct amount, have computers to write code on, and so on—in the broad picture, when forced to choose between investing a dollar into the company infrastructure or into a client or consultant relationship, most healthy consulting companies choose the latter.

> **Michael Hugos**   The consulting world started to make a lot more sense when I understood these metrics and saw how they applied to me. In each consulting engagement I need to know these metrics and use them to help me make decisions.

The Cobbler's Shoes Problem

The aspiring consultant needs to understand overhead, in particular, because most technology consultants, even those at very good consultancies, are surprised when they come to a new company and find that the infrastructure is dated. It is common for the programs on which the consultancy runs to be two or three versions behind what that same organization is suggesting to clients. More than one consultant has achieved cognitive dissonance when confronted with this fact. However, when you understand the investment priorities of a consultancy are its consultants and clients, not its infrastructure, the idea becomes a little more clear that the sign of a consultancy in which all its systems are "latest and greatest" might be either overinvesting in its infrastructure or it has consultants that are not building solutions for clients, but rather building solutions for themselves.

> **Chris Williams** The problem that you can run into here is when clients visit the consultancy (this doesn't happen often, but is more likely with first-time clients) or when the salesman spins his laptop around on the table to show a prospective client some numbers and hears "Whoa ... you guys are still on Office 97?" Proceed with caution here.

We can be thankful that rare is the case in which technology consultancies are judged by their internal technology. It is not uncommon for consultancies to suffer from what is known as "The Cobbler's Shoes Problem": The cobbler is so busy making shoes that his own children go around barefoot.

Take Overhead Positions with Caution

The best advice for a consultant is not to take an overhead position at all. From time to time, you might even be presented with an opportunity to join with the infrastructure group of a technology consultancy. Generally speaking, you should view offers to do this with extreme caution, especially in cases in which you do not already have a strong network connection with the senior management and/or owners of the company. When utilization in a consulting company is going down, overhead positions are the first places that a consulting company will look when seeking to "chop heads." Without a strong connection with the company leaders where you are seen as an essential part of the company (that is, *deeply trusted*), being overhead in a consultancy is very risky.

Do We Need Overhead?

After all is said and done, all technology consulting firms need a certain number of things done that are not directly related to the bottom line. Without a payroll department, or at least someone to manage a payroll provider who does most of the work, it is hard for employees to get paid. There is an internal technology infrastructure to maintain, and you need managers to make sure that issues between employees on engagements are handled.

This section does not intend to make the case that all overhead is bad because, clearly, you need some to operate. However, as an aspiring technology consultant, you would be wise to understand why company management will be very slow to spend a lot of money on people and equipment that does not directly result in the company attaining more revenue.

> **Jason Bock**   Some consulting companies don't even invest in a physical space, or they have a very small office with only one or two conference rooms and a couple of small cubes/offices. Either employees are working from home (usually overhead positions), or they're billing at a client. This is fairly rare; the biggest barrier to this idea is the lack of trust some people have in letting their employees work from home, but it's another way to keep costs low.

⮞

The Profession of Technology Consultant

Overall, being a technology consultant is about making your skills recognized on a continuous basis in the open market and realizing the rewards that come with that. That said, this is not a place for slackers! The benefits are great—in terms of the expanded network with its job security, the opportunities to continuously develop not just your technology skills, but your people skills. Not to mention the higher salaries. But this profession requires a certain personality oriented toward self-improvement and a predisposition to being proactive in managing your career. If your goal is to find a secure place and do the same thing over the next 20 years, this is probably not the place for you.

That said, you are probably not that person because if you were, you would not choose an occupation that causes your current skills to become obsolete every five years. Assuming you are interested in doing this kind of work, it would probably be a good idea to read on and learn more about the different firms you may end up working for.

⬱
Summary

In this chapter, I explained the idea that technology skill is great but is not always the most significant predictor of job security. I demonstrated how networking skills have a good deal to do with success in the technology business and how consulting is ideal for not just building networking skills (you can do that in lots of technology jobs), but also building networks that have diversity across industries and disciplines that can help you fight off the negative effects of a recession.

From there, I went further to cover the basics of why consulting firms exist, the basics on how consulting firms measure themselves, and lastly, the reasons your rates are what they are, relative to your salary. Understanding the economics of your career is critical, and one of the aims of this chapter has been to give you a broad overview of the topic.

In the next chapter, I take "a walk through the swamp" and look at some firms you may want to avoid as you look to either start a career in consulting or consider changing firms that you already work for. Consulting is a great line of work, but there is a small number of unscrupulous players or otherwise incompetent ones who, if you go into consulting with them, might leave you worse off, not better.

CHAPTER TWO

THE SEVEN DEADLY FIRMS

When you make the fateful decision to join the ranks of technical consultants, you will at some point start to think long and hard about whom you would want to work for, evaluate each company's strengths and weaknesses, evaluate your own, and choose one that is the best fit for both you and your employer. At least that is what you *should* do. Sadly, however, most people, including me on more than one occasion, choose on different criteria, namely

- Is the economy bad? Take the job. It's money. Rent is due on the 15th.

- Is the economy good? Which of the many companies you are talking to is offering the highest salary? Good, take *that* one.

This decision, as you would expect, results in a great deal of disappointment on the part of legions of technology consultants about their careers. Make no mistake, money matters. But numerous other factors affect how happy and productive you will be working as a technology consultant, such as

- How secure you feel in your position

- How much autonomy you have

- How much you are treated more like a professional and less like a glorified typist
- How well the culture of the firm matches your own personality fit

These factors, among numerous others, affect how satisfied you will be working in technology consulting. Your satisfaction is especially important because of the nature of the consulting business; that is, often you will be called upon to enter situations working for clients who are, on occasion, highly dysfunctional, politically charged, and otherwise unpleasant. If you are going to go through all that, you want to at least be able to count on a culture "back at the mothership" that makes you comfortable dealing with the occasional difficult client. Put another way, if you are going to do hard work in difficult terrain, you want to do so with a strong sense of purpose that carries you through.

Sadly, not every company is going to be that kind of company. In fact, a good number of firms will lie, cheat, and swindle you into employment situations that are highly beneficial to them and only of marginal benefit, if not outright harmful, to you. Some employers will tell you, with a straight face, that business is great the same day they miss payroll. Others will lie by omission when they fail to inform you that all consultants are expected to log extra unbillable hours on a routine basis—and make it part of their business plan. This chapter provides you with a way to recognize and understand these situations so you can avoid those that will make your life miserable.

≋

Brief Descriptions of the Seven Deadly Firms

Indeed, life would be much easier if these firms went by the names we suggest in this chapter. Unfortunately, most firms say a lot of the same things: They have great intellectual capital, the benefits plan is great, they have a process that makes them unique, and all their people are valued. In the realm of technology consulting, as in life in general, you have to look past what people say and more at what they *do*.

Table 2-1 categorizes dysfunctional firms based on how they go about treating consultants, securing customers, or the combination of the two.

TABLE 2-1

Dysfunctions of the Seven Deadly Firms

Firm	Dysfunction
BOZO Consulting	Sales-driven culture that lacks the ability to leverage any sort of delivery capability it accidentally hires.
FEAR Consulting	Firm founded on its ability to motivate software developers by fear. Micromanagement, abuse, and/or Machiavellian management techniques are the tools this firm uses to generate mundane and uninspired results for clients.
The Body Shop	Contracting firm that pretends to be a consultancy. Sadly, not all the consultants involved have been informed of this "minor" detail.
CHEAP Consulting	Some firms compete on quality. CHEAP consulting isn't one of those firms. This is a great place to work as long as eating and having a roof over your head are not huge priorities for you.
Personality Cult Consulting	The only drink that this firm has in the company refrigerator is kool-aide. And if you refuse to drink it—that is, decide not to indulge in the cult of local hero worship— you might not have a future here. Critical thinking skills are not the highest priority.
Smelzer and Melzer Accounting	Even the owners of this place, an accounting partnership, wonder how they ended up in the "computers" business. They know they make money from it but are unsure why, and frankly, they are not sure they trust these "kids" who have a lot of scary ideas.
"Push the SKU" Consulting	"Services" arm of a product company that ends up acting as a de facto sales force for the product, while at the same time, getting paid by the hour from the client to sell…ahem, I mean…"provide independent advice."

Note that not all firms are going to fall neatly into one bucket or another. Some are a combination of some of these (that is, companies that operate a fear-based culture and also happen to harbor personality cults), whereas others resemble one of these but perhaps not completely share each characteristic. This chapter details how each of these firms works, what life is like for consultants there, the prognosis for the survival of the firm, and most important, how to know if you are interviewing at such a place so that you can know whether the risks to your mental health are worth taking a paycheck from such a place. Of course, you still may decide to work there, knowing the risks, but you can't say that you weren't warned!

> **Michael Hugos** In my experience most consulting firms fall into one or more of these categories, and over time firms often drift from one category to another. This isn't good or bad; it just means you need to know which categories your firm falls into and make appropriate decisions based on that knowledge. For instance, don't argue with the sales people at BOZO Consulting and don't try to build a career at FEAR Consulting. On the other hand, if you agree with and admire the local hero at Personality Cult Consulting, it might be a great place to work for a while.

BOZO Consulting

If there is a firm that exists in spite of itself, you would point to BOZO Consulting. Let's be clear: BOZO is a place with well-intentioned people who really want to please their clients. The only downside to BOZO is it doesn't have the slightest clue about how to achieve that goal. BOZO was founded by a single charismatic individual with some innate sales skills. The CEO of BOZO then got together with a couple of his golf buddies and decided to move from a one-person operation employing a couple of programmers on a small project to something larger and grander.

The story of BOZO starts with an initial project that, because of various circumstances, happens to work out. Unfortunately, like the person who hits the jackpot on the first trip to the casino and somehow attributes the success to skill rather than luck, the organization is forever bound to think that its success is due to its own cleverness and not the circumstances around the initial success.

And what does BOZO think made it successful? Well, it says yes to everything—no matter how ridiculous or unrealistic, as in, "Yes, of course. We will cut the estimate.""Yes, of course, we will lower our bill rate.""Yes, of course, our people have an average of 15 years of experience in Ruby on Rails. In 2004." In other words, saying yes is all about getting the deal, no matter what you have to agree to in order to get it.

A cornerstone of sustainable success in technology consulting is to have both a great sales organization to help generate demand for software development services and a great delivery organization to fulfill that demand. BOZO, at best, has only half of the equation. The error of BOZO is that it generates demand for products that usually don't exist, such as

- Software developers with years of experience in technologies that are not yet in general release

- The ability for a team to replicate the entire functionality of a complex product that cost a large software company tens of millions of dollars to develop—in six months

- Software that does something mathematically unfeasible, such as break 128-bit encryption in less than 20 milliseconds

The problem is not that the sales staff of BOZO are snake oil salesmen on purpose, but the end effect is nearly the same. BOZO has sold something that, for various reasons, is impossible for you, as a consultant, to deliver.

Life at BOZO Consulting

Life at BOZO Consulting is certainly not boring. Sadly, what happens at BOZO is that the culture is all about the sales organization. The software developers and other professionals who must deliver what is being sold rarely have a say in anything, notably the estimation process. Remember, the favorite word at BOZO is *yes*. Not "Yes, but if you want us to build a competitor to YouTube that runs on a wristwatch, you might need to increase your budget," but simply "Yes." You, the diligent professional software developer, are then responsible for delivery to always-escalating expectations.

So fine, you say; you will just work extra hard to meet those expectations. Well, in the first project BOZO ever won, that is exactly what everyone did.

That is, at the end, the expectations were only somewhat beyond what was reasonably possible in the allotted time frame—say, 20 percent. Thus, by requiring work on Saturdays and/or late into the night, the team was able to please the client. The CEO of BOZO discovered that because he was paying people salaries, he could just make people work more to meet expectations. He would call it "an expectation to go the extra mile" and make it part of the corporate mantra. This was all well and good for the first couple of projects, and because the economy was bad, people didn't complain.

Now, fast-forward a year or two. Two things happened. First, over time, the CEO hired people with slightly less sales skill. Those with less sales skill did not sell as many projects, but when they did, they didn't do so with a 20 percent gap between reasonable expectations and promised expectations, but more like a 40 percent gap. Whereas a company may be able to overcome a 20 percent gap with extra hard work for a short period of time, a 40 percent gap is on the verge of hopelessly overpromised.

The second thing that happened was that the economy got better. Suddenly, the really good developers, that is, the ones who could stretch to cover a promise 20 percent over what is realistic, got tired of constantly working overtime in exchange for nothing and found greener pastures. Over time, whatever talent base that BOZO started with turned over, and what remained were mediocre people who, no matter how many extra hours they worked, would never meet the expectations. This led to firings (when things got bad), more turnover, and a general downward spiral.

The result is a company with little culture (because of the turnover) and little success (because of the unrealistic expectations). Such companies tend to have a great deal of turnover in their client base as well because naturally, companies that are overpromised and underdelivered tend to seek better firms. This lack of a culture in everything but the sales organization leads to a firm that acts in a transactional manner, meaning other than your exchanging your time for our money, we have zero interest in you.

Signs You Are Interviewing at BOZO Consulting

One of the first clues you are interviewing at BOZO, especially a "late stage" BOZO, is that the job ads it puts up become very specific and unrealistic, similar to the projects it sells. When you go to the company's Web site, generally speaking, you are not able to determine the names of any of its consultants—for a couple of reasons. One, BOZO fears to death (because of its turnover) that a competitor will steal away one of its people and that showing the name of a consultant will lead to that consultant's being lured away by a competitor. Two, and more fundamental, turnover is so high, few consultants are around long enough to justify the expense of setting up a blog or profile page. For the same reason that fast-food employees below the managerial level usually have nametags where the name is replaceable using a label maker, the consultants are not deemed important enough to have a presence in any of the marketing material.

Beyond the surface level though, BOZO is easily identifiable by its level of client and employee turnover. If you're thinking of working for BOZO, it is a good idea to ask about both employee turnover and client turnover in your in-person interview, *not* the phone interview. The reason is that you not only want to know how the prospective company answers the question, but also see the interviewer's body language while answering the question, especially the client turnover one because most people forget to ask that. You should watch for the common signs for determining whether someone is lying (such as shifting the eyes when answering, fidgeting, and so forth).

That said, you may not even need that much. One of the most significant accomplishments of BOZO is always its large client list. A typical mark of a BOZO Consultancy is a large set of clients, say 30 or 40, of which only 4 or 5 are current clients, especially if the company is only seven years old. In fact, I use a measurement I like to call "The Bozo Index" to determine the BOZOness of a consultancy:

BozoIndex = HistoricalClients / CurrentClients / YearsSinceFoundingOfCompany

For example, an eight-year-old technology consultancy that has 10 current clients out of 15 it has had over its entire history will have a BOZO Index of

15 / 10 / 8 = 0.1875

On the other hand, a typical BOZO consultancy that has 3 current clients and 25 total over its entire history of 3 years:

25 / 3 / 3 = 2.7777

The higher the number, the more likely it is that you are dealing with a BOZO. Because most BOZO consultancies are proud of their accomplishments, at least with total clients over time, they usually volunteer this information in the interview process. Asking the number of current clients is usually considered an innocuous question as well, as is number of years since the company was founded.

Prognosis

Most BOZO consultancies rarely ever grow beyond the skill of the initial founder's sales capabilities. Occasionally, a firm like this will land a large project and may even get to around 60 billing consultants, but that growth will be followed by a contraction just as swift after the big project's expectations fail to be met. Sometimes, in a larger firm, a BOZO branch office can survive for a short while, but even then, such a condition can last only for as long as the parent organization funds the money-losing ways of the wayward branch.

In either case, BOZOs tend to self-destruct, by either going bankrupt or, in the best case, being bought out by an unsuspecting buyer who is typically the last victim of a sales job of the original founder. And even in the buyout case, you end up working for the kind of company that can't grow by more traditional means, the kind of firm I like to call FEAR Consulting.

⮑

FEAR Consulting

Whereas BOZO may be a place that can be described as bumbling, well intentioned, but nevertheless ineffective, FEAR Consulting is a much darker place. It is the Gulag of software development shops. Although some technology consulting firms engage in a management style that is about empowerment of the consulting staff, retention, and at least try to appear as though working there is a reasonably pleasant experience, it is safe to say that the management of FEAR thinks all those kinds of practices are a sign of weakness that only results in "uppity consultants asking for more money." If Machiavelli were going to start a consultancy, he would have started FEAR.

Companies like FEAR Consulting usually don't start out that way. A company can start out as a great place to work, but as the result of a crisis—be that crisis external (such as the 2000–03 tech bubble bursting) or internal (loss of a couple substantial projects)—that company can devolve into FEAR Consulting.

The typical catalyst for this devolution, after the initial "glory years" period, is the hiring of a high-level executive savior who, while adept at looking the part and showing confidence as an executive, has a manner with the service delivery part of the organization that is nothing short of abusive. Such a person works his or her way into an organization by either bringing on a few initial clients and thereby increasing internal credibility or, more commonly, uses the Machiavellian tactics to generate some good short-term results.

Of course, the key term here is *short-term*. Management by Fear, as I like to call it, can indeed generate great short-term results. Especially in a slowing economy where there are few outside options for employment, fear is a powerful motivator because it kicks in the biological "fight or flight" response.

Life at FEAR Consulting

Imagine a world where

- "Bathroom time" must be reported on your time report.

- Cell phones are not allowed on the premises; you are here to work, not talk on your cell phone.

- No outside Internet is allowed at all; if you need to look up something, do it on your own time at home.

- "Flexible hours" means "choose the 20 hours you want to work each day."

- Anyone who bills less than 2,400 hours in a year is considered not pulling his or her weight and is a candidate for termination.

These are all true stories from various people I have met in the world of technology consulting. You probably wonder why anyone would tolerate such bad working conditions, especially given the costs in mental health, marital problems, and general self-respect that working in such conditions can bring forth.

> **Chris Williams** Sadly, I worked for these guys once upon a time. They embodied the worst aspects of most of your seven deadly consultancies, but fear and intimidation were their way of life. I watched a seemingly sweet PM go positively rabid over timesheet discrepancies and saw her practically disembowel a consultant who was late on task completion.

Stockholm Syndrome

The best way to describe how FEAR stays in business despite such deplorable working conditions is to reference what is known as the *Stockholm Syndrome*. This affliction occurs when the captives of a kidnapping become loyal to their captors. The trick that abusive managers employ in this situation is to make sure that the people who work for them have the lowest possible self-esteem. This can be done several ways, such as publically embarrassing the subjects, making sure the subjects know that they are valuable only because of the abusers' own goodwill, and making sure to tell the subjects that they have zero value outside this particular organization (that is, without them, you will be begging for change at the nearest freeway intersection). As a rule, such people refer to their employees as *resources*, to underscore how replaceable they are (see Appendix B, "A Consulting Lexicon," for further definition of the term *resources*).

Amazingly, this situation can be true in good times as well as bad. In fact, in many FEAR shops, the level of captivity is such that the people who work there are so broken down by the systems in place that they think they are worthless to other better consultancies. And although some do escape, the politics of FEAR work such that those who do are considered traitors to the cause, often escorted out by security guards on the day they tender their resignation so that everyone else can see what happens to people who dare try for something better. In fact, even the suspicion that you are looking outside the camp will often result in your receiving consequences, such as higher levels of micromanagement, more verbal berating ("How dare you consider leaving us after all we've done for you?"), and even higher levels of social ostracism within the walls of FEAR.

Other Working Conditions

You would think that at FEAR Consulting consultants would get together and band against this kind of thing happening to them. Sadly, that does not tend to happen either. The reasons for this are twofold. First, there is no cohesive culture because nobody is allowed to do anything that does not involve sitting at a desk and typing. Second, much like in Soviet Russia, the level of fear at FEAR Consulting is so high that people don't talk about the problems of the organization, lest they be terminated, which, as previously covered, is the worst possible fate.

> **Chris Williams**   I've witnessed this firsthand. One company I worked at regularly read through employee emails, and anyone who complained about working conditions was brought into HR and given the "we know you're not happy" talk and then threatened with firing. More than one of my coworkers narrowly avoided termination by promising he or she was just "blowing off steam" just to buy time to look for a new job.

In such organizations, there are stories that, just like cigarettes are the currency of prisoners in a death camp, the right to bill a billable hour to one client or another is treated like currency. For example, friends have told me that if you wanted a favor—say, someone to spend 15 minutes with you to understand some legacy code received from a client—you would have to offer some multiple of that time, perhaps as much as two chargeable hours for that person to help you. Not only was this behavior encouraged, it was *policy*, designed to limit interaction between individual "resources" such that any sense of cooperation even with teams was discouraged.

How FEAR Consulting Sustains Business

You can be thankful that, despite what might seem like an evil yet effective technique for controlling people, FEAR typically does not scale. Such firms tend to run on low margin, competing on the basis of price against other companies like CHEAP consulting (see the following section). These other companies will meet FEAR on price, yet at least get more out of the underpaid and inspired than you get from the fearful and cowering. Typically, FEAR does work for like-minded clients who want a firm that will give them very controlled, mediocre work, such as straight porting of an application from one framework to another, without any real creative thought involved.

Although a certain amount of this work is still available in the United States and other first-world countries, economics dictates that much of this work that is of any substantial size will be done in places like India and China or other places where the work, which is not client-facing and does not require a lot of interaction, can be done for lower cost. The work that remains is limited to cases in which a savvy salesperson working for FEAR can sell to an audience where cost is less important than control. Again, you can be thankful that this is a limited market.

> **Jason Bock**   In my experience, FEAR Consulting firms are usually rare. It's the clients that have the FEAR factor as *the* driving force of their culture. Consulting firms have employees who thrive on technical challenges without a lot of boundaries. Truth be told, a fair number of the people I know that joined consulting companies did it because they were fleeing FEAR-based companies!

Signs You Are Interviewing at FEAR Consulting

You would never work at such a place as FEAR Consulting, right? And truth be told, nobody in his or her right mind would ever work for FEAR Consulting if that person knew what he or she was getting into. That is, of course, when the alternative is not working at all, which is precisely when times are best for FEAR; this is when it is at its most effective. For then is the only time when something beyond only the most desperate people will consider working for such a company. That said, even in the worst conditions, when you consider the long-term career damage, costs to your mental health, and general cost of being *unhappy*, there is really no amount of money that should make you want to work for a place like this.

Thus, to filter out companies like this, make sure you *never* accept a position without having a chance to see the workplace. One of the biggest reasons this advice is true is that a place like FEAR has a certain look to it. Because the only way to control the employees of FEAR is to have them work in a development facility, you will walk in and see a very drab workplace. The developers will work not just in cubicles, but tiny cubicles that offer no storage space, no place for personalization, but only a meager, tiny desk with a keyboard and the most inexpensive office chairs that you could possibly buy.

What is difficult about FEAR Consulting is that when people interview there, the only people you will meet are the owners and possibly others (often sales, but managers as well) who benefit from this situation. It is in their interests to put forward a face of the firm that hides to the degree possible the level of depravity the office runs under. One trick to get around this is to leverage your personal network to find one or more people who work there in a non-management capacity and see what they think. Whereas one person may just have an axe to grind with even a good company, getting, say, three out of four who paint a picture of the company as something that looks like FEAR is probably a good way to know you should be very careful about going there.

Other possible though not definitive indicators are

+ Very aggressive annual billable hour targets (1800 or higher)
+ Bench policies that reduce your salary while on the bench

- Strong embrace of Waterfall software development methodology, with a strong aversion to Agile or other methodologies that emphasize people over process

- Few, if any, current members of the company are ever seen at software development community events

Prognosis

The ability of FEAR Consulting to survive is countercyclical; that is, when the economy is bad, these shops can thrive for the same reasons that sweatshops survive in places where there are no better alternatives. They typically do not become firms with a global presence. The reason is that at certain sizes of a professional services company, one person can't control all aspects of the company, and thus, the ability to have a reign of fear breaks down. Sometimes FEAR grows by acquisition (that is, "if we can't hire them, we can buy them"), but such gains are short-lived because most people who come from somewhere else won't tolerate the conditions at FEAR and go away within the first year.

The Body Shop

For the same reason that when a restaurant wants to charge higher prices, it changes the name of its "food" to "cuisine," the Body Shop is a contracting firm posing as a consulting firm. Body Shops are perfectly reasonable places to work if you know exactly what you are getting into and understand the terms of the transaction. But working there isn't consulting; it is short- to medium-term contracting. Hence, if your desire is to be a consultant, this isn't the firm you should be working for. Unfortunately, a number of these shops thrive on hiding the terms of the transaction and preying on unwary consulting professionals who have not had the benefit of reading this book.

The economics of a Body Shop are not difficult to understand at all. They are vastly simpler than what Chapter 1, "Why Consulting?," describes. A Body Shop takes orders from clients who need a short- to medium-term software developer, searches through a pool of resumes of people—some of whom they know, but most of whom they don't—and submits resumes to the company. Often, a dozen or more Body Shops try to fill a single short-term need in a company. A hit occurs when the Body Shop submits a resume that the buying company likes. At this point, the Body Shop can charge a relatively low hourly rate (say, $60 per hour), take $10 off the top, and offer

- $50 per hour for a short-term project (if it is ethical)
- A salary of "$100,000 per year" and pretend it is a consulting company that will place you in your next gig after this first project is done but then "fire" you because it has no work for you at the end of the project

The first case is entirely reasonable; the organization is acting as an agent, finding the work, and you are doing the work, which the agent accurately describes. The second case is really the anti-pattern because it misrepresents the risk that you are taking on by accepting the position. The second case is what lures someone from a relatively secure $80,000 per year job to a more exciting "$100,000 per year" job that has a hidden surprise for the new "consultant."

> **Chris Williams**   Wow. Been there, done that. I got lucky because my 6-month gig ended up lasting 18 months. When it ended though, they didn't have anything for me, nor did they even really look. I got sent on a couple of interviews that I was completely unqualified for (at the time) and was eventually let go altogether after a short time on the bench. Quite the eye-opener.

Life at a Body Shop

At first, life at a Body Shop isn't that bad, depending on the client with whom you have been placed. Because the Body Shop isn't really a consultancy at all, the culture you experience will be that of the company where you are placed, which is as variable as there are companies. One thing you will notice, and quickly, is that the Body Shop itself has zero corporate culture. No corporate events, no infrastructure, and no interaction with fellow "consultants."

Contractors and Consultants

In fact, to call a Body Shop a consulting company is really somewhat of an embarrassment. The reality is that it is a contracting company. One way to think of the difference is that in contracting, you are strictly exchanging time for money, whereas in consulting, you are exchanging ideas for money. The act of contracting is highly focused on rate per hour and set of skills brought to the table. No other factors matter in the context of contracting, such as the intellectual property the firm as a whole brings to the table or the broader capabilities to staff a team of professionals and provide leadership to a project.

Consulting, on the other hand, not only sells individuals the time for money, but sells a whole host of technical capabilities, intellectual property, and leadership to achieve an outcome that simply hiring individuals to do a specific task will not be able to achieve. Because consulting delivers a lot more value, if hourly rates are involved at all, they tend to be higher to reflect the value that the consulting package brings to the table.

Contracting firms, in an attempt to get higher rates, frequently either misrepresent themselves as consulting organizations or simply have aspirations to become consultancies, which causes them to overstate their market position. This, of course, leads to a great deal of marketplace confusion, which is a factor that the bad version of the Body Shop tries to use to its advantage.

The Day Your Gig Ends

For the person who takes a "salaried" position at a contracting firm like Body Shop, there are a couple main versions of what happens when you "hit the bench." In the best case, your salary continues up to about a month, while the shop furiously moves your resume around town in an attempt to place you somewhere else. Sadly, this is what the more charitable ones do—particularly if you have a skill set that they think they can easily place. The less scrupulous ones, on the other hand, change the story in the two to three weeks leading up to your end date, and inform you that "times are bad" and that they can no longer afford a "bench."

While this outcome is not a shock to the person who came into the contracting firm knowing what to expect, for the person who thinks he or she is going into a salaried position, this is a shock indeed. Nothing is worse in a job market than not negotiating from a position of strength, that is, being able to walk away from a job that is offered because you have a current position. In fact, it is often the case that a person ends up at a worse company, such as FEAR or BOZO, because he or she was snookered into working at a Body Shop that failed to tell him or her that, in all likelihood, the gig was of limited duration.

Signs You Are Interviewing at a Body Shop

Knowing whether you are interviewing at a Body Shop is actually pretty simple. Most of the time, your real interview will not be with someone at the shop itself, but at the company it is contracting with. Thus, what occurs is that the interview sequence is something like this:

- Interview 1: The Checklist
  - Check that you have a pulse
  - Make sure you have reasonable interviewing skills
  - Make sure you can spell the name of the technology that you are working on (that is, make sure you can spell *VB*)
- Interview 2: The Real Client Interview
  - Actually check your technical skill
  - Make sure you will work well with the team
  - Do other typical stuff more common for first interviews

The bottom line is that Body Shops are easy to spot because they never hire anyone that they don't already have placed somewhere. If your getting an offer depends on passing an interview with a client, there is a strong chance you are dealing with a Body Shop.

Prognosis

Body Shops have a place in the market. In fact, many successful businesses of substantial size are Body Shops. Most of the large ones are open and honest about the temporary nature of the work. It is likely that these kinds of companies will be around for a very long time because they fill a niche at the lower end of the market.

The more dishonest ones—the ones that claim you are going in for a salaried gig when, in fact, you are contracting—tend to be the results of late-stage versions of BOZO Consulting and thus are on a downward trajectory anyway.

CHEAP Consulting

Whereas a Body Shop tends to operate in the world of low-cost *contracting*, CHEAP Consulting firms execute entire projects using hordes of low-cost developers, rather than small numbers of good ones. Ironically, this makes their projects, after all is said and done, come in far more over budget than the firms they competed with in the first place.

CHEAP Consulting takes advantage of the tendency of some organizations to buy services based on rate-per-hour, to the exclusion of all other considerations. This frequently occurs when the agent purchasing professional services is separated from the person who is responsible for the outcome of the professional services. In such a case, the former, often called a *vendor manager*, is compensated on getting average hourly rates low and does not have a meaningful stake in project outcome. The latter, often a development manager, is left with the results and often lives a very frustrating existence trying to get useful software built using the lowest bidder per hour.

This scenario occurs because there is a mindset in some quarters that a developer-hour is a universal unit of exchange in software development. Of course, history shows us that the output of one developer-hour of a person with a particular skill set can vary drastically from person to person (Brooks 1975, Curtis 1981, Mills 1983, DeMarco and Lister 1985, Curtis et al. 1986, Card 1987, Boehm and Papaccio 1988, Valett and McGarry 1989, Boehm et al 2000). However, despite all this overwhelming evidence to the contrary, some organizations continue to be blind to this reality, likely as a result of the influence of a long tradition of thought in industrial engineering—starting with the work of Frederick Taylor—that seeks to minimize variation in personnel performance.

Life at CHEAP Consulting

The main feature of CHEAP is the heavy use of the word *resource*. More than in any of the seven deadly firms, the fact that you are one resource of many, pluggable from one project to another, is the chief feature of CHEAP Consulting. That said, life at CHEAP isn't bad, per se; it isn't FEAR, where the goal is to keep you there by sheer intimidation. Nor is this BOZO, where the projects that are sold usually end up being done for a loss. If anything, CHEAP Consulting is a place where you do mediocre projects for mediocre money for mediocre companies.

The problem for consultants at CHEAP is that the work is of low value, requires comparatively low skill, and frequently features technology several generations behind what would be considered current. Conformity is a core part of the culture at CHEAP. Because of this culture, the primary attributes that cause growth of a software developer—chiefly using the creative urge to overcome technology problems—tend to be selected against.

This, of course, is just fine if your main goal in life is to simply collect a paycheck and put in your time. And for people for whom software development is merely a means to an end, working for CHEAP is a perfectly acceptable solution. At least for a while.

The problem, however, is that if you become a commodity, you become very easy to outsource. The kind of work done by CHEAP Consulting can also be done very easily anywhere in the world. Thus, the main problem with CHEAP Consulting is that it becomes CHEAPER Consulting over time. Thus, over time, your ability to make a consistent living becomes more and more difficult, and you are constantly prone to job loss.

This brings you to the next feature of working at CHEAP Consulting: constant fear of being outsourced. Because you know you are a commodity (unless you are blissfully ignorant of what is going on around you), you likely lose a lot of sleep that your consulting gig will be shipped to India, or nowadays, somewhere even less expensive than that, such as The Philippines or Vietnam.

Last, the salaries at CHEAP Consulting represent where this firm sits in the marketplace. Because CHEAP competes on price, it is highly likely you will be in the bottom 25th percentile of wages for your given skill set. Furthermore, advancement is going to be slow, and because you are working on technology several generations behind what is current, your ability to market yourself is going to be limited to other similarly situated companies. It becomes something of a downward career spiral that can be tough to recover from.

Signs You Are Interviewing at CHEAP Consulting

If job ads in consulting came with salary figures attached to them, knowing who CHEAP is would be real easy. Unfortunately, rarely is this the case. As a result, you have to look for the signs that point to what will ultimately be a low job offer.

To get an initial sign you might be at CHEAP Consulting, first ask the prospective firm how it gets business. CHEAP Consulting tends to get business through what are known as *vendor management programs*. Not all vendor management programs are bad or dysfunctional, but many are, and seeing a prospective firm primarily working through said entities is usually a sign that such a firm primarily competes on price.

A second sign is to ask what technology you will be working with. Of course, asking this question can be difficult because the technology stated in the job ad can describe what the firm wants you to know, which frequently has nothing to do with what it wants you to do. The actual work you will be doing may end up being on technology several versions behind what is current, which is a good indicator you are working for this kind of firm. The question to ask, then, is "What kind of technology will I be working with on day one?" The manner in which this question is answered should tell you a lot about this firm.

Prognosis

I would like to think this kind of firm is likely to fail over time. But cynically, I suspect that there will always be people who believe that people are "plug compatible" and, thus, will have services purchased at the lowest possible price. Especially because there is always going to be a sector of this business doing work with only marginal economic value (higher than zero, but not by much), there will always be a place for this kind of firm. Given that some of the largest firms out there are like this, the economics are going to dictate that they will stick around.

That said, while such firms may be good stock investments, they are lousy places for creative-minded technology professionals to work. Although marginally better than the more dysfunctional cousins, BOZO and FEAR, CHEAP Consulting is, nonetheless, not somewhere that most people will ever go to work on purpose.

> **Chris Williams**   Being Devil's advocate here, Cheap Consulting is certainly not the sort of place that someone would want to go mid-career or later, but could be a decent "foot in the door" experience for young technologists looking to get a start in the industry.

⤳
Personality Cult Consulting

The firms profiled so far primarily have dysfunctions of the ethical or human decency variety. Personality Cult Consulting (a.k.a. PC Consulting) has different problems more due to a certain level of success of its initial founder. Frequently, a person who combines charisma with a good measure of talent finds himself or herself able to start a consulting company that capitalizes on these traits. What first starts out as a small group of like-minded people with a mission grows into a creature called PC Consulting.

The chief problem of PC Consulting is a distinct lack of critical thinking among its rank and file and fear and loathing of those who do. This, of course, causes later waves of creative people who might enter such a firm to experience short and brutal careers there. What the particular leader of PC is promoting as part of the firm is less important than the fact that at PC, there is no substantial debate about how to move the business forward. Discussions in such a place are rife with appeals to authority; that is, if the cult leader says something, it not only is given a lot of weight, but is treated as gospel, unchallenged even when evidence exists that might be to the contrary of what the leader is claiming.

Life at PC Consulting

How life feels at PC depends on whether you are a member of the cult or someone who happens to have critical thinking skills that ends up there. Given that many software developers tend to have highly developed critical thinking skills, this tends to lead to problems. That said, for those who get caught up into the hero worship aspects of life here and just go along with it, life will probably be pretty great, at least for a while. Being around like-minded people feels wonderful in the short term. However, not being challenged—truly challenged—intellectually leads to atrophy of exactly the same thinking capabilities that make you a good software developer. A software developer who does not regularly exercise critical thinking skills is less likely to have the acuity to look at a code base as critically as he or she could. This brings us to the chief problem of working at PC: intellectual stagnation.

What happens at PC if you are one of the true believers is that, over time, your network becomes isolated to people who think like you do, which is dangerous if the particular school of thought that PC espouses goes out of favor. Also, because true believers tend not to read or keep up with developments that are contrary to the vision of the leader, they stop growing intellectually.

For the person who does not fall in line, however, life is often much worse. People with critical thinking skills can suspend disbelief only so long without losing their minds. When you realize you are in a company like this, assuming you don't bolt for the door on your second day in the office, you start to think you might be able to change the organization. This path is alluring because it allows you to be the hero that saves the firm from itself. This idea—changing the nature of a firm that has started down the path of hero worship—is almost certainly doomed to failure. Although you might get one or two people or even a few dozen to change their minds and see things your way, you are up against a figure in your company who has most of the client relationships or controls those who do. Like the Greek tragic hero Sisyphus, you continue to try to push the boulder up the hill, no end in sight, as the effort to change one person's mind is greater than the effort that the organization will have on the masses you might have already converted.

> **Chris Williams**   Having witnessed this Greek tragedy firsthand, I compare it to Prometheus bringing fire (enlightenment) to the mortals (other developers in the company) only to be caught by Zeus (the owner) and punished for all eternity by being chained to a rock and having his guts ripped out and eaten by birds, only to regenerate and be devoured anew each day (made an example of). In this particular case, people who tried to "bring fire" were summarily dismissed, and then their "crimes" were detailed in a companywide email, branding them traitors or heretics.

In other words, the problem is not unlike trying to boil the ocean; that is, even if you experience some local success, the greater body of water will likely overwhelm you and shut down your valiant attempts at change. This eventually takes a serious toll on your mental health, and usually within a year, you get up and leave in frustration.

Regardless of whether you decide to try to change the organization or simply tolerate it, PC Consulting is a miserable place to work. It typically is one of those places that look great on paper and might even look good on a resume, but working there costs your own mental health far in excess of the benefits of working there.

Signs You Are Interviewing at PC Consulting

Companies like PC Consulting often name themselves after their founder. But even if this isn't the case, the people with the most power in such an organization tend to be close friends and family. The About Us page on the company's Web site will reveal a few too many people who have the same surname.

But beyond this, when you read the company materials, much like a religious cult, they all speak to the vision of a single individual. Pictures of the founder are everywhere, yet finding out about anyone else who works there, save perhaps the executive team, is impossible. To an outsider, the in-person interview will give a feeling that loyalty to the founder is one of the most important values.

While it is true that when evaluating any company you should go out of your way to speak with current and former employees, if you suspect you are interviewing at PC Consulting, this is doubly true. Most former employees of PC Consulting will be more than willing to share the war stories that working at such a place will give you.

> **Jason Bock** I once worked at a small company (no more than 30 employees) where I was told by the founder the first week I was there that there was a "circle of trust" that existed within the "higher-ups" at the company. He literally made the "circle of trust" motion with his hands. While it wasn't a true "PC" firm as Aaron describes it, it was pretty close, and within a couple of months my level of misery was skyrocketing.

Prognosis

Companies such as this have limitations on how large they can grow. In my experience, I have rarely seen PC Consulting type companies growing to larger than, say, a couple hundred people. Larger than this and it becomes harder to control the masses and enforce cult orthodoxy. The best hope in such a situation is that the company gets sold to a larger, more competent consulting organization, and the initial founder leaves. Sadly, for many who are the true believers, getting bought is the worst thing that can happen to them because they suddenly go from a world that was easy to understand to one that requires critical thinking again.

〰

Smelzer and Melzer Accounting

In many firms technology consulting occurs almost entirely by accident. These firms, typically accounting firms, happen to have a set of partners who have a number of relationships that are conducive to doing work with computers. Thus, this is the genesis of the technology consultancy embedded within an accounting firm that we are calling Smelzer and Melzer Accounting, a.k.a. S&M Accounting.

Not every company in this situation is a bad company to do work for. These companies can be structured in many ways, some of which allow them to take advantage of the C-level relationships that accounting firms have, while retaining the capabilities a technology consulting firm needs. That said, in many cases this firm is dysfunctional.

Accountants are nothing if not generally savvy with money (probably why they went into accounting!). Accounting and audit work tends to be standardized under Generally Accepted Accounting Principles and, as a result, such businesses tend to have profit margins around 5–8 percent. On the other hand, a well-run technology consulting firm can have much higher margins, closer to the 12–20 percent range. Although the revenue from accounting activity is more regular—public companies need to be audited at every quarterly report and have constant and mostly predictable activity—those same companies tend to have more volatile technology spending. Having different kinds of work (some with more revenue volatility, some with less) makes for a good balance of revenues that give these kinds of companies a further advantage in the marketplace.

So what's the problem? Well, in most cases, accounting firms are run by accountants. And accountants frequently have significant issues with the way software tends to be developed. Software development, even in methodologies that pretend to plan everything up front, is frequently a nondeterministic process that makes even the best-laid plans not terribly useful. Over time, unless expectations about how a software development project can go are very carefully managed by the person who owns the top-level relationship (typically an accountant), it is going to end up looking bad when the content and budget of the project change significantly, as happens over 50 percent of the time.

Needless to say, these are conditions under which adversarial relations can develop between the consulting and accounting organizations.

Life at S&M Accounting

When adversarial conditions occur between the accounting and technology organizations, life becomes about doing everything it takes to please the partners. The result is a lesser, more distributed version of PC Consulting, insomuch as "Pleasing the Audit Partner" is the main goal of all interactions that the technology consultants have with the client. Software development methodology is chosen, in such cases, based on what is perceived as predictable (even when it's not), and developers often become the scapegoats when the expectations of predictability fail to materialize.

Needless to say, this is frequently not the kind of place software developers are likely to get the benefit of the doubt. Because the technology consulting organization often is newer, less powerful, and less connected, it is starved for resources and blamed when things go wrong. It is not the kind of place where you are likely to find cutting-edge technology because, again, the premium at this kind of company is predictability, not agility.

For you, as a software developer, the picture is mixed. On the upside, in the organization that has not yet established its own identity as a technology consultancy, this isn't a horrible place to build some relationships at some point in your career. But it is important to understand that rarely in a place like this will you advance very far because the reality is that the company you work for is, at its core, not a technology company at all. At some point, you will likely consider either joining a pure technology consulting firm or at least one of the firms that is tied to an accounting form (currently or historically) but has since formed its own identity.

Signs You Are Interviewing at S&M Accounting

In most cases, the tipoff that you are interviewing at S&M Accounting is that the name of the firm has two or three last names in it. If you go to the Web site, it lists a series of services, most prominently accounting, audit, business advisory, and tax, and to a lesser degree, technology. By the time you are interviewing, it becomes obvious that technology is a mere adjunct to the main action that occurs here.

If the technology consulting firm happens to be connected to an accounting firm, on the other hand, there is a good chance that the technology consultancy has grown to the degree needed such that it has its own identity and is not overly tied to the accounting side of the business. At this point, it becomes much more likely you are going to avoid the problems alluded to previously because at this stage, demonstrated by the name change, there is at least a chance that enough power has accumulated on the technology side of the organization to be able to effectively negotiate with the accountants.

The key to interviewing at one of these firms is to look at the size (large tends to be less risky) and the company culture. Determining the latter in the interview process is always tricky because, like with dating, everyone is on his or her best behavior in the first few meetings. You might ask some pointed questions, such as

- Who owns the client relationship? (Technology projects should be owned by the technology organization.)

- How are conflicts between business units handled? (There should be a collaborative process, and the answer should be convincing and not defensive.)

- How is business generated? (It should not be 100 percent dependent on the accounting side.)

One key to determine whether such an organization supports technologists—and not a bad way to vet any potential firm—is to see whether that firm employs any prominent consultants who have a reputation at an industry level.

Most such people will rarely stand working in a place where the mantra is "When things go wrong, blame the technology people." Although not 100 percent dispositive, it is a good sign you are considering joining one of the more reasonable varieties of this type of firm.

Prognosis

A quick scan of the market finds a lot of these types of S&M organizations. Early stage versions of these organizations do not have to be bad places to work, in the event that both sides have implemented a strong company culture that places a high value on collaboration and emotional intelligence. Such organizations can be great places to launch a career and have the best chances of becoming large versions of these organizations. The largest of these organizations are well-run public companies that, in some cases, have long thrown off the chains of their former accounting masters, such as Accenture.

Push the SKU Consulting

Like S&M, SKU Consulting is a firm that, although it does consulting, often has an agenda that makes consulting a secondary concern at best. At Push the SKU, professional services exist primarily to help sell software licenses or some other product. Although such places can be fine places to work, make no mistake, the incentive system tends to make this not the place for development of software that works independent of a particular product.

That said, such a place is frequently not miserable per se. In fact, Push the SKU is a great place to get experience with software products in a manner that is almost impossible to attain outside the company.

Long-term, however, it can be risky—for many, unacceptably risky—to tie your career to a single software product or even software company. For example, there are legions of former consultants who worked for mainframe software companies and, while able to find work on some of these archaic systems, became overspecialized; they then faced either catching up on sometimes over

10 or 20 years of new technology and taking the attendant pay cut in the process or further living off the carcass of previous overspecialization.

Life at Push the SKU Consulting

Push the SKU comes in a number of forms. In many or even most of the smaller cases, the services arm of the software company serves as the implementation and customization arm, making it more obvious what the agenda of the organization is. As mentioned, life here is a good way to get some experience on a specific product. The more sinister version is the firm that pretends to be an independent consultancy but in fact is somehow incentivized to sell solutions of the parent software company.

Such an organization is not always a good place for software developers who have the interests of the client at heart first and foremost. Frequently, architectural decisions are informed not on what is best for the client, but rather what will push the most Stock Keeping Units (hence, SKU). Arguments between sales and delivery are legion at this kind of company, especially if and when the salesperson who owns the account is behind on his or her quota. The adversarial relationship that occurs between a technologist who is acting in the role of client advocate and the account executive who is selling SKU poisons the atmosphere of many projects. This does not make for a particularly enjoyable work experience and often breeds a certain early-onset cynicism in consultants who work for such an organization.

The best of these organizations make sure to put up something of a "Chinese Wall" between the account executives who work for the product division and the account executives who work for the services division. There is no reason a software company could not operate a successful technology consulting organization if the sales relationships from product and services can be cross-leveraged at the sales level. However, it is critical that delivery considerations are isolated from sales considerations in the opposite division; otherwise, the lack of independence results in unsatisfied clients, unsatisfied consultants, and frustrated account executives.

Jason Bock   SKU firms also have a quasi-PC feel to them as well. You're forced to sell their products (either through subversive or direct ways), and you really can't question this because the SKU company relies on the success of its product. In other words, it almost feels like a cult because you have to sell the SKU at all costs, which requires you to minimize critical thinking.

Signs You Are Interviewing at Push the SKU Consulting

Chances are, if you thought you were interviewing at a software company, and you suddenly find out that you are interviewing for a "consulting" job, you are interviewing at some version of Push the SKU. Because the consulting organization wants to take advantage of the software brand, it would almost be impossible to not know you are interviewing at this sort of organization.

That said, the bigger key is to determine what variety of Push the SKU you are interviewing at. The following questions need to have good answers when you are in the interview process:

+ Does this firm sell consulting services under the expectation that the consultants have independent judgment about product selection when designing solutions?

+ Does the sales staff have any incentive to challenge independent judgments of people on the delivery team?

+ What processes are in place to assure independence of delivery?

The quality of the answers to these questions should give you a fairly good sense about the level of independence under which the particular firm operates. Of course, nothing will stop a firm that operates independently in good times from changing in bad times when there is more pressure on product sales. If that is a concern, you should probably not work for a product company at all, regardless of how independent the consulting division of one claims it is. In practice, even in the best case, there is pressure to push product if for no other reason that when a company becomes part of your identity, it is not unusual to be biased toward your own products.

Prognosis

Consulting divisions of software companies will almost certainly always exist. There are too many cases in which a company, desperate to get specialist product knowledge, decides to source its services from the same company that produces the products it uses. In fact, the margins on this work tend to be a great deal higher than what an independent company charges because of the implicit assumption that the consultants on site have direct access to the product teams that built the product.

⌒

Summary

After reading this chapter, you might start to get cynical and wonder whether there are any places that are not run by swindlers, psychopaths, and jerks. The organizations described in this chapter, especially the more sinister versions of them, are a minority of the world of software consulting. Companies that do not engage in one or more of these modes of dysfunction tend to have competitive advantage mostly because they tend to have more engaged consultants, which in turn results in a better service climate and happier clients.

The majority of consultancies are reasonable places to work. Some are actually fantastic, winning "Best Places to Work" awards and having employees who, when you meet them, can't stop talking about how cool it is to work for their company. The most creative and inspired technical work gets done by people who are engaged, happy, valued, and secure enough to be able to feel as though they can be candid with their bosses when something isn't going right.

The following chapters explore how the better companies work and how you can get into the better companies, all while avoiding the bad ones covered in this chapter.

Works Cited

Brooks, F. (1975). The Mythical Man Month, Dept. of Computer Science, University of North Carolina at Chapel Hill.

Curtis, B. (1981). Substantiating programmer variability. Proceedings of the IEEE.

Mills, H.D (1983). *Software Productivity*. Little, Brown & Co., Boston.

DeMarco, Tom, and Timothy Lister. 1985. "Programmer Performance and the Effects of the Workplace." Proceedings of the 8th International Conference on Software Engineering. Washington, D.C.: IEEE Computer Society Press, 268–72.

Curtis, Bill, et al. 1986. "Software Psychology: The Need for an Interdisciplinary Program." Proceedings of the IEEE 74, no. 8: 1092–1106.

Card, David N. 1987. "A Software Technology Evaluation Program." *Information and Software Technology* 29, no. 6 (July/August): 291–300.

Boehm, Barry W., and Philip N. Papaccio. 1988. "Understanding and Controlling Software Costs." *IEEE Transactions on Software Engineering* SE-14, no. 10 (October): 1462–77.

Valett, J., and F. E. McGarry. 1989. "A Summary of Software Measurement Experiences in the Software Engineering Laboratory." *Journal of Systems and Software* 9, no. 2 (February): 137–48

Boehm, Barry, et al, 2000. *Software Cost Estimation with Cocomo II*, Boston, Mass.: Addison-Wesley, 2000.

CHAPTER THREE

How Technology Consulting Firms Work

The Universal Consulting Mission Statement: "We Convert IQ Points into Money."

Technology consulting is a business that is not all that complex. In fact, it could be said that the average software developer, who is used to dealing with complexity, would probably be surprised how simple the technology consulting business is.

Chapter 1, "Why Consulting?" covered the basics of why consulting firms exist, what the key metrics are, and why you should care about them. This chapter digs a little deeper so we can further understand how different people who work for a technology consulting firm contribute to the metrics described earlier.

Technology Consulting: Two Pipelines

A lot of businesses involve conversion of one kind of good into another kind of good that is in a more finished state. The basic premise is that the costs to acquire the raw good, plus the cost to process and sell that good, leave enough money left over to make a profit. If you are in the business of selling cars, you are likely spending a lot of time and money marketing and selling to consumers so that they will purchase your cars.

Technology consulting is a bit different: You are selling to two main constituencies. Of course, you have to sell to customers the idea that your technology consultants are able to help achieve the customers' goals for a given price. However, these goals are usually only barely defined and sometimes so vaguely defined that they defy even the best estimation efforts you could throw at them.

That is hard enough; there are few people who are skilled in selling custom technology solutions to clients, given how difficult and risky technology projects can be. Technology consulting organizations, however, have a second sales task that can be just as daunting, depending on the phase of the economic cycle. That task is selling scarce technology talent on the idea that a given technology consultancy is a good enough place to work that they should change from their current employer to a new one.

Explaining the Pipeline

In the management halls of almost all consultancies and, for that matter, any organization that sells anything these days, you are highly likely to hear the term *pipeline*. A pipeline is a way of visualizing the progress of potential opportunities to sell a project to a client or sell a career opportunity to a consultant. Figure 3-1 shows a typical sales pipeline.

For a consulting company to create the desired environment for a technology consultant—that is, cool, interesting work with competent colleagues—someone has to convince someone else who has money to spend that a group you might work for is capable of producing the desired result. Sadly, this task of knowing who needs work done; convincing said organization, including all people who might impact the decision, to move forward spending money; and then actually getting them to sign a contract to pay you and your group to write software is as far from trivial as you can imagine.

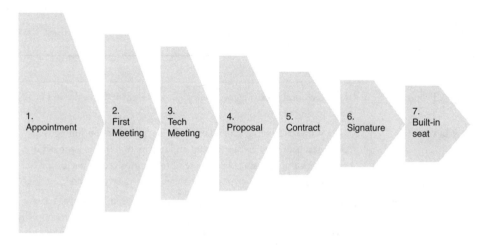

Figure 3-1 A typical pipeline structure used in consulting to differentiate where a prospect or recruit is in the sales cycle.

Many books have been written about how to successfully execute a sales process; thus, the details are beyond the scope of this book. However, it is important for a technology consultant to understand typical steps in a funnel to gain an appreciation for all the work that happens before the "cool work" can even start (see Table 3-1).

TABLE 3-1

Typical Steps in a Sales Process

Stage	Description
Stage 1: Appointment	Just getting someone to pick up the phone and talk to you about possible technology solutions is a huge challenge. At this point, you have a chance to talk to someone about a technology solution.
Stage 2: First Meeting	Movement to stage 2 typically means you are meeting someone face to face and, ideally, relating a business problem of the client to a technology solution that you may be able to build for the client.
Stage 3: Technical Meeting	You have a decision maker interested enough for a second meeting, where the goal is to have someone find out enough information to generate a proposal. This person doing discovery for the solution usually needs to be technical because the goal is to determine overall scope and initial budget from the discussion.

(continues)

TABLE 3-1

Typical Steps in a Sales Process (continued)

Stage	Description
Stage 4: Proposal	If the technical meeting goes well, you may be invited to submit a proposal to do the work.
Stage 5: Contract	If the proposal is accepted and everyone decides that continuing is a good idea, contracts are written up and negotiated. If it is a project of consequence, at this stage lawyers tend to get involved to make sure neither side agrees to something that isn't in either party's interest.
Stage 6: Signature	After the decision maker signs a contract, you are in this stage. You are almost home-free. That said, sometimes you get a phone call to stop the project while you're on the way to the project site after a signature has occurred.
Stage 7: "Butt-in-seat"	When you have a person working at the site, unless the firm is taking a risk and letting work start before contracts are done, it generally means you are in "delivery"; that is, work has started, and the sales process is complete.

Stage 1: Appointment

People who have decision-making power to spend money on technology consulting usually have a great number of people calling on them to help them with their problems. Breaking through and having something different to say—different enough such that a person will pick up the phone and talk to someone he or she doesn't know—is a huge challenge.

Needless to say, the chief obstacle at this stage is to get someone to pick up the phone and listen to you. Of course, it helps to already have relationships with decision makers to lean on, and in fact, as noted in Chapter 2, "The Seven Deadly Firms," entire technology firms have been founded on the strength of pre-existing leads from sources other than picking up the phone.

Most firms source appointments through three primary means:

+ Current relationships and partnerships
+ "Dialing for dollars," that is, cold calling
+ Marketing (advertising, webinars, trade shows, and so on)

Of course, the way a particular firm does this depends on the strength of its demand generation, that is, sales and marketing organization. Almost all places do some of each in varying amounts with varying success. For a consultant, however, the important takeaway here is that relationships do not come cheap; they are typically the result of either (1) building a relationship over a long time; (2) a ton of cold calling (sometimes 30 calls for a single appointment); or (3) a good deal of money and effort spent on marketing. No wonder those sales folks get so irritable when the project isn't going perfectly!

Stage 2: First Meeting

On first glance, the difference between appointment and first meeting simply should be a matter of showing up. Unfortunately, a lot of things can go wrong between having an appointment and having a meeting. It is not uncommon for meetings with decision makers to be delayed because of more pressing priorities, which sometimes are as trivial as "my lunch went long and vendors are a dime-a-dozen." Because in many situations you have not demonstrated your value at this point, simply going to the meeting, from the buyer point of view, is seen as a favor to you. Frequently, fewer than half of all appointments produce an actual meeting with a real decision maker.

Given these odds, actually getting a substantial meeting with a technology decision maker is quite a triumph! This, however, is just the start. When the face-to-face meeting occurs, you typically have less than an hour to convince this decision maker that he or she should decide to take a risk and even consider spending money with your firm. The goal of this meeting is to find some sort of pain the decision maker is experiencing (for example, "we are losing customers" or "if this project isn't done, I don't get a bonus") and seed the idea in the decision maker's head that your company can solve that pain. In other words, create a reason for a subsequent meeting where someone more like you will be able to help solve his or her problems.

Stage 3: Technical Meeting

In most well-run consultancies, the technical meeting is the first contact that the client will have with the technical talent of the firm—that is, someone like you who will actually do the work. This type of meeting can take a lot of forms but is usually characterized by fact gathering on the part of the consulting firm such that a proposal can be developed.

If you are invited to a meeting in this stage of the relationship, you need to realize that this is a very high stakes meeting. For every meeting like this that occurs, great expense in demand generation has probably taken place to get to this point in the relationship. If you work for a firm that generates leads through cold calls (yes, some do generate leads this way), there is a good chance that more than a couple hundred calls had to be made to get to this single meeting. Needless to say, doing well here can be very good for your career, but on the flip side, performing poorly in this task can be a limiting factor.

A consultant who is seen as a good presence resource—that is, someone who can be depended on to make a good impression on a client—tends to have more job security than someone who does not have that skill.

Chris Williams   This is what separates the coders from the consultants. You can be a brilliant developer or a world-class software architect, but if you dress like the Unabomber, nobody is going to take you seriously. Certainly not a prospective client.

This meeting is all about the important exchange of information in two different directions. The client learns a *lot* about the level of talent of the technical people through the intelligence of the questions asked, listening skills, and general business acumen demonstrated. That is the goal: "Can these people help me?" is the question that the client generally wants to ask himself or herself at the end of this meeting.

You, on the other hand, have a goal of not only impressing the client, but getting enough information to generate a proposal that, in all likelihood, contains a reasonable cost estimate for the solution to be developed. In many instances, you will be able to engage in additional discovery sessions before being asked to draw up an estimate, but these meetings are far from guaranteed, and it is critical you get enough information to at least get a broad idea that puts "the right number of digits" on the price.

> **Derik Whittaker** If you are the technical person sitting in on this meeting, my advice is to ask intelligent questions, listen very intently, seek clarification when needed, but most importantly do not make any promises of any sort. It is entirely too early in the process to make any promises, and trust me, the client will hold you to them.

The way this stage is conducted between different companies is a key differentiator between the good firms and bad firms described in Chapter 2. In bad firms, although a technical person may be involved, the sales team draws up the estimates. Or even more sinister, the technical person draws up an estimate, but said estimate is ignored so that the proposal can be "priced to win"—that is, priced at a level where you end up working a ton of unpaid overtime to make good on the promises made by the sales staff.

A consultancy that allows the sales staff to pressure the people doing the estimate into reduction of the estimate is almost certainly one you do not want to work for.

> **Jason Bock** I was recently at a client where we were required to give an estimate for a project's work. Our estimate was considered too high by the client, but my employer trusted our numbers. That spoke volumes to me. Having a company stand behind your decisions is vital.

Of course, even good firms have different methodologies for estimating, most of which depend on the project management methods typically used by the firm. At the time of this writing (2009), there is a vibrant debate whether Agile or plan-driven methodologies provide better results. Regardless of method used, though, it is important to understand that the word *estimate* means exactly that: It is an estimate. In virtually all projects that last longer than a few weeks, plans and priorities change, causing the estimate to change. As such, it is important to make sure everyone understands the assumptions on which the estimate is based so that when those assumptions change, everyone understands why the price might change as well.

Stage 4: Proposal

After you have done all the discovery work, painstakingly worked on the best estimate you can muster up, and managed to get the client to agree to let you present, you are ready to give a proposal. The proposal presentation is the point at which your firm presents the solution to the pain that the client perceives. Often this is the real test by which you will find out how serious the client is at pursuing a solution.

Of course, all sorts of things can screw up this stage. For one, you typically have a great deal of competition. In most cases, you have competing firms, some of which already have relationships with the company you are targeting—the dreaded incumbent. In fact, especially if these firms have a good relationship with your prospect, that prospect often has every opportunity to put up defensive measures, such as installation of fear, uncertainty, and doubt about your firm. Certainly, the more competition you have, the more acute is the need for your proposal to be effective.

Every proposal has at least one competitor: the option of doing nothing.

Even without other firms competing, every proposal always has at least one competitor. That competitor is, of course, the fact that your client may choose to do nothing at all. Unfortunately, for reasons that may or may not be the fault of our industry, software development projects are seen as risky endeavors that have substantial risk of failure. Because of this perceived risk, it is imperative that you make a clear link for your project to demonstrate that the money invested has potential to generate a substantial return.

We cannot stress enough how important it is to have your proposal be a demonstration of your best work and attention to detail. You have enough to worry about with competition, potential to overshoot the client's budget, and other uncontrollable factors. The factors that you can control—getting to the meeting on time, making sure there are no obvious grammar errors, and making sure you are appropriately dressed for the occasion—should be clearly under control.

Stage 5: Contract

After a proposal is agreed to in principle, consulting firms tend to draw up contracts that allow the work to proceed. The most important contracts are the *master consulting agreement,* or simply *consulting agreement,* and the *statement of work,* also known as a *work order.* The first of these defines the rights and responsibilities in the broader relationship—for example, "client can't offer direct employment to the consultant" and "consultant can't recruit any employees of the client"—as well as payment terms and other details that transcend any individual project.

The work order, or statement of work, defines legal details related to the project itself. The number of hours that consultants are allowed to bill before the contract has to be renewed is almost always a component, and depending on the project, the work order might include other items such as acceptance criteria, roles and responsibility distribution between the client and consultant, and a general description of the work. In some cases, there are references to other, more detailed documents that describe acceptance and payment terms; this is especially true in projects where there is a fixed bid. The various types of consulting contracts are described in Table 3-2.

TABLE 3-2

Types of Consulting Contracts

Contract	Description
Master Consulting Agreement	Governs terms of the overall relationship between a client and the consulting firm. Covenants that dictate that neither side can hire each other's employees for a period of time, payment terms, and other cross-project concerns are typically defined here.

(continues)

TABLE 3-2

Types of Consulting Contracts (continued)

Contract	Description
Statement of Work or Work Order	Project or time-limited terms of engagement. Typically defines how much will be billed, hourly rates, and project-level roles and responsibilities.
Nondisclosure Agreement	Often entered very early in the process, establishes responsibility not to disclose trade secrets one may learn about in the discovery and engagement process.
Letter of Intent	In certain cases, both sides are ready to agree, but the legal teams on either side of the relationship have not agreed to all terms. A letter of intent allows work to start without all the other terms of the engagement to be in place. It has more limited terms that address both sides making a good faith effort to come to agreement in some limited period of time.

In the Contract stage, contracts are defined by attorneys on both sides of the relationship and sent to the appropriate signing authority on either side. Depending on the firms involved, this process can be very fast if neither side has issues with each other's contracts or painfully slow if either side has problems with terms of the proposed contracts. In the latter case, if some subset of the terms are agreeable, a *letter of intent* can be established that allows work to start before all the details are finalized. This latter option usually requires that all the big points are agreed to and that contract negotiation is making good progress toward settlement.

Stage 6: Signature

On that glorious day when the client decision maker signs the contract, you have officially moved to stage 6, Signature. When you are here, you are ready to start, and if you have not done so already, you begin getting people together and planning the first day of the actual project. At this point many people on the sales side of the organization start to open the champagne bottle and celebrate the win.

Chances are there is good reason to celebrate. When the signature occurs, it is highly likely the project will start and the people like you, the technology consultants, will get to do what you do best. However, occasionally something happens between the Signature stage and next stage, which I like to call the "Butts-in-Seats" stage (or less colorfully, Delivery). The buyer could discover that the person who signed the contract lacked authority to sign said contract, and the project could be canceled before it starts. And, of course, you can never underestimate buyer's remorse, especially if, on Friday night, the company announced a bad quarter to Wall Street.

In technology consulting, the expression, "You ain't there 'til you're in the chair," exists because sometimes things happen that can cancel a project, even after the work order is signed. The event could be something completely unexpected, such as a company bankruptcy or someone signing a work order who lacked the authority to sign it. Thus, it is often said that a project does not really start until there are "butts-in-seats."

> **Jason Bock**   The more time I spend in consulting, the more appreciation I've gained for the pre-"butts-in-seats" phases. That said, as a consultant, you are usually responsible for making that last phase succeed, and that's where you'll spend the bulk of your time. I've always said that I really don't believe anything that happens in the pipeline (because so much is up in the air) until I'm at the client, sitting at my laptop and working.

Stage 7: Butts-in-Seats

In the final stage of the sales process—when primary responsibility for the project outcome, in most firms, is handed off from the sales team to the delivery team—the work actually starts. From this point forward, if something occurs to end the project prematurely, it is the people doing the work, not the people working in the demand generation organization (a.k.a. sales), who will likely be asked, "What happened here?"

That said, the sales process never really ends. In consulting, you are always selling, whether or not you are formally part of the sales organization. The formal sales organization sells by convincing an organization that it should invest in a given technology. The delivery organization sells by effectively delivering the technology and doing so in a way that makes the buyer—the person who took the risk and hired you—look good. Although there are good, high-minded reasons to want to achieve success on projects, reasons that should not be discounted, it is a fact of life in this business that the better you make the buyer look, the more likely your company is going to be able to build the relationship.

In fact, building a current relationship into a bigger one can be even more effective than simply getting new relationships. Your goal is to make your company be perceived as the low-risk option when thinking about the next project or beyond that and getting into a position where you can scout out opportunities on behalf of the client. These kinds of activities are known colloquially as *making rain*, a term we use to denote the act of growing opportunities for not just you, but all those around you. Rainmakers like this tend to be the most successful people in consulting, as covered in more detail in Chapter 7, "Thriving."

Michael Hugos   Working in computers and programming is tough and demanding, but if you really want a tough job, go into sales. For me, figuring out computers is a challenge, but figuring out sales is an absolute mystery. Blessed are the rainmakers.

The Second Pipeline

The business of technology consulting would be challenging enough if there were a nearly unlimited supply of great technology consultants you could procure like a commodity, the same way you would with steel or coal. Fortunately—for you at least—people are the furthest thing from commodities you could possibly conceive of.

This is not to say that businesses have not tried to commoditize people. If you have ever read the classifieds, you have likely seen a job ad like this:

Looking for an experienced developer with 15 years of Ruby-on-Rails in a financial services company, who also has a master's degree in fine arts and graphics skills, along with 10 years of experience maintaining ActiveDirectory, who has experience working at both Microsoft and IBM, and lives within 2 miles of Bismarck, North Dakota.

In this case, the recruiter is mad because he received only 20 applicants, of which only three have all the qualifications (and, of course, all three are lying—no programmers live in Bismarck, North Dakota).

The attempted commoditization of talent in the technology business has never materialized; there is simply too much variability in people to allow for it. Talent in this business is scarce, which is the reason there is a market for expensive consultants in the first place. Thus, recruiters in technology consulting organizations also talk of *pipelines*. The stages are similar to the sales pipeline; the only differences are the tactics and the nature of the contracts.

Technology consulting firms operate two pipelines because software developers are in short supply. The chief difficulty of operating a consulting firm is coordination of these dual pipelines—matching volatile supply with volatile demand (see Figure 3-2).

Figure 3-2 Dual pipelines.

Your involvement in the recruiting pipeline is often as early as stage 1, which in this case means sending your friends and colleagues to your firm through the referral program. Through this mechanism, you can make some extra money by providing leads to the company. Barring that, you will often involve yourself as the counter-party of stage 3—the technical meeting, which in your case, means you will be doing technical interviewing.

It is important not to discount this particular responsibility. If you give someone a pass on a technical interview and that person joins up and causes your company to lose a client, you are suddenly in the circle of blame. Generally, you need to make sure you recommend people who not only have the technical chops to make it, but make good consultants; that is, they show a lot of the traits referenced in Chapter 4, "Getting In: Ten Unlisted Traits That Technology Consulting Firms Look For."

Of course, this responsibility is tricky because other people—namely, recruiters on one hand and potentially a colleague who provided a referral on the other—often pressure you to be easy on certain interviewees, for reasons of short-term self-interest. This can be true especially if your company has just landed a contract that it does not have enough staff to handle and is in an "emergency staff up" situation.

Managing Dual Pipelines

One of the most challenging aspects of managing a professional services company that deals in technology is matching up supply with demand when both sides of the equation require a significant sales effort. A mismatch on either side of the equation can spell problems. Too much supply (people) and not enough demand (work) means that the company either doesn't make a profit or possibly runs at a loss. Too much demand and not enough supply might cause the firm to turn down work, which is a very efficient way to demoralize a salesperson who probably worked hard to generate that demand. Or even worse, it might require that the firm go out to the open market and pay spot rates for talent—talent it may or may not know a lot about. This latter situation is almost certainly expensive because independent contractors usually cost more, sometimes 50 percent higher on a tax-adjusted basis to cover their own business expenses. It is also risky because you often know less about what the contractor is actually good at—unlike your own employees who work for your consulting firm—and thus take on risk to your own reputation as a firm.

The Players

The business of technology consulting obviously consists of a great number of, well, technology consultants. In addition, there are numerous people about whom you might wonder exactly what they do. This section helps you understand exactly what everyone around the office does. Although I certainly can't vouch for the idea that every person in every single consulting firm serves a useful purpose, this section gives you a sense of what the various people do. Table 3-3 introduces you to the coworkers you will have within a technology consulting firm.

TABLE 3-3

People You Will Meet in a Technology Consulting Firm

Role	Description
Account Executive or Sales Person	The person who, through a personal network, marketing leads, or simple cold calls, generates demand for technical consulting services and ultimately closes deals that allow you to start doing actual work. Also known as the *hunter*. Generally makes a commission from work sold that represents the majority of his or her income.
Engagement Manager (EM) or Client Partner	The person who manages the client relationship in some firms (in some firms, this is an account executive role as well). Typically has some combination of business, project management, and technology skill. Tends to be less commission-based than pure account executives.
Recruiter	The person who works the recruiting funnel, generating a supply of technology consultants that are then sold by the demand generation portion of the firm. Part of income is derived from the number and quality of candidates sourced and hired.
Consulting Manager (CM)	The person who, rather than billing, spends all his or her time supporting consultants, particularly in firms that can support a separate person whose job is to act as a mentor/supervisor/career coach to consultants. In some firms, this role is handled by a billing engagement manager or a commissioned account executive. In smaller firms in particular, this role is handled by senior management or a director/GM.

(continues)

TABLE 3-3

People You Will Meet in a Technology Consulting Firm (continued)

Role	Description
Presales Specialist	The person who is dedicated to supporting the sales team. Provides technical credibility to the sales pursuit and makes sure deals are technically feasible.
Marketing	Folks who generate demand by means other than "one-to-one" communication, such as advertising, hosting events, arranging for podcasts and other consultant publications, and performing general lead generation activity that eventually can be passed onto the account executives.
Industry Guru	An industry figurehead who acts in the role of walking, talking, marketing arm of the firm, especially in larger firms that can support the overhead. Usually someone who is published and has some measure of gravitas in the industry. Such a person tends to provide the firm a halo effect.
General Manager (GM) or Director	The person who owns profit-and-loss responsibility for a region or business unit. Makes hiring, firing, and most other major decisions that do not have a companywide impact.
HR, Accounting, Finance, and so on	Folks who typically work in support functions that, while important, are not considered key investment areas in technology consulting firms.
Senior Management	Usually the owners of the firm. Usually have CxO titles and tend to work *on* the business rather than *in* the business; that is, they make decisions about opening new offices, acquiring smaller firms, and generally establish companywide policy.
You	The person at the center of all this activity. None of these people would have a reason to exist without you.

The Account Executive

Account executives, also known as VPs of sales, salespersons, business developers, and numerous other titles, are the people responsible for generating demand for consulting services from individual companies. In nearly all consulting firms, people in this role derive most of their income from commission;

that is, they are paid a percentage of the revenue they generate. As such, they are highly motivated to get you working at a client.

The personality profile of this job is certainly that of an extrovert. Account executives are folks who, generally, are not afraid to strike up a conversation with a random person looking for business. They usually excel at small talk, golf, eating at expensive restaurants with clients, and generally schmoozing.

The most prized possession of any good account executive is his or her contact list. Account executives who do their job spend a lot of time looking for opportunities for software developers to do good work. This means that they are making calls, trying to get appointments with decision makers so that the first stage of the sales process can start. Account executives often spend months getting that elusive first meeting. You, as a technology consultant, need to understand this point is critical: Without understanding the role, you might come to think that the chief job of the account executive is to eat lunch and collect a commission.

Dealing with Account Executives

Technology consultants frequently have run-ins with account executives. One reason is that when you make a mistake (and it *is* a matter of when, and not if…nobody's perfect), there is a distinct possibility that your mistake can cause a direct hit to the account executive's income. Most account executives recognize this as a job hazard, but when this kind of thing happens more than a few times, it can have a career-limiting effect. When word gets around to the various account executives for whom you cause commissions to shrink, you may find that no account executives are willing to sell your services anymore.

Worse, there can be times when it seems like an account executive is taking advantage of you. Specifically, you might think that the account executive sold you down the river and collected a commission at the expense of your sanity. If you are working 60-hour work weeks with unpaid overtime because an account executive pushed for an estimate that was too aggressive, you will probably start to harbor hard feelings for that person.

Needless to say, the most common flashpoint for drama in consulting tends to be between consultants and account executives. This is why working for a firm that balances these forces is so important. Firms that let account executives run wild with promises tend to devolve into the BOZO Consulting archetype described in Chapter 2. On the other hand, if consultants are not performing for the client and said incompetence is widespread (perhaps because of bad hiring practices), these companies can devolve into bankrupt companies. This happens because no revenue means nobody, not the account executive nor the consultant, makes any money at all.

> *Learning to build a positive relationship with your account executive is one of the most critical skills you must master as a technology consultant.*

It is imperative you build a healthy relationship with account executives. This does not mean being a yes person to them, but it does mean doing everything within your power to build a healthy relationship where you can disagree and negotiate through issues that occur. One way to do this is to serve them well during the sales process if you are invited and by doing everything you can under their guidance to help close deals. Becoming someone that account executives can depend on gives you the credibility you later might need to spend when they receive the bad news you have to occasionally deliver that, no, the client won't be able to get a perfect replica of Google.com for $15,000.

> **Michael Hugos** When dealing with account executives, I always try to understand the six key metrics (revenue, margin, utilization, hourly rate, backlog, and overhead) as they relate to me and the other consultants from the firm who are at this account. Remember, "Money talks and bull---t walks."

The Engagement Manager

Engagement managers, also known as partners, client partners, or even account managers, are differentiated from account executives in a few important ways.

Notably, they are usually not responsible for sourcing new business outside their assigned clients, are not paid on a commission, and most importantly, tend to have specific and direct responsibility for project outcomes. Of course, there are similarities as well. Specifically, engagement managers typically are responsible for growing the business by expanding a relationship within a client, hence, the nickname *farmers* in comparison to the nickname *hunters* for account executives.

Good engagement managers combine the schmoozing capabilities of the extrovert account executives with a level of competence at project management, people leadership, and business acumen that allows them to effectively work within a client to significantly expand the relationship. The chief goal of an EM is to become the trusted advisor for technology matters to the C-level person in the client organization that your firm is working with. This means someone who takes pain—that is, organization problems disclosed over the course of months during a project—and works to identify those cases where a technology person or team can address those problems.

Dealing with Engagement Managers

As a consultant, you have a common interest with the engagement manager; that is, expanding the relationship makes both of you look good. Because engagement managers are usually considered directly responsible for day-to-day results, they should be your best advocates for getting the resources you need to successfully complete projects.

By becoming a trusted ally of your engagement manager and making that person look good, when said person is doing the right stuff—that is, finding opportunities within the client and advancing the client's and consultancy's agendas—it is likely you will find your own advancement opportunities in his or her wake. Because good EMs expand engagements, they tend to move to new clients so that new relationships can be grown, and this move provides a nice upward path for you if you are interested in working in this kind of role. (See Chapter 8, "Your Career Path.")

However, in the event your relationship with your EM becomes adversarial or negative, it is probably a good idea to make sure others on your team feel the same way before attempting to resolve the problem with higher management. Not all engagement managers are terribly competent; the variability of capability in this job isn't that different from any other one where some are very good and some are not so good. A bad EM, however, can cause some real serious problems due to the combination of daily client and consultant exposure; incompetence is hard to hide in this role. As such, if things are going wrong, and you can't solve a problem with your EM directly, make sure you gather facts and allies and then go to higher management. Going to senior management only with opinions in this case is certainly doomed to failure. The reason is that people who are entrusted with the EM role almost by definition have enough credibility with management to overcome all but the most fact-based cases against them.

The Recruiter

Recruiters are, in effect, the account executives who work on the recruiting funnel rather than the sales funnel. Also extroverts by nature, recruiters are tasked with finding talent and making them want to join your firm. Most recruiters work on a base plus commission structure that pays them for the number and quality of hires they make in a year. The job of recruiter is literally to schmooze software developers and other people who need to be hired by a technology consulting firm and get them excited about working for your firm rather than the employer for whom they might currently work at the moment.

Of course, not all recruiters are good. Some recruiters simply put advertisements out on job boards and hope that people will call them. This behavior creates a façade of competence because, surely, putting out advertisements and responding to the resulting email and phone calls can create a lot of work. Sometimes they score hundreds or more resumes from people who often lack the basic qualifications for the job, much less have what it takes to be great technology consultants. However, as Joel Spolsky talks about in his famous essay, "Hitting the High Notes" (www.joelonsoftware.com/articles/HighNotes.html), it takes a good amount of work to find great candidates, particularly, the "A" players, who currently have jobs and who, frankly, don't need the work. This model of recruiting "passive" candidates takes a lot more work but has been shown to produce superior results.

> **Derik Whittaker** When you are new to the consulting game, it is very easy to be wooed by recruiters, as they have often been compared to drug dealers. They will tell you anything they think you want to hear to get you in the door. Make sure you ask quality questions during the recruiting process and always take everything told to you with a grain of salt.

Because finding passive candidates is a lot of work, most companies have a role for the technology consultant in this task. Many firms have referral programs such that you can receive a lucrative bonus in the event that one of your friends or former colleagues is hired. Of course, the whole business of referrals has its own set of risks you should be aware of.

> **Derik Whittaker** If you find yourself working for a firm that does not have a referral program of some sort (which could be a fat bonus check or as little as dinner on the company), then you may be working for a CHEAP firm. If it is not willing to extend some form of bonus to you for helping the company, what else is it going to try to slide by with?

> **Chris Williams** In today's sagging economy, many of these referral bonuses have dried up and blown away. When this happens, and the referrals keep coming in, it's a good measure of the person doing the most referring. It's a safe bet this person has your company's interests at heart because there's no immediate monetary gain.

Dealing with Your Own Company's Recruiters

Unlike your work with the engagement manager and account executive, your work with the recruiter will mostly be limited to your experience when you are being hired. The major exceptions to this are when you are asked to interview incoming candidates and when you refer a friend or colleague to the company. In the latter case, it is important not to refer just anyone who has a pulse and an email address. Having your company hire someone who loses money for the company through a bad engagement can not only put the candidate, possibly your friend, in a situation in which he or she gets fired and no longer wants to be your friend, but it hurts your own credibility because it was partially your fault for helping hired the person who didn't work out!

Outside that case, though, you also will frequently be asked to participate in the interviewing process. Again, it is critical that you defend your company against hiring incompetents because even an incompetent person screwing up a team working for a different client than yours hurts your company and your office. In addition, if you interviewed someone who got kicked off a client and thus caused a problem for an account executive or engagement manager, there is a good chance someone will ask, "Who interviewed this Bozo?" The answer, of course, leads back to you! Not good for you at all.

> **Jason Bock** One lesson I learned early on with respect to interviewing candidates is this: *Never* give a yellow light. Either say yes or no. If you say maybe, the recruiter will see the yellow light, and as we all know, everybody hits the gas to get through the intersection. The recruiter is on commission, and if he sees an "in," he'll take it. If you have any doubts about someone you're interviewing, just say no. Remember, you may end up working with that person on a future project!

Dealing with Other Companies' Recruiters

Of course, as you advance and gain experience, word will get out that you are a good consultant. This means that other recruiters are likely going to become very interested in your skills and capabilities. As a result, you will start to get phone calls from recruiters with all sorts of pitches about how the grass is way greener on the other side.

On one hand, it is important to be very skeptical of claims made by recruiters. Although most of them are well-intentioned, recruiters tend to have very little interest in providing you with the downside to changing companies. That said, especially if you happen to be working for one of the Seven Deadly Firms described in Chapter 2, it is a good idea to at least be polite and listen to what they have to say. Remember that recruiters are people too, and you never know when you might find yourself in need of a recruiter to help you get into a position during hard economic times. If you are rude to recruiters, word may get around, and you might suddenly find yourself without any options in a bad market.

That said, you would be wise to make sure you deal with these folks through non-work-related email addresses and take their calls outside business hours if possible. If you use LinkedIn or other similar social networks, you should be careful about linking to recruiters, especially if you are linked to your own company management. Flagrantly demonstrating to your bosses that you are on the market puts your loyalty in question, which tends to lead to a decrease in their confidence in promoting you or putting you in a position of responsibility. That said, it is certainly a good idea to keep a list of good recruiters handy and even go out to lunch with them from time to time. Just being polite can do wonders for those times when things go wrong and you need a way out of a position.

Practice Lead/Consultant Management

In firms that have business units that reach a certain level of scale, the idea of having separate consulting managers becomes viable. In some firms, particularly firms where the engagement managers do not take on a "people management" role, consulting managers become the official persons that consultants report to on the organization chart. In firms that have CMs, it is rare that they would solely perform consultant management. More typically, they take on various roles, from recruiter to presales to engagement management, depending on what the director/general manager needs at a given time.

In most cases where this position exists, it is a step on the path to management of a business unit, in the form of a director or general manager position. Generally speaking, it is a position provided as part of a career path for consultants who demonstrate maturity and management skills, frequently as a step after operating as an engagement manager for some period of time. One common element in this position seems to be that a PL and/or CM is usually responsible for developing staff, working with consultants on training plans, and generally retaining consultants, for example.

Dealing with Your Consulting Manager or Practice Lead

If you report to a consulting manager or practice lead—that is, someone who is not on your billing engagement yet to whom you report—it is generally advisable that you keep in touch with this person once per month and let him or her know what you are up to. Because a CM/PL often has client responsibilities in all but the largest firms and usually comes from a technical background and is not always an extrovert, it is usually a mistake to assume that this person will be taking on responsibility for forming the relationship. Like most things in life, the more responsibility you take on for managing the relationship, the more successful it is likely to be.

A good CM/PL is a natural ally. This relationship is usually one of the key performance measures to assure you are retained and can continue to advance in your career. However, it is incumbent on you as a consultant to not just expect your CM/PL to do all your self-development work for you. If you do not take proactive steps toward furthering your own career, such as keeping up on technology trends, attending user groups, and so on, there is little a CM/PL can do to make you take those steps. On the other hand, if you are doing those things, you make it possible for such a person to enhance those efforts by scouting out opportunities for self-development.

Presales Specialist

Companies that sell solutions with some level of complexity usually need someone around to support salespeople who are good at selling but generally do not have a skill set that includes deep technical knowledge. The person who acts in this capacity, if given a separate role at all, goes by several different titles, including sales engineer, technical solution specialist, and technical sales specialist. For purposes of this conversation, we'll simply use presales specialist.

The typical activities of presales usually involve working with a group of three to six account executives on activities between stages 3 and 5 in the sales funnel. Presales usually orchestrates development of estimates, involving billing consultants in the process so that estimates are not overly optimistic. (Estimates developed by sales are almost always aggressive because of the overwhelming pressure to try to win deals on price.) Other activities include conducting demos if solutions include packaged software, writing proposals, handling other contractual matters such as work orders and consulting agreements, and generally, making it such that the account executive can focus on selling.

In some firms, presales specialist isn't so much of a role as it is a responsibility that you have when you are on the bench. In cases like this, becoming perceived as a valuable resource in presales is a great way to increase your chance of not only surviving when times get bad, but thriving when times are good and you want to establish your promotability. Given most positions in consulting above that of billing consultant involve some aspect of being able to sell, being perceived as competent in this area is certainly not a bad thing.

Dealing with Presales Specialists

A presales specialist is usually someone you work with on a pursuit team trying to win new business. If you are on the bench helping a sales pursuit, it is usually a presales specialist who will pull you into the estimation process. If the presales specialist pressures you into reducing an estimate, be wary but be prepared to back up your estimate with supporting facts. Most consultancies do not question estimates too much, but there will always be cases in which a pursuit team is eager to get a deal done, and estimates come in higher than expected, resulting in questions.

If you are reducing an estimate, one of the best things you can do is make sure you have assumptions in the proposal that provide a basis for the reduction (such as "using a pre-built library should reduce this from three days to two days"). There is usually much less push back to adding content to an assumption section than there is to an estimate increase, and you can use this in your favor.

In the event that you get a lot of pushback on an estimate you believe to be very credible, you may be in a no-win situation. The best way to deal with a problem like this is to make sure your concerns are documented by the stakeholders on your pursuit team and then move on. At the very least, if the aggressive estimate being put into place does not work out, you are not as likely to be blamed for the result. However, if you find yourself in this position alone, you may be working for a firm like BOZO Consulting profiled in Chapter 2, and it might be advisable to brush up on your resume, given the prognosis of those types of firms.

The Industry Guru

Whereas some organizations work on the strength of their salesforce, some companies enhance their image by hiring someone with some level of celebrity in technical circles. This person, the industry guru, has an enviable job that mostly is composed of leveraging his or her status for the good of the company. Certainly not a bad gig if you can get it!

Sometimes, this role is given a more mundane title like chief technical officer. In other firms, it might be chief evangelist, chief scientist, or some other title that reflects the position of the particular person in the industry at large. In any case, this person's responsibilities are part marketing, by enhancing the image of the firm by association; part sales, by meeting with individual clients to close deals; and part delivery, by working with teams to provide technical or process advice across the company.

The personalities of industry guru types vary as much as the general human population does. The ideal industry guru is someone who is at ease with himself or herself, uses his or her credibility to further the careers of those with whom he or she works, and generally makes things better for everyone. However, in some cases this person may be narcissistic and/or Machiavellian, and his or her presence can easily cause a firm to devolve into a version of Personality Cult Consulting, covered in Chapter 2.

Dealing with the Industry Guru

The way you, as a consultant, directly interact with the industry guru will vary a great deal. In some firms, you might only rarely work with this person because the activities of an industry guru tend to be broad and shallow across different project teams. However, in certain cases, you could get a real up-close look at such a person if the guru in question is suddenly on your project. In the latter case, there is usually a good reason—either the project is high profile/high stakes (big initiative for client, one of the bigger engagements in the company) or is in serious trouble (the guru was brought in as a "Hail Mary" pass to save the project.)

In either of these cases, the best course of action is to probably just treat the guru in a manner similar to that of an engagement manager. Do not be afraid to engage, but be aware of the politics and build the relationship before spending credibility by taking up an argument with such a person. This is doubly true if the guru has a bit of an ego such that challenging the person might seem like an affront to his or her own perception of his or her capabilities.

Michael Hugos As a self-appointed industry guru myself, I can say that a bit of ego usually comes along with the guru. Being a guru is nerve-wracking because there is always another guru looking to push you aside and take your place. So let the guru know you admire him or her and respect his or her knowledge, and you will start your relationship on the right note. Gurus are always interested in new information about their industries, so structure your conversations in the form of information sharing instead of arguing, and that will also help build your relationship.

Derik Whittaker If you are able to work with a guru, do yourself and your skills a favor and attempt to learn as much as possible from him or her. This person is not the guru for nothing and in most cases will be able to teach you something new and useful.

Director/General Manager

Director/general manager is the role through which most individual hire/fire, budgeting, and staffing decisions ultimately get made in larger firms. Directors or general managers are generally accountable for the profit or loss of the business unit that they manage, usually organized by region, particular subspecialty, or in some cases, a combination. It is a role with a great deal of responsibility because decisions made at this level generally affect the employment status of numerous individuals, not to mention have a substantial effect on the profitability of the consulting organization overall.

When directors/GMs work in the organization, they tend to play a lot of different roles, depending on what is needed at a given time. They can be called upon to close deals, help in presales if needed, help manage the careers of consultants (taking on some CM-type tasks), and build relationships in the broader business community to improve the business standing of the company. Most GMs have key performance measures around not only revenue, like an account executive, but a broader set of sometimes competing measures, such as pointed out earlier in this chapter. In many cases, they are effectively CEOs of a portion of the organization in larger companies.

Smaller consultancies, especially ones with fewer than 100 billing consultants, may not have this role at all, with these functions being performed by the senior management team. However, larger ones, especially ones passing the 150-consultant mark, are past the point where the CEO can effectively manage an organization that large—hence, the need to create a position like that of the GM.

Dealing with the Director or General Manager

As with all relationships covered in this chapter, your relationship with the director/GM is one you need to nurture when you have the opportunity to do so because this person tends to have a good deal of decision-making authority, some of which can positively or negatively impact your career. The GM tends to be the person who authorizes your raises and promotions and makes the final decisions about which clients you go to. Therefore, it is critical that you build credibility with this person.

Does this mean you brown-nose? Certainly not. It is much more important to, in your first year, simply perform very well and predictably so you can build credibility with your GM. After you have built up a good reputation, you can use that so if you ever have to disagree with the GM in a discussion (say, you disagree about a staffing assignment or an estimate), you have a well of credibility to draw from. After you have gone through a few instances of productive discussion and debate, and managed to do so without making the GM look like a jerk, you start to become more of a trusted advisor to this person—something you definitely want. By doing so, you also demonstrate that you can become a trusted advisor to clients. Demonstrating the ability to not only deliver to clients but to gain their trust as well is the best possible way to become indispensable to a director/GM-type person.

Senior Management

In smaller consultancies, senior management *is* the director/GM role; however, in larger ones, usually a few executives are responsible for the strategic direction of the company. The senior management team is that group. The titles of the folks in this group are usually chief executive officer, chief operating officer, VP of sales, president, chief financial officer, and so forth.

The senior management of a consultancy is usually a small group of three to six executives, most of whom have significant equity ownership of the company. They decide which markets the firm will enter, what strategic alliances will be started, and what new business units will be created. Although they do spend a lot of time working with the business units to close deals, handle interoffice problems, and recruit certain high-level talent, for example, their main job is to work *on* the business rather than *in* the business. In fact, most people at this level feel as though they are doing their jobs if they are spending more time making decisions about how to grow, and not doing the day-to-day work of selling individual projects, hiring/firing individual consultants, and addressing other more tactical concerns.

Typically, the general managers report to the senior management team, which gives the GMs the goals for the year and measures progress against those goals. In this structure, you can think of the senior management team as managing a portfolio of individual businesses, each of which is headed by a GM or director.

That said, senior management does dictate a sort of personality about the company overall. If senior management harbors personalities that are, well, aggressive and not particularly people-friendly, that cultural trait is likely to show up in the GMs and, thereby, is likely to filter down to where you work as a consultant. It is important that you understand the values of your senior management team because for good or ill, it is likely to impact your day-to-day life in a meaningful way.

Dealing with Senior Management

Most of the time, as a consultant in a large company, you will not deal with senior management directly (this is *not* true in smaller companies, where senior management and the general manager role, described previously, are the same thing). The most common direct interaction you will have is either at companywide events, particularly if you happen to operate from the same location as the company headquarters or perhaps if you are in a branch office when the executives come to town to visit.

When you have this opportunity to interact, generally speaking, you should be prepared to ask a couple of good questions about how the company is doing. If nothing else, these folks generally love to talk about the company that they have likely had a hand in creating. Demonstrating interest in the company is a good way to get noticed in a positive way by these folks. Most good senior management members are happy to answer your questions as long as you are not overly aggressive and sending email every two days and becoming super high maintenance.

On the other hand, getting the negative attention of senior management can obviously be a career-limiting move. This can occur by, as mentioned in Chapter 1, causing an engagement to prematurely end and thereby reducing the backlog by a considerable amount.

Chris Williams   One consulting company I know of has a tradition of taking a group of new hires out to dinner with the senior management. These dinners include an open bar, and the consultants are left to their own judgment on how much to indulge themselves. The unspoken catch is that these dinners are a test. How a new consultant behaves at one of these dinners is a good indication of how he or she might behave in a similar situation with a client. Senior management might be drinking as well, but they are also watching very closely. More than one career at this company has been abruptly terminated after the new hire dinner.

HR, Accounting, IT, and Other Overhead

Of course, there are various other folks in supporting positions in the company. Whereas Human Resources in particular may be of some importance in some companies, HR in consulting tends to be a little more distant. It is best to think of HR, Accounting, IT, and these other functions as services there for you to utilize if they can help you get your job done more effectively, but not as big departments that have a lot of power. Given that these are overhead positions in a business that runs on what are sometimes fairly thin margins, these folks tend not to have a ton of resources. As such, patience is a virtue with any of these folks, who tend to be overworked and underappreciated.

Complaining About Overhead Not Recommended

It is almost a cliché that consultants and sales people have a negative view of overhead because both tend to think of these other folks as taking dollars from them—by their mere existence—that could be used for more "useful" things. In almost all cases, you are best served not to fit into that stereotype. Even if it is true, remember that senior management probably put those people in those positions for a reason, and even if that reason is wrong, going negative on that decision is a good way to gain negative attention from people from whom you almost certainly don't want that kind of attention. If the situation is really so bad—bad enough to impact profitability—it is probably a good idea to consider changing firms. Otherwise, given that being a jerk about overhead has almost no upside and a ton of downside, it is probably best to just let the situation be.

You: The Nomadic Developer

Of course, we saved the best for last. The technology consultant, the *nomadic developer*, is the product that is lured, sold, and ideally, nurtured. Technology consulting can't exist without you, and thus, your career and your interests are going to be of great interest to, we hope, every other person we have talked about in this chapter.

Your own career path can lead to a lot of different roles, which are described in Chapter 8. Dealing effectively with other people like you is a critical success factor for your career. In fact, most of your day-to-day interactions will be with other technology consultants.

Dealing with Other Consultants

Technology is one of those fields where people often hold strong feelings about technology—sometimes so strong that it starts to resemble religious fervor. Perhaps proof of this is the fact that the term *Language War* is used in common parlance. Indeed, different methodologies, work styles, and design preferences can be real issues between technology consultants. Although we can't possibly give you advice for how to handle every disagreement, some general principles are important:

+ Argue the principle, not the person.
+ Allow for the distinct possibility you might be wrong.
+ Acknowledge the value the other person is bringing to the conversation.
+ When in doubt, rely on facts, not opinions.

- Shun use of circular logic or confusion of cause and effect.
- Exit discussions with people who do not respect these principles, if possible.

The last point can be difficult and counterintuitive. Passion can sometimes turn into not being able to "disagree without being disagreeable" and can ruin teams if you are not careful. Sometimes it is best to acknowledge someone else's argument and, if it is not on a critical decision, move along and allow that person to be right, even if he or she is not. That said, if these disagreements are occurring in more high-stakes contexts, you might need to escalate matters to your engagement manager or other person responsible for the engagement when logic and facts cease to work.

> **Chris Williams**   Beware of those consultants who have made a name (if not an entire career) of publicly attacking contrary opinions and the people who hold them. These people will never see your side (because they delight in the argument itself), and arguing with them publicly only damages your own credibility.

Challenges You Will Face as a Consultant

The preceding section described interpersonal challenges that can afflict your relationship with your coworkers. However, you will face other challenges, so you need to have at least a basic plan of action as you progress in your career. Although this list is not exhaustive, it does cover some of the typical problems you will run into.

Project Running Late

If you meet technology consultants who say they have never been on a project that was running late or over budget, they are either very inexperienced or almost certainly lying.

If you notice you are running behind, ideally make sure the person responsible for the project knows this early. Although people don't like deadlines being missed, being surprised about such situations is almost always far worse. If you report early, the project can still be salvaged by adding more people or resetting expectations. On the other hand, resetting expectations late in a project is almost always difficult and can often lead to projects being canceled or the consulting firm being asked to work free to get back on track.

> **Derik Whittaker** If you do have to report that your project is running behind schedule, make sure that no one on your team panics or starts to create a negative vibe. This will most likely only cause the project to fall even further behind.

Generally speaking, report progress early and often, and make sure that, ideally, you are reporting only whole deliverables, not 90 percent done on a long-term task where you lack sufficient means to know for sure the percentage complete.

> **Jason Bock** No matter what the client or even your employer says, always be transparent. At the very least, fill out a weekly status report. It doesn't take longer than 10 minutes to state what you did, what you're going to do, and what roadblocks you currently have. Make sure all the stakeholders get the report. At least you can say you did what you could to state when a project was going back. Don't go dark; keep everyone informed to minimize blown schedules.

Someone Else's Code Sucks

One of the primary axioms in programming, particularly in cases in which there is no shared ownership of deliverables, is that your code is awesome, and everyone else's code sucks. Complaining to the management about this problem is always going to start out as an uphill argument.

Nowadays, we have better ways of actually measuring code quality than we had in the past. We have metrics like code coverage, cyclomatic complexity, and numerous others that can give us some facts by which code can be measured. And in the realm of code criticism, these metrics are always going to be more important than opinions. Should you find these quality problems repeatedly, it should not be too hard to get the problem solved by bringing the matter to the attention of the lead, who can deal with the person who isn't writing code to the required standard.

Scope Creep

Of course, one of the problems you will find when you are doing a good job, particularly if you are working closely with clients, is that they will want every possible feature they can throw into the project once they find someone who can do good work. This can be a good thing on some projects, particularly if your project has a change-embracing methodology like the ones in the Agile family of methodologies. However, if you are on a project being run from a contract where scope needs to be managed by a change control board, you are going to have to learn how to say no, but in a manner that provides the client with a means to get the change.

Sometimes, getting client approval for a change is as easy as saying, "Great idea, let's get the project owner on board with this and see if we can get funding." Other times, you get personal pleas of, "But it's just one little feature. Come on, you can sneak it in." These situations are harder because you are dealing on the front end of a dynamic where someone is doing an end-run around a change control board. Unless you have project-level responsibility, it is best to stand firm and escalate the issue to the lead or engagement manager, who, if doing his or her job, should be able to get the sponsor involved so that the change can go through the correct channels.

Allowing the scope add generally will make the person come back for more once he or she figures out this way around the system. Do everything you can to avoid that because it will tend to come back to bite you, especially if there are bugs in the "freelance" feature you added and people start asking why you are adding stuff not in the specification.

> **Michael Hugos** My ability to deal with the infernal dynamic of scope creep is one of the most valuable consulting skills I have. It is far more involved than just saying no to client requests. It is learning to balance the need to please the client with the need to avoid working for free. It is learning the fine art of negotiating change orders to the original system specs.

"I Know How to What?"

The problem that occurs when you suddenly find yourself sold for a project where your skills have been misrepresented is what I call the "I know how to what?" problem. It tends to occur in more transactional firms that don't have much of a clue what their people can do or, more sinisterly, in those that just change the resume to say whatever the client needs to see. In the latter case, it may be time to consider going to another firm if this change was made on purpose.

However, if you give the company the benefit of the doubt and assume there was a misunderstanding, it is probably a good idea to bring this up with your engagement manager and possibly a practice lead/consulting manager or general manager. This is particularly true if you have been sold into something you have no hope of doing (such as selling a database administrator as, say, a user experience expert).

Many problems in this category occur when an account executive or salesperson somehow misreads your resume (that is, takes your Oracle 8 experience and confuses it with Oracle Financials because both have the word *Oracle* in it) and somehow, the misread makes it all the way through the sales process. Such cases, while embarrassing, become far more embarrassing the longer the situation is allowed to persist, so early communication of the problem is vital.

Derik Whittaker I was once sold as a C++ expert, when the only expo-sure I had working with C++ was during my college courses. The client asked whether I could take a look at an existing C++ issue and was stumped when I said that I was not the best choice for that task. I later found out that my company resume had indeed indicated I had advanced C++ skills. Fortunately for me and my firm, this was not a C++ project, and the client was not too upset.

Chris Williams This situation is probably more common than most folks (and companies) would like to admit. It's also a warning flag that a company may be getting desperate (due to a decreasing sales pipeline) to staff people to avoid a large bench. As a consultant, you can easily be flattered by this ini-tially. After all, if you pull this off, you're a hero. Of course, you're also set-ting yourself up for it to keep happening.

Summary

Understanding the whole picture of how a technology consulting firm works and where you fit into the picture is a key factor to being successful. However, none of that matters if you don't find a good firm to work for—one that does not fall into one of the categories described in Chapter 2—and manage to get into that company. The next chapter provides you with the tips and tech-niques you need to break into this business.

CHAPTER FOUR

GETTING IN: TEN UNSTATED TRAITS THAT TECHNOLOGY CONSULTING FIRMS LOOK FOR

MOVING FROM THE world of university into the actual world can be shocking. When you get close to the end of your high school career (at least in the United States), you go forth, take a test, such as the SATs, and get a number that represents the sum total of your accomplishments. Depending on how you do, you might be able to leverage that score into getting into the college of your choice. Sadly, there is no comparable test you can take when you get past that point in your life.

Getting into a consulting company depends on factors that are much more subjective and, frankly, not always as fair as the selection criteria for your getting into college (and that is saying a lot because selection criteria for getting into college are hardly the most fair in the world). Some things, like having good technical skills, are going to be obvious. Others are factors you probably always suspected, but rarely do people actually admit (see Table 4-1).

TABLE 4-1

Tips for Breaking into Consulting

Tip	Summary
Tip #1: Appearance	As much as we hate the fact that this is true, clients don't just buy a set of skills, but rather they buy an image. Looking the part matters.
Tip #2: Be Really Good at Being Interviewed for Jobs	One of the biggest competencies of a consultant is to be very, very good at the job interviewing game because when you're a consultant, it is actually part of your job.
Tip #3: Always Be Learning (Have a Reasonably Broad Skill Set)	The more you read, the broader your knowledge base and the more likely it is that you will get into consulting, where there is a premium on players who not only have good skills, but have a reasonably broad skill set (but not too broad—there are only so many things you can know at a useful level). It is especially relevant to expand expertise beyond technology and into industry verticals.
Tip #4: Be a Scarce Commodity	All other things being equal, having skills that are in short supply and high demand will always open doors for you.
Tip #5: Be Active in Your Technical Community	People who are active in their technical community are seen as very attractive consultants.
Tip #6: Be Easy to Work With	Generally speaking, consulting firms tend to avoid prima-donna types who bring outsized egos to the table. Being perceived as a team player who works well with others is very helpful.
Tip #7: Energy, ENERGY, Energy*$&%!	Although by itself having energy doesn't mean a great deal, combining all these things with a good deal of energy and enthusiasm is a great way to set you apart from the crowd.
Tip #8: Demonstrate Great Writing Skills	It's not just code you need to be able to write. You need to be competent writing documentation and even email. Being able to write in complete sentences is a big win in the consulting business where clear communication is a critical success factor.
Tip #9: Develop Your Network	The more people you know in technology consulting, the better chances you will land a position that isn't one of the Seven Deadly Firms from Chapter 2, "The Seven Deadly Firms."
Tip #10: Live a Balanced Life	Being one-dimensional (all about technology, for example) can make you quite a bore. If you do nothing but technology, you will burn out, and burnout is not difficult to spot by people who make hiring decisions.

Tip #1: Appearance

Sadly, most people make decisions based on packaging—that is, how a product looks. When you think about this concept for a second, it really isn't that controversial. Think about houses rather than people. When you meet a real estate agent to put your home up for sale, the first thing the realtor does is give you a list of projects you need to do to spruce up your house to add curb appeal. You are asked to keep the lawn mowed, remove the clutter, and generally make the home look really nice. And should you ever have someone come through the house and you accidentally left out the kids' toys, you definitely will hear it from your real estate agent.

These human tendencies do not change just because you are in the technology consulting business. When you realize that, you will determine how marketable you are by what skills you have, how well you seem to work with others, and, right or wrong, how you present yourself.

Let's think about this from a buyer's standpoint. Many people who buy technology consulting services are doing so to reduce risk. Coming into an initial meeting or interview without having paid some attention to appearance—be it coming in with a stained shirt, rumpled attire, or otherwise ungroomed—sends the message that even on this most important day when you are probably trying to impress us, you didn't even bother. This, of course, is generally true, since the day of the interview, the day when you make the sale, tends to be the one when most people put forth their greatest effort.

In other words, the buyer wants to see a polished product. Especially if he or she is being asked to pay handsomely for this product, which is usually true, at least in the eyes of a buyer of consulting services. Now, "good looking" here comes with some caveats. Keep in mind that there is something to be said for "looking the part." Walking into the interview wearing a three-piece suit, when you are interviewing at a tech company, is likely to send the wrong message. The best tip here is to understand the culture of the consultancy where you are interviewing. If most of the clients on the client list seem like technology-oriented companies, perhaps the big power suit is not the right attire. On the other hand, if most of the clients are known for how conservative they are or have names that end in *Bank*, *Financial*, or *Trust*, the suit is probably a good idea. (Frankly, for tech people, the three-piece with the vest is never a good idea; nobody believes the idea that a real technologist would wear a three-piece.)

Of course, one of the best ways to know what is acceptable is to simply ask the person scheduling the interview what the dress code is. Then generally go on the more conservative side of what that person says. The minimum standards should be, on the clothing front, to make it neat and make sure it doesn't smell bad (wearing the clothes you slept in is not good).

Looking good really goes further than this though. Although dressing well is a first step, you can take additional steps to make it more likely you will not miss the short list of candidates. Over the longer term, being fit, meaning working out regularly, will do wonders for your ability to walk in to interviews with confidence. Does this mean body fat percentage implies employability? No. However, almost all people who have studied the link between exercise and career success have demonstrated that the benefits of working out—being active regularly—have significant effects on your own self-confidence. This self-confidence spills over into your interactions with potential employers, which leads to a tendency to succeed.

Does this mean you have to be in perfect shape, have great hair, and have a wardrobe filled with expensive suits to make it? Certainly not. It is more of a matter of making sure you make no huge mistakes, such as showing up to the interview at the bank wearing a t-shirt that says "I'm With Stupid" and jeans with holes in them. If you have questions, consider buying an outfit or two at a higher end retailer, where the salesperson will often give you some frank advice for what works for you and what doesn't.

> **Chris Williams**   It should go without saying that this advice isn't really limited to just the interview. It should, but it doesn't. Many times, I've seen consultants rapidly adopt the dress code of the lowest common denominator at the client. Just because some of the guys on your new team like ThinkGeek t-shirts doesn't mean you should bust yours out. Stay professional. Make an impression with your work, not your wardrobe.

With respect to appearance generally, this tip really comes down to the fact that people would rather work with folks who are physically, mentally, and emotionally well than people who are not. If it is at all within your control to remove the "packaging" variable from the equation, you should do everything you can to do so if it is your intent to work in technology consulting. Although there will always be counterexamples of people who have made it despite coming into work every day with wrinkled clothes and a general sense of unkemptness, doing so is like starting a game of football and giving your opponent a seven-point lead to start. You can get there, but chances are you are going to have to work a lot harder. Given that this is one of the easiest factors to control, there is no reason not to make sure you do everything you can to not leave anything to chance.

⮡

Tip #2: Be Really Good at Being Interviewed for Jobs

It is not lost on the author that this advice on being good at interviews is a little like saying, "The best way to become rich is to be really good at making money." It might be true that if you are good at this, you probably don't need to read this chapter much.

There is something to be said for emphasizing that in technology consulting, more than technology jobs in general, being really good at interviewing matters. In a general technology job, the chief purpose of the interview is to ascertain whether you have the required technical skills and, perhaps, reasonable enough interpersonal, or "soft," skills. On the other hand, because part of your success in technology consulting is your own ability to sell yourself, the interview is usually seen as an audition that demonstrates how you will do in the *client* interviews that, as a technology consultant, you will partake in very frequently.

Volumes have been written about succeeding at the game of job interviewing. Starting with *What Color Is Your Parachute* by Richard Bolles, and going from there, you can get a lot of great detailed advice on how to become good at interviewing. Beyond those general tips, Table 4-2 shows some more specific tips.

TABLE 4-2

Tips for the Consulting Interview

Tip	Explanation
Understand the reason why the consultancy where you are interviewing is different.	Interviews are part information exchange but also part exercise in flattery. Being able to explain to potential employers what makes *them* special not only demonstrates understanding, it makes the interviewees feel better about themselves—not a bad thing for you!
Be ready to explain how previous projects have achieved their return on investment (ROI).	This tip is generally a good idea but is especially important in consulting, where the ability to communicate a message about return on investment really can help land projects.
Ascertain which technical areas you will be interviewed on and be ready to answer even detailed trivia questions.	You will almost certainly be technically interviewed by people who are presently consultants. And because most places do not train people in how to interview, these people generally are not very good at it. Be ready for ridiculous trivia questions.
Demonstrate how you learn new material.	Better consulting firms will ask a question about how you go about making yourself a better software professional over time. If your answer is limited to "company-paid training," you are probably in trouble. Be ready to talk about what you read and how you learn in a way that shows you are a self-starter.
If coming from a position not in consulting, demonstrate you have an understanding of what consulting is.	You are reading this book, which is a good start. Generally, companies prefer to hire technology consultants who won't be surprised by the nuances of how this business works. The reason is that consulting firms are often burned hiring people who later quit because they didn't know what to expect.

Derik Whittaker One thing to watch out for is selling yourself as having more knowledge or abilities than you really have. If you mention a term or a technology, make sure that you are able to explain what you mean. If the company thinks you are simply throwing around buzzwords, it is likely not to want to hire you.

Understand the Reason Why the Consultancy Where You Are Interviewing Is Different

Showing interest in why a given firm exists, including what it does to distinguish itself from the competition, is a great way to demonstrate your interviewing competence. Doing so shows that you spent some time doing research, which is never a bad thing. It also shows that you have probably thought about what your specific skills can bring to the table. Demonstrating that you do your due diligence preinterview is a way to show that, as a technology consultant going on a client interview, you are probably going to be someone for whom management does not have to cajole into doing research. This means you will be a lower-maintenance hire, and when you are dealing with a firm that might be managing an office of 20, 30, or even 50 consultants, that isn't a bad thing at all.

The other reason why this technique works is that it appeals to the ego of the interviewer, but in a subtle way. All the people who work at a company, particularly those who make hiring decisions, want to feel good about their company. Having someone from the outside who validates why a given company exists flatters the person doing the interview by flattering the company that person was smart enough to work for.

Be Ready to Explain the Return on Investment for Previous Projects

There is a sense, possibly unfair, by people who manage software developers that most software developers just want to write code and really don't care about such "Pointy Haired Boss" issues like return on investment (ROI). Although the truth of this assertion might be debatable, the perception persists. Being able to run counter to this perception and clearly explain how the investment in your previous project translated to either the company saving money or adding revenue is a great way to demonstrate why you should be hired.

Why would a technology consulting firm care about this skill? Remember that when you interview, the firm is asking you this question to see how well you will answer it when you are presented to a client. Having a consultant who can clearly state how technology can add value to the bottom line is a huge asset to a technology consultancy. It creates a sense that you are a business-savvy developer, a much easier sell to clients than someone who fits the stereotype of software developer who just wants to keep his or her head down and code.

Ascertain Which Technical Areas You Will Be Interviewed on and Expect Trivia Questions

Few resources show technology consultants how to conduct effective technical interviews. And it shows. Although some buck this trend (ThoughtWorks, in particular, having a fairly well-thought-out process), the process at most companies is as follows:

+ See who has time to interview (who is on the bench and so on).
+ Schedule an hour to talk on the phone.

That hour is frequently an "anything goes" conversation in which the poor interviewer is being asked to ascertain someone's technical skill. Because most technology consultants are not terribly good at interviewing, and because most learned what technical interviews are from *others* who were terrible at it, these interviews tend to resort to getting a list of technical questions and asking the candidate the questions, one by one, checking off whether he or she got them right or wrong.

This process tends to lead to the trivia question effect. The test might start out as reasonable, but somehow a bad hire slips through, so some effort is made to make the test harder because the test itself is blamed for the result. Of course, not a lot of thought goes into what harder means, so rather than introduce better questions that test for the real factors that matter (logic and reasoning skills, knowledge of what a given technology can do), the test is oriented toward specific trivia (what method do you use to do X, where X is some obscure thing almost nobody does). This "harder" test appears to work because it screens out heavily, which reinforces this bad result.

Chris Williams This approach is extremely common at body shops as well. If the interviewer appears to be resisting any attempts at a technical conversation or discussion, instead slavishly adhering to a scripted set of tech trivia, you may want to consider looking elsewhere.

Because of this dynamic, it is likely that you will need to cram and study ahead of the interview so you can pass the trivia challenge. To give yourself the best chance of this, it is a good idea to know what areas are going to be tested. You should already know a good deal about these areas because you are probably claiming knowledge of them on your resume. The point here, though, is to use the time leading up to the interview to perhaps brush up your knowledge of specifics, as silly as that might seem.

Remember, clients will likely be interviewing you too; and even in consulting firms that have sane technical interviewing processes, not all clients will. Having the capability to take a deep dive on specifics of a technology prior to an interview will serve you well.

Demonstrate How You Learn New Material

Technology consulting firms prefer people who are self-motivated and who are able to learn something without having to be sent to a training class each and every time. This is not to say that technology consulting firms never send people to training, conferences, or other opportunities to learn things. They frequently do, especially when people are on the bench, so they send people to learn something that would make them more marketable.

If you do not demonstrate that you are able to be engaged in your occupation to the point where you go out and learn stuff on your own, if only for your own employability, you are likely going to be seen as someone who will stagnate. This is why most good employers ask, "What do you read to keep up?" or some question along those lines that gets at how you keep up with the industry.

A frequent answer to this question from many interviewees I have talked to is, "Oh, I read blogs," or, "I keep up by reading magazine articles." Although these are good places to start, it is even better to be able to say which specific blogs and magazines you read and talk about what is interesting about them at length. Maybe you read an article that you thought was particularly insightful; talking about something specific that you read recently and how it can apply to a real business problem is a good way to demonstrate that you are constantly learning. It also helps you strike up an interesting conversation in the interview about the topic. This can be a great means of establishing rapport with your interviewer, which tends to be a good harbinger for getting to the offer stage.

Generally, technology consulting companies look for people who take responsibility for their own training plan, rather than make demands on the company to "show them the way." Although some companies and managers provide some level of guidance, all things being equal, they would rather hire self-starters than people who rely on others to motivate them to improve.

Demonstrate That You Have an Understanding of What Consulting Is

One of the biggest causes of turnover in the technology consulting business is hiring a new consultant who does not have a real understanding of what he or she will face when entering this business. The consultant comes on and decides either the travel is too much or gets a client that results in a bad commute for a while or for some other reason decides that consulting isn't for him or her. This happens frequently enough that many firms work hard to make sure that the people they hire are going to be okay with the way this business works.

Given this, it does not hurt to make sure that during the interview process you demonstrate an understanding of what the work and commute conditions actually are in the technology consulting business. Of course, reading this book is a good first step to understanding, but more importantly, you need to demonstrate what you learn here during the interview. When asked, for example, what you would do if you had two weeks of bench time, you will know that "sitting in the office playing XBox" is probably the wrong answer. All things being equal, most technology firms will select the person who has a working knowledge of technology consulting over the one who does not.

> **Jason Bock**   If you're interviewed at a client and placed there, remember the style of the interview so you can share it with other consultants from your firm if the client needs to ramp up staffing. The questions I've been asked at clients can be mundane, bizarre, obtuse, and so on, so letting others know what you were asked gives them an advantage.

⤳

Tip #3: Always Be Learning

The 1980s movie *Glengarry Glen Ross* has a famous line in it when the sales manager is pumping up the sales force: "ABC—Always Be Closing." The idea is that no matter what the current prospect is talking about, the direction of the conversation should be toward getting clients to sign on the dotted line.

Thankfully, in technology, we don't have to have that kind of pressure to "close the deal" on a daily basis. In tech, we are better served by "ABL" or "Always Be Learning." The reality is that this is a fast-moving business, one that either (depending on your opinion) is constantly innovating new things, or more cynically, sometimes innovating but at least frequently re-inventing. In either case, to keep up, you must Always Be Learning.

So how do you go about this? This section covers the main techniques you use to keep up with the rapidly changing world of technology (see Table 4-3).

TABLE 4-3
Resources to "Always Be Learning"

Resource	When to Use It
Books and Whitepapers	If a topic has piqued your interest, investing in a quality book on the topic that explains the concepts well is always a good start. Whitepapers can be good ways to introduce yourself to a topic in more of a long-form setting.
Magazine Articles	Even though generally fewer software professionals are subscribing to trade magazines in recent years, there are still publications worth picking up and reading on a regular basis.
Blogs and Forums	Blogs are helpful in a couple of ways. By subscribing to a diverse set of blogs, there is a good chance you will become aware of technologies you would not otherwise. Blogs and forums are also useful as a resource for learning from others when they post solutions to common problems.
Conferences and User Group Meetings	Attending technology-focused events is a great way to not only learn something from a talk, but also get a chance to ask questions, face to face, with leaders in the field. That said, the knowledge gained tends to be shallower and more introductory.
Paid Training	If you can afford it, or your company will send you, paying for training is a good way to take a deep dive into a technology.
Downloading the Bits and Trying Them Out	All these resources can't beat actually downloading the new technology, writing a "hello world" application, and going from there to try to build something useful with it. Nothing will make you learn faster than doing.

Books and Whitepapers

Nothing can replace having good reference material when you are learning a new technology. Certainly, a lot of material is available out there, and you probably do not have enough hours in your life to read everything. But for select topics that seem important based on your research on blogs or other reading, finding the best book and then reading it is a good way to complement some of the things this section discusses.

Finding the book that is at the right level is key. It is probably not terribly helpful to pick up a detailed reference book when you need an introduction.

Do not be afraid to ask around and get recommendations on what the best current book is to learn a given technology.

Whitepapers are a good way to get introduced to a concept so that you can at least be briefed on why a technology is important. Generally considered a middle ground between shorter magazine articles and books, whitepapers can usually be read (not just scanned) in an hour or two, somewhat consistent with most people's attention span for taking in this kind of material.

Magazine Articles

As the world moves toward online media, the footprint of magazine articles on the desks of software professionals has been on the decline. However, there still are some very good resources that come in print form as well as online form. Although they do not have the detail of books or whitepapers, they provide a moderately deep dive on a technology that someone thought was worthy of publication.

Magazines have a nice added advantage in that you can easily take them with you on planes, into the bathroom, or simply read them separately away from the distraction of your computer. There is definitely something to be said for reading an article without your email notification icon flashing at you.

Blogs and Forums

Books, whitepapers, and magazine articles are more broadcast-style forms of learning: One person writes something with the intent of distributing it toward a large audience. Blogs and forums, on the other hand, provide many more chances for interactivity. The advantages of blogs are that you can build a blog feed using feed-readers like Google Reader or Bloglines; they aggregate the posts of hundreds of people who are so interested in technology that they bother to put their thoughts out to the world online.

There are two main advantages to learning via this method. Subscribing to a few dozen high-quality blogs gives you a chance, every single day, to learn about topics you might want to take a deeper dive with. Through the comment function, you have a chance to interact with the thought leaders in a way that simply reading a book does not.

Of course, blogs are probably not the place for a deep dive on a given technology, though there are exceptions. But they do frequently contain good nuggets of information that are useful in the debugging process.

Forums, especially forums populated by strong communities of people who post frequently, are also great places to learn new things and have a chance to interact online. Particularly, places like stackoverflow.com, infoq.com, and other similar news/forum combination sites are great ways to learn about new technologies as well as interact.

Conferences and User Group Meetings

Further up on the interaction continuum, attending conferences and user group meetings is a great way to get introductions and tips on using new technologies, while getting a great opportunity to network. Presentations at these kinds of events tend to be around 45–75 minutes and are either focused on a narrow topic for technologies that have been around or more general for newer technologies that are just being introduced.

Of course, it is probably too much to expect that in 45 minutes you will become an expert in a technology. Most of these kinds of forums seek to accomplish getting you enough information to know (1) what the technology is, (2) why it is useful, and (3) where to go to dive deeper. In most cases, you will get a chance to ask questions and discuss the topic at hand with an expert as well, which is a great way to network and get some great information.

User groups, in most cases, are no charge. Certain regional events also fall into this category, such as code camps. That said, if you have a week to spend, going to national events like QCon, TechEd, JAOO, and VSLive is a great way to get in a lot of talks from leading experts on technology. It is usually definitely worth the investment.

Paid Training

Paid training, which features your working in a classroom setting on labs to take a guided deep dive in a technology, is an effective way to learn a lot in a short period of time. Although not the least expensive way to learn a new technology, if you can get your company to sponsor it, it is a great way to go. Of course, if you feel strong enough about its applicability to you that you want to fund it yourself, you should consider that option as well. Remember that you will need to recoup an investment of around $5,000 and up for some of the better classes.

Downloading the Bits and Trying Them Out

Although all these methods are useful, there is nothing better than simply downloading the technology you want to learn and using these other resources to help you take it for a spin on your own. Most programmers start by getting to "hello world" (writing a trivial app that puts a message on the screen) and go from there, acquainting themselves with some of the more useful features of the technology. This learning-by-doing approach allows you to move from abstract knowledge to practical knowledge.

Of course, this approach assumes a couple of points. First, it assumes that either the maker of the technology offers introductory, trial, or learning versions so that you have a version to learn with or that you are using open source software, so cost isn't an issue. It also assumes you will probably enhance this technique by using resources like blogs, forums, articles, books, and some of the others mentioned here to help you.

After you get the basics done, try writing an application in the new language that has some utility for you or at least is fun to write, like a simple game. Something that not only exercises the technology, but exercises how the technology integrates with databases and such is best. The reason is that it will take you through most of the paces of actual uses in a professional setting.

All these methods tied together will make it such that you have a much better answer to the, "What do you do to keep current?" interview question. They will also help you maintain a broad enough skill set that you will be attractive to consultancies eager to hire people with broad technical backgrounds who might be useful to a diverse set of clients.

Jason Bock   One of the de facto rules I've learned being a consultant is that you are pretty much expected to stay current, even if that means doing it on your own time. Your employer will usually help out with paying for training expenses, but at the end of the day you need to drive your own career and spend time learning when you can.

Michael Hugos   When I started in consulting, there were people who believed their existing skill sets would see them through their entire careers because those skills comprised the great majority of IT consulting work (in the 1980s, those skills where COBOL, CICS, and MVS). It may seem hard to believe that .NET or Java or PHP won't still be in demand five years from now, but don't count on it.

⁓

Tip #4: Be a Scarce Commodity

Learning a broad set of technologies and keeping in front of the technology curve are great ways to leverage this fourth tip, becoming a "scarce commodity." Let's face it, a lot of people can write mediocre programs that push data to and from simple forms using well-known languages like Java and C#. The key to this tip is to have something about you that sets you apart from the crowd. Doing so, having something extra, makes you more valuable to your consulting firm because people who have harder-to-find skills tend to be placed faster (have higher utilization) and bill at higher rates.

The goal for you is to add scarcity to your resume. Scarcity can be done through soft skills, such as being very presentable (see Tip #1). But also it can be done by picking good specializations and being very good at them. The trick, of course, is to pick specializations that (1) are valuable in the marketplace and (2) you are actually interested in working with. In cases where the former is true, but the latter is not, you stand a chance of putting yourself into a miserable project (did you really want to be the world's top FoxPro specialist?). On the other hand, you could specialize in technologies that are a lot of fun, like niche languages, but also have a limited market.

Specialist or Generalist?

I have always believed the question of being either a specialist or generalist to be a false dichotomy as it relates to technology professionals. You can have a broad skill set such that you have a good understanding of all the technologies required to architect a system but also have a few technologies where you add specialist knowledge. In fact, doing so, especially with technologies that are particularly in demand or have a perception of being difficult but important, are ways to greatly add to your marketability as a consultant.

Of course, doing so requires a lot of work. Some of the things we talked about earlier in Tip #3, "Always Be Learning,"—particularly the need to read a broad set of blogs, books, and other information sources on a regular basis—help you stay on top of the general picture. For gaining a good specialty, that is a bit trickier. You could go the path of simply doing a survey of the most in-demand skills by looking at job postings, doing a little research on what skills pay the most, and doing everything you can to learn the subject. That approach can be effective to a point, but sometimes the market works against you because lots of other people might be going into the specialty and decreasing the marketability of it. In other words, the market does, in fact, work from time to time, with the increased rates drawing more people to the field, which means that later entrants will not get the same benefits that early entrants do.

Selection of Early Technologies to Specialize In

To become the early entrant is somewhat trickier. To do that, you have to anticipate where the market is going to go and try to learn the technology while it is still in its emerging stages. While this is difficult, it is not impossible. Good candidates for specialization are usually new technologies coming from large software vendors where there is a significant marketing spend (that is, lots of advertising, lots of buzz, solutions for a large class of problems). While there are technologies worth specializing in that do not meet these criteria, the less they are in this category, the more you need to consider that you could spend a lot of time learning something that may or may not have economic value. This is perfectly okay if it is something you are interested in and would do even if it wasn't a career move. However, when you're prioritizing what you spend time on, this issue is definitely something to consider.

$\approx$

Tip #5: Be Active in Your Technical Community

Among software developers generally, only a percentage invest their time in attending user groups, code camps, or other events where people in the technology business get together and share ideas. While this says something for those who do not go to these events, it presents a great opportunity for you because you can likely increase your chances for getting into technology consulting simply by attending and participating in these user groups.

User groups and other local gatherings of technology professionals help you accomplish a number of related goals. First, they usually have presentations of new and interesting technology that has a reasonable chance of being directly applicable to your job. If nothing else, you will learn new things at these events. Second, these venues are terrific for networking. Most of a typical software developer's workday is interaction with people within the same company. Going to community events therefore gives you a chance to meet and collaborate with people in your industry, giving you a much broader set of networking opportunities than you would likely otherwise have.

But more important, one of the main sponsors of community events tends to be *technology consulting companies*. In fact, it is not that unusual for the technology consulting firm that runs the user group to judge incoming resumes on whether the person has been an active user group participant. Getting in touch with a hiring manager at a technology consulting firm may be pretty tough a lot of the time, but at the user group, you can easily talk to the same person—largely because he or she is there to talk with potential consultants and network.

INETA (http://www.ineta.org) is the main organization that sponsors user groups in the world of .NET development. JUGs (http://community. java.net/jugs/) is the analogue for the Java community. Other technical communities can easily be found by searching the Internet for whatever technology you are interested in, followed by "user group."

> **Chris Williams** Don't be afraid to start a community as well. Lots of folks bemoan the lack of events and options in their local technical community, but few do anything about it. Nothing screams initiative like getting out there and doing it yourself. It's a lot of hard work, but it comes with a lot of rewards: Not only does it look great on a resume, but you will also increase your own knowledge and personal network in the process.

Tip #6: Be Easy to Work With

Being a prima donna (someone who generally is irritable, hard to please, and has an overly high opinion of himself or herself) is a good way *not* to get into the technology consulting business. There are some very good reasons for this, starting with the fact that people who are inflexible to different environments and afraid of criticism rarely make very good consultants. Said people either leave on their own because various clients almost always fail to live up to the prima donnas' expectations, or their huge egos alienate their clients and other developers and lead to their being removed from their engagements.

Derik Whittaker Although technical skill is always very important, it alone may not land you every job. I know that when I interview someone for a position on my team, I use what I call the "beer test." What is the beer test? I ask myself or others if the person being interviewed is the type of teammate they would like to have beer with after a long day. If I or others would not want to socialize with this person after hours, he or she may not be the right person for the team because this person may not fit in.

Let's assume for a bit that you can hold your ego in check and understand that technology consulting requires that you demonstrate some level of flexibility about your surroundings and your coworkers. By doing that, you will get a leg up over lots of candidates who try to enter technology consulting but have an unrealistic view that all clients give you an office with an ocean view, free soda, foosball, and free lunch. You demonstrate one of the most important traits of a technology consultant, namely the ability to go into situations that are less than ideal yet still produce great results.

Chris Williams There is an aphorism in the entertainment industry that "the smaller the star, the bigger the pain in the rear." The same applies in the tech industry. Don't embarrass yourself (or your employer) by being "that guy." There is always going to be someone smarter, faster, or better than you, and he or she just might work at your new client.

People who are able to roll with the punches and not get caught up too much in the day-to-day politics tend to be the kinds of people technology consultancies look to hire. There are some important reasons for this: Perfect environments that do not have political problems tend to attract some of the best and brightest to work for them directly. As such, fewer perfect potential clients need consulting services (though some do—and these are *great* clients!).

Furthermore, in many situations the consultants are called in to save projects that already are failing because of personal and/or political problems. In these cases, the consulting firm is called in to use its expert skills to "right the ship." In these situations, not only are technical skills being asked for, but great people skills; cooler heads, if you will, are what the client is really buying.

> **Chris Williams**   And if you do get called in to "right the ship," please have enough sense not to blog about it in excruciating detail for all the world to see. Even if you massage some of the details, if your client sees the blog, it will know whom you are talking about, and more importantly your *next* client will (rightfully) assume you'll do the same.

The people who run technology consulting firms know this; they deal with these realities every day. And because they do, they know that they have to hire not just for technical skills, but for the ability to be easy to work with and adaptable to change and environments. As a candidate, you need to convey your ability to work in tough environments and deal with less-than-ideal people; doing so demonstrates you are the opposite of the prima donnas that the people who run technology consulting firms see on a frequent basis.

> **Jason Bock**   At the same time, though, don't get rolled over by the punches. As a consultant, you're brought in for your expertise, and sometimes you need to raise your voice to get the client to understand when it may be going down the road of failure. The trick is to make that criticism effective rather than destructive.

Tip #7: Energy, ENERGY, Energy *$&%!

If you are looking to break in, or for that matter, if you are in an awful project with one of the Seven Deadly Firms from Chapter 2, doing whatever it takes to have energy and enthusiasm about the company you have landed the interview with will go a long way toward increasing your chances of landing the position.

Although I would certainly not recommend having six cups of coffee and washing it down with four cans of Red Bull before your technology consulting job interview, it is equally important to demonstrate a high level of energy and enthusiasm about technology and projects you have worked on in the past. Showing a readiness and willingness to jump in and start solving problems is a good way to put you in contrast with a lot of the people who consulting management deal with on a day-to-day basis.

This, of course, is natural, just as in any long-term relationship; excitement about your job will fade over time. Having a new person showing a lot of energy and enthusiasm is frequently what hiring managers in tech consulting firms are looking for when bringing in some new blood. Let's face it, most of us become cynical at times, especially on those occasions when working through the darker months of a difficult project. You too will likely go through this when you get into the midst of your technology consultant career.

It is important to note that it helps to have genuine enthusiasm here. You need to have enthusiasm about technology, and more important, what technology can do for clients. This should not be confused for enthusiasm to start collecting a salary. The latter—an enthusiasm that is more self-serving—is typically pretty easy to spot because the whole conversation is about what getting the gig will do for you, rather than being about what it will do for your clients. Of course, you will look after yourself and position yourself for success; in fact, that is what this entire book is about. In the interview, however, you need to be excited about what you can do for the consulting firm and the client, rather than the converse.

Enthusiasm About Business Results over Technology

Being enthusiastic about technology is all well and good. But to really demonstrate your value as a consultant, you should focus your enthusiasm on what technology can do for your clients, especially in the areas of improving financial performance and return on investment.

Speaking of enthusiasm, it certainly is good to be enthusiastic about technology. The fact that you enjoy technology is, we hope, one of the reasons you sought to work in this business. That said, if you are looking to communicate the right kind of energy, enthusiasm about tangible business results for your clients is probably the best kind of energy you can project. When you are talking about your prior projects, it is usually a good idea to save the heavy arm-waving part of the presentation for when you talk up the results—the $1 million saved per year because you and your team worked with the business to identify and execute on the opportunity.

Having enthusiasm is another way to demonstrate engagement with your career, your industry, your colleagues, and your clients. Companies generally look for employees who are engaged, active participants, particularly when times are not as good and they are looking for the folks who will steer them through rougher waters. Showing energy focused toward the company goals is a great way to position yourself not to only survive during rougher times, but to actually thrive.

> **Michael Hugos** While working for a very successful boutique consulting firm, I learned that it is not only important to work hard, but also important to be *perceived* as working hard. As an engagement manager there explained to me, that means arriving onsite 30 minutes before the client arrives and staying onsite 30 minutes after the client goes home.

Tip #8: Demonstrate Great Writing Skills

Unfortunately for people who got into this business to simply write code and only write code, technology consulting, like most careers that involve doing a task and working with others, requires competence in written communication between humans, not just from human to computer.

Let's think about the term *consultant* for a moment. One of the things that separates a contractor from a consultant is the former is there to do a specific job for a specific amount of time. The latter, the consultant, is there to provide other humans with advice and guidance in addition to doing work. Although some of this guidance is going to be hands-on or verbal, the vast majority of this guidance tends to be passed around in written form, in emails, or in actual documentation and reports.

One way to demonstrate this is to pay lots of attention to your resume. Although a seemingly obvious piece of advice, it bears repeating that the first writing sample that your potential employer will see is this piece of work, and having gratuitous errors in such a high-stakes document generally does not reflect well on your writing skills. Having a few people proofread this document for consistency and basic grammar is one of the fundamental steps you should always take, whether or not you want to be a technology consultant.

In addition to this, though, early in your career, you should start accumulating some of your best writing samples. Realizing that writing skills are as much of a success factor as technology skills are, many of the better technology consultancies ask for writing samples as part of the recruiting process. Generally, you will want to scrub samples and remove any trade secrets or other proprietary information. Nothing is a bigger turn-off than a candidate who demonstrates a willingness to break a nondisclosure agreement. But assuming you can do this, you should always have a few good samples of your writing available.

That being said, some of you are going to have some great writing samples out there by virtue of, perhaps, a professional blog. Assuming you carefully edit and make sure the grammar in your posts isn't horrible (and this, of course, is a mighty big assumption!), being able to point to a professional blog is not a horrible way to demonstrate both your writing skills and your excitement about the technology business in general. On the other hand, pointing an employer to a personal blog, as high as the writing quality might be there, is almost always a bad idea, particularly if the pursuits you talk about might be the least bit controversial or lascivious. Not that those things are inherently bad, but drawing attention to your personal life during the recruiting process has a good chance of negating the advantage of showing what a good writer you are. Keep it professional, however, and it is probably a good move.

As you progress to the higher levels of your consulting career, the effect of your writing skills on your career success will only increase. The more responsibility you have, the more likely you will be writing status reports, findings reports, recommendations, and other documents whose goal is to inform and frequently to persuade as well. When you are on the bench as a consultant, it is very likely you will be asked to help write proposals, which are high-stakes documents that help determine whether your consultancy will win a project. This is why, as a general rule, firms that hire not just for skill, but for aptitude as well, almost always have submitting a writing sample as part of the hiring process.

You may wince at this aspect, particularly if writing isn't exactly why you got into this business. And it is true that you can be quite successful in technology consulting and not be a terrific writer. However, developing this skill can only increase your chances of success and is certainly yet another way, all things being equal, to increase your employability and your ultimate success as a consultant.

⌒

Tip #9: Develop Your Network

In Chapter 1, "Why Consulting?" you learned a great deal about how building out your personal network is a key reason to get into technology consulting. And it is true that a good reason to enter the technology consulting business is that it can drastically expand the network of individuals you know and work with. However, it is also true that to get into technology consulting in the first place, it is an excellent idea to preemptively develop your network by being active in your community (see Tip #5) and, as important, working to keep in regular touch with those you have worked with in the past who have moved on to other companies.

For the person entering technology consulting, building out a good network has three primary benefits. First, a larger network increases the chances you will be able to know which firms are good and which ones are not. Being able to get the word-of-mouth war stories about who the technology consulting players are in a given city will help you avoid ending up at a Deadly Firm. Second, there is a good chance that, with a broad network, you will have either a friend, or at least a friend of a friend, who might be in a position to hire you and thus give you an inside track on a position. Third, having a broad network makes you more valuable to the consultancy that hires you because a "connected" potential consultant will have much more valuable contacts for both sales and recruiting than one who isn't as connected. By every objective measure, having a good network makes you a much better candidate than one who does not.

That said, networking isn't just showing up at parties and engaging in small-talk over chardonnay. Developing and nurturing a good network take a good deal of organization and effort. It is relatively easy to have a shallow network of people with whom you met once and have since not paid attention to. The more challenging bit is making the effort to reach out to your circle of current and former colleagues on a regular basis, investing the time and energy required to keep in touch, and actually be interested in what's going on in their personal and professional lives. However, it is definitely worth doing, especially when you don't need something. People are suspicious of others who network with an agenda; nobody wants to go to lunch just to be "sold." Building a network when you don't need one is the best way to have one in those times when you do need one.

The best investment you can make in your own career security is building and maintaining a great network. A good goal is to do one thing per week, be it a lunch or even reaching out to someone in an email to catch up, just to see how people around you are doing. You will frequently be surprised how useful it is to not be stuck on an island by yourself as you progress through your career.

Michael Hugos In my career, the most effective ways to build my network have been to participate regularly in relevant professional associations and to be a good writer. I spend a lot of time writing and learning to be a better writer, yet it is through my writing that I often get noticed and invited to speak or invited to participate in projects. These invitations turn into good networking opportunities.

Tip #10: Live a Balanced Life

Although the previous nine tips are all useful ways to make your case for breaking into consulting, none of it will matter if you forget that nobody ever went to his or her death-bed wishing to have spent more time at the office. If you do nothing but work, in your networking attempts (see Tip #9) you will find that most of your networking conversations are all about work. Although the topic can be interesting for a while, a conversation that is nothing but shop talk tends to become boring. Having interests outside work, be they family, hobbies, travel, or other diversions, gives you experiences that form the basis of more interesting conversations.

One of the best pieces of advice in this area is to have at least one frequent activity that is "away from the screen." Not that video games, movies, blogging, or Internet surfing are bad things to do; they are actually all very good things. However, having something that is more active than passive will not only keep you in better shape and reduce your chance of developing eye strain, but it will open you up to a set of activities that are shown to reduce stress and promote emotional health.

People in the technology business who do nothing but work tend to become burned out and lose the energy and drive that made them good in the first place. When these things set in, it is hard to fake the energy (see Tip #7), the willingness to Always Be Learning (see Tip #3), and the general desire to succeed that it takes to launch a technology consulting career. Over time, the passion fades, and you find yourself watching the clock and not caring much about your career at all. Not a terribly great way to live. Nothing is worse than hating what you do for eight to ten hours per day.

> **Michael Hugos**   Living a balanced life is easier said than done. I find that my best hope of balancing my work life and my private life is to do work that I am interested in and that I like so much that it is okay if it spills over into my personal life. I do not believe it is possible to advance in your career if you keep a strict separation between work life and personal life. So if you do work you love, then you won't mind so much that at times it takes up all your time.

> **Jason Bock**   That's not to say that there aren't developers out there who truly live, breathe, and eat code. There's nothing wrong with that, nor should it be discouraged. However, I've personally found that a diverse set of beneficial experiences in life always helps me grow in ways I didn't expect.

⁓

Summary

These ten tips are oriented toward launching your career in technology consulting, but they are also critical for surviving and thriving in the long run. They are oriented toward making you the best possible candidate for joining a firm. Of course, not all firms are equal, as Chapter 2 discusses. The next chapter covers the questions you need to ask before you join so you do not end up in a Deadly Firm or a company that is unlikely to be a good place to work.

CHAPTER FIVE

What You Need to Ask Before You Join a Technology Consulting Firm

There are lots of places to work; few are truly rewarding.

As everyone who runs a technology consulting firm knows, there is no shortage of competitors in this business. In fact, the cost of entry into this business is shockingly low. You only need to sell a project with more than one person involved, and suddenly, you can call yourself a technology consulting firm. And frankly, many do! Although not bad inherently, and in fact good if you are looking to start into this business by owning one, it does make for a lot of mediocre-to-bad firms out there doing business.

This chapter focuses on specific questions you need to ask any technology consulting firm you may ever want to work for during the hiring process. You should not be afraid of asking these questions, even if they seem hard and/or privileged information. On balance, if a company does not want to disclose an answer, that company probably has something to hide—which should itself present a large red flag. Your goal should be to work for a consultancy that operates in a transparent manner so that you can know when things are good, bad, and ugly, rather than be surprised.

☙

Interviews Are Not Just for the Employer

Probably one of the first points to understand, right off the bat, is that job interviews are not a series of tests to be passed so some employer can throw you some table scraps. You need to treat the interview process as an opportunity to make sure you are not putting yourself in a position that leaves both you and your potential employer worse off. Getting into a company ill-suited to you—too much travel, wrong technology, wrong culture, and so on—usually ends up being a disaster for not only your career, but your piece of mind and sanity.

> **Derik Whittaker**   Be strong here. It is perfectly acceptable to walk away from a positional firm (and is highly recommended) if the firm is not able to answer your questions to your liking. Remember, this interview is a two-way street; you too have some power and control.

The problem most people face is that they view "snagging an interview" a huge win. At this point, they have not only a personal stake in the process, but probably some hopes that the interview will go really well. This leads to over-looking flaws, just to keep the momentum going. If you think about it, most of us have been taught from an early age to be deferential toward potential employers. We work really hard to make the resume perfect; we do all the things described in the preceding chapter to make sure we are marketable, and we certainly make sure not to make simple mistakes like being rude to the secretary on our way in. All these things that you condition yourself with on the way to the interview turn you away from asking questions that may either break the deal or seem impolite.

For the good of your career, once you have gotten far enough through the interview process that there is at least a sense of mutual interest, it is absolutely critical that you knock the angel from your shoulder telling you not to ask any hard questions of the nice person at the other end of the table. The

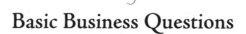

consequences of joining a company that will make you miserable, unemployed, or otherwise worse off are typically far higher than the consequences of not getting a particular position. And frankly, any company worth working for will realize this and respect you for asking these kinds of questions.

One caveat here that applies to each of these questions is to make sure you look not only at the answers given, but also *how* the interviewers answer the questions. Look for signs of evasiveness, like fidgeting, a change in timbre of the voice of the person answering, and other body language that shows the signs that someone is either stretching the truth or lying to you. This method isn't foolproof because some people are very good liars, but on balance, being on the lookout for what *is* said versus what *isn't* said is a good way to know where to probe deeper, at the very least. For example, if someone gives an evasive answer to a sales pipeline question, this may be a place where you want to probe more, not less.

> **Jason Bock** When you're interviewed by the technical personnel (and you will be!), interview them at a technical level. You want to make sure you're joining a company that has consultants with the same (or better) technical abilities as you have. If the interviewer asks all sorts of hard technical questions that are coming from a cheat sheet, a couple of probing technical questions from you may uncover a firm that doesn't meet your technical expectations.

Basic Business Questions

Table 5-1 lists some basic business questions that are good starting points for understanding the employer you are evaluating. Rest assured, these are the most basic questions any investor would ask when considering investing in a company. Given that you, as a consultant, are investing yourself into a company by becoming an employee, it is critical you get these questions answered to your satisfaction.

The audience for these questions is typically someone at the general manager (GM) level or above. Even if people lower on the organization chart have answers to these questions, you need to understand how voluntarily and honestly the people who are in real power in a company will answer the questions.

TABLE 5-1

Basic Business Questions

Question	Why Ask It?
What is your annual revenue?	You probably should know whether you are dealing with a large company, small company, or something in between.
What is your net profit? What is your Earnings Before Income Taxes, Debt, and Amortization (EBITDA)?	A company can have a good deal of revenue and still be unhealthy. You want a company that not only generates revenue, but has some left over for its investors.
What is your target for profit margin? Why not higher? Why not lower?	Knowing the target margin tells you a good deal about whether the company is meeting its goals when you consider actual margin that you can calculate from the preceding two measures. It opens a conversation about the strategy under which the firm operates.
How many billing consultants do you have? What is the mix of subcontractors to consultants?	This information allows you to estimate revenue per consultant if you know the revenue. It also tells you indirectly how many hours you will need to charge per year when combined with other answers. The sub-to-consultant ratio tells you whether the organization really invests in people or acts more like a broker.
What is your target growth rate? How do you plan to achieve it?	This information helps you understand *how* and *how much* the company intends to grow. Be wary of overly optimistic growth targets or overly pessimistic ones.
Are consultants allowed to see the sales pipeline and other operational reports?	You want to work for companies that work in a transparent manner. This question helps establish how transparent they are.
What is the exit strategy?	Do the owners have a plan? They asked you where you want to be in five years. This is a good opportunity to turn the tables and see whether they have a realistic plan.

What Is Your Annual Revenue?

Asking about annual revenue tells you some important information. First, it gives you a sense for the size of the organization. Your career tactics in different consulting organizations will often vary by organization size, so knowing the size is important. Smaller companies, defined here as less than $10 million in revenue, are usually structured such that everyone outside those in a strict sales capacity is billing in some capacity. Companies like this tend to have less tolerance for bench time, tend to have more expensive health plans (in the United States), and are inherently riskier. But they offer more rewards: If the company is growing, you will be one of the people on the ground floor, potentially with a better shot at really good leadership opportunities as the company grows. Many in this range offer equity participation as well, which allows you to profit if the company ever gets sold.

Mid-sized companies ($10M to $200M) offer more of a balance. You are not on the ground floor anymore, and by now, company politics are a fact of life. If there is equity participation, it is usually much less significant for all but the most senior hires. But there is also more stability, more bench time, and probably bigger projects. Whereas small companies tend to either strictly do staff augmentation, or live and die by particular projects, mid-sized companies are more diversified, such that one client leaving does not devastate the company. These companies are large enough so that you benefit from having your brand attached to them, but not so large that you become just another number.

Large companies ($200M and up) often offer more stability in exchange for less opportunity. In better large companies, you have a client base that is diverse—in different industries, different technologies, and different regions of the world. In the event that demand is weak in your region, your worst case is that you may have to travel to another region and work there for a time. In a properly managed large consultancy, if you are doing your job well, at least better than the lowest 10 or 20 percent of your colleagues, you are pretty well provided total job security.

However, large companies are not always this stable. Some larger companies are simply collections of a number of smaller units that act like small companies. At some large technology consulting organizations, bench time is either paid at reduced salary, or after two weeks, it is standard procedure to let you go. Because large companies are less likely to provide you opportunities to really have the management/investors understand your value, you will more likely be viewed purely through the lens of "personal utilization"—that is, your ratio of billing time to overall time. And if that falls short, some larger companies will be more severe in cutting you out than small companies. The section titled "What Do You Do with Bench Time?" delves more in depth to give you means to separate good large companies from bad.

The nice thing about this question—what is your annual revenue?—is that it is simple. The answer should be "Our revenue is *X*." In technology consulting, unlike income or other financial measures, there are no real ways to spin this question, with perhaps the exception of "revenue or revenue net of reimbursements." Your follow-up would be to ask "after reimbursements are taken out" because it makes little sense to count as real revenue what does not come from actual work performed.

What Is Your Net Income? What Is Your EBITDA?

Just like you personally have a net income after taxes, companies have net income after payment for costs of goods sold (in consulting, this means consultant's salaries), rent on office space, salaries for sales, and other overhead expenses. To make sure the company you are considering joining is healthy, you need to ask about net income. As mentioned in Chapter 1, "Why Consulting?" a technology consulting firm should have enough earnings left over after all expenses that the investors in the company make a reasonable profit to compensate for their risks.

When you ask about earnings, I always recommend asking the question about net income first, without modifiers. The response will either be a number or, if the person you are asking has more of an operations or finance background, might be, "What type of income?" Your answer in such a case should be "EBITDA" (*ee-bit-dah*), which means Earnings Before Income Taxes, Debt, and Amortization. In the event that you are not asked, "What type of income?" your follow-up response should be, "Is that EBITDA or some other measure?"

EBITDA is typically what accountants and analysts use to judge earnings from one company to the next. Although being able to demonstrate you know what EBITDA means is a good way to demonstrate business acumen during a job interview, the answer to the question is actually pretty meaningful. Companies that make money tend to have more of a war chest to invest in their people, invest in pursuit of more clients, and spend to keep consultants on the bench longer than they would otherwise.

I recommend asking this EBITDA question of the most senior person you are scheduled to meet with during the interview process. The answers to this question that should give you the most pause are "I don't know" or the more sinister twin, "We don't disclose." The former speaks to incompetence: No real decision maker would not know how much money the company actually makes. The latter speaks to a lack of transparency, especially given that the company's making money is such an important indicator of your own job security.

What Is Your Target for Profit Margin? Why Not Higher? Why Not Lower?

Although you can infer what the actual margin is from the previous questions (revenue, EBITDA), it does not hurt to understand what the company has as a target for profit margin. Although the previous answers are fact-based, this question about profit margin speaks more toward in what direction the managers and/or owners want to take the business.

The number provided should tell you about how much risk the company is willing to take on. A company looking for a mid to high single-digit percent margin (6–9 percent) is potentially competing on price (lower margin) or looking to sacrifice some margin to pursue a higher growth strategy (sell some consulting at close to cost to increase sales). A company looking to operate at a higher margin, on the other hand, might be taking a market position to not compete on price, but rather use its leverage and/or brand to achieve higher margins.

Frankly, there are a lot of reasons why margin will be targeted a certain way, and all of them make great conversation starters! This is especially true when you ask follow-up questions like, "Why not higher?" or "Why not lower?" By asking these kinds of *why* questions, you are engaging the senior management in a conversation that gets at the heart of the strategies the company is employing. Should you decide to join, you probably have a good deal more information about how you can help the firm achieve its margin target.

How Many Billing Consultants Do You Have?
What Is the Mix of Subcontractors to Consultants?

There are multiple aspects to this question of billing consultants, especially when combined with the answers to the other questions, that make this really, really important. To start, though, size itself is a good measure of what employee number you are. Even more than revenue directly, this number gives you a visceral sense for how much of an impact you can make on the company directly. There is a big difference between being 1 of 10 and being 1 of 10,000.

The raw count by itself, however, is just the surface-level reason this question is important. If you know the revenue and profit of an organization, knowing the number of billing consultants gives you enough information to derive the *revenue per consultant* that you will be expected to generate. This number is critically important because it provides one of the key numbers that goes into the equation, "How many hours must I bill to have a good year?" When that answer is combined with the answer to the question, "What do you anticipate as a billable rate for someone with my skill set?" you will have enough information such that you can derive what the expected number of billing hours are per year, without even having to ask directly! Simply divide your revenue per consultant by the expected hourly rate:

Revenue / Billing Consultants / Expected Hourly Rate = Hours You Need to Bill Per Year

The resulting number, the hours you need to bill per year, tells you a little about what the company really thinks about work/life balance, not to mention its perception of reality! If the number is 1,900 or higher, you might think about getting up immediately and walking out of the interview. After thinking about this number, rather than do anything rash, you should ask a couple more questions but do nothing to extend the interview. At this point, you know you are interviewing someone who assumes you never take vacation, never get sick, never have bench time, and this person probably wants you to work a good deal of unpaid overtime to get to the 1,900 hours. It is probably a good idea to turn down any offer that subsequently comes your way from such an organization.

The follow-up question—how many are subcontractors—is really aimed at getting a different piece of information. The independent contractor-to-employee ratio (divide the number of independent contractors by the overall number of billing consultants) is something I call the *body shop ratio*. A body shop ratio below 0.1 generally means that the company uses subcontractors only when required for certain specialist needs that it could not fill otherwise. A body shop ratio of over 0.3 means that either a substantial minority or possibly even a majority of the consultants are independents and that this company isn't really serious about being anything other than a "broker for bodies"—a la The Body Shop from Chapter 2, "The Seven Deadly Firms."

What Is Your Target Growth Rate? How Do You Plan to Achieve It?

Different technology consulting firms have various plans for how fast they want to grow, based on the market opportunities they see and the level of investment they have. There are few right answers to this question, given both good and bad firms will have target growth rates that vary because of overall market dynamics. That said, you should be very careful about numbers higher than 50 percent in all but the best times and numbers lower than 5 percent in all but the worst times because such numbers are almost certainly either too optimistic or too pessimistic.

The most important part of this answer is that the senior person you are interviewing should have a coherent and realistic plan for achieving these growth rates. If, say, a large technology consulting firm with 2,000 billing consultants and annual revenues of $500M claims to have a target growth rate of 40 percent, you should rightfully ask exactly how the organization intends to put up such aggressive numbers. Similarly, if a small company that makes $2M per year with 8 billing consultants is only looking to grow 5 percent during a boom cycle, you should ask why the projections are so low! Have an open mind, but make sure the answer makes sense.

Are Consultants Allowed to See the Sales Pipeline and Other Operational Reports?

Rumor mills, politics, and general negative work environments flourish when information about how the company is doing remains a deeply guarded secret. Although there are excellent reasons to keep this information from competitors, how much this information is guarded from consultants tells you a good deal about the actual level of trust that the firm has with its own people. You should be rightfully wary of companies that go out of their way not to communicate how the company is doing. Your potential employer is asking for your trust. You should demand that level of trust in return.

Working for a company where the sales pipeline, staffing report (which tells you who is working for which client, who is on the bench, and so on), and utilization forecast are a secret can be miserable. You have your own career to manage, and what you ask for in terms of training, getting moved from one client to another, or whether to consider going to another regional office normally depends on being able to see this operational data on an ongoing basis. Without access to it, you are much more limited in how you can navigate your career.

> **Michael Hugos** In my experience, many firms do try to keep this information a secret sometimes because they fear it will fall into the hands of competitors. These fears are valid only if their consultants are not being treated well; consultants who are being treated well by their firm will not give this information to competitors because it would only endanger their own good deal. So if firms keep this information secret, it usually tells you something.

What Is the Exit Strategy?

It is not unfair to ask the question, "What do you plan to do with the company?" This is particularly true if you are interviewing with someone who is either the owner or at least is in senior management. The answer to this question can and often does have great bearing on what your future may hold with the company. The main answers to this question are either, "Eventually look for a buyer," "IPO," or "Nothing; we are happy growing this company on our own for the time being." Any one of the three is a good answer, but the content of the answer really isn't the most important part. What you really want to see with the answer is (1) whether the company is willing to share with you the exit strategy and (2) whether it seems to have a realistic plan.

In 1999, it might have been realistic to take a technology consulting company public. Since that point, however, it has been a very uncommon path. The way that technology services companies are valued by Wall Street tends to make the IPO path not terribly attractive. Valuation is lower when you have a broader number of investors who don't have a strategic reason other than "need to generate return" for owning you. A more attractive exit option for managers is selling the company to a larger firm, which, for reasons of regional expansion or expanding expertise in a specific technology, is a better reason to buy your company. For those with an exit strategy, you will find the option of "sell to strategic buyer" much more common.

The best way to think about "sell to strategic buyer" is to remember that not all buyers need the same things. There is no such thing as a "generic" technology consulting firm; each one has a different mix of people, skills, management, and clients. A company looking to grow via acquisition is going to be looking for a firm that complements its capabilities, regional coverage, or development process. In recent years, particularly since the 2000–03 tech bubble, this is the most common exit strategy.

However, if the person either won't answer the question or answers it in a way that seems not terribly credible (such as betting the ranch that Microsoft will buy the company), it may be a good idea to think about your own exit strategy … from the interview. As with other general business questions, if the senior management team of the company is being evasive, it probably means these people either have something to hide or have not thought much about these very important topics. Joining a firm without knowing the business is like investing in a stock without doing research. You would be taking a huge risk with your career.

⁓

Sales-Related Questions

In technology consulting, as stated previously, "you are what you bill." If there are not good future prospects for billing work to come out of the sales organization of a technology consulting firm, none of the other stuff really matters much. Companies that have a weak sales process tend to be miserable places to work because it is very likely you will spend a lot of time on the bench worrying about your contribution. The questions in this section get at the core of how the prospective company will make it so that the only real thing you have to worry about is how well you do *your* job, rather than worrying whether other people are doing theirs (see Table 5-2).

TABLE 5-2
Sales Pipeline Questions

Question	Why Ask It?
What is the value of the sales pipeline? How do you value your sales pipeline?	You want to make sure that the sales pipeline can support the revenue the organization wants to realize. You want to then dig deeper and make sure the pipeline is measured in a reasonable way, given that some organizations look at the pipeline too optimistically.
What is your sales process?	There should be one. If the process is "wing it," there is a good chance you will be dealing with a lot of boom and bust cycles within the firm.
Does the delivery organization work with sales to make sure estimates are realistic?	It is not a bad thing to ask directly whether delivery is consulted during the estimation process. A "no" answer is a big red flag.

Question	Why Ask It?
What are the basics of the commission structure for sales? Commission only? Base plus commission? Straight salary?	Most technology consulting firms pay salespeople base plus commission. If the firm varies from that equation, you should know why.
How are leads generated? What happens if a consultant generates a lead?	This question helps you understand the theory under which the firm generates new business. Some do it through "partner-sales," depending on relationships; some do it more through "cold calls." Asking what happens when you, as a consultant, generate a lead is a good way to signal you will go the extra mile to help the company.

What Is the Value of the Sales Pipeline? How Do You Value Your Sales Pipeline?

Asking about the value of the sales pipeline is good because you want to get a sense for how the company is doing and how well the salespeople are doing their jobs. Most sales pipelines are measured over time, so you may want to clarify by asking "What does the sales pipeline look like over the next 12 months?" The number you get will vary depending on how the pipeline is weighted. However, it should be a number that results in sales equal to the current year's revenue plus a certain amount for growth. If the given pipeline number does not reflect the answers given for revenue and growth rate (see the basic business questions earlier), you should ask why there is a difference.

It is also important to ask how the pipeline is valued. Most companies value a pipeline using some variation of the following:

1. Broadly estimate the value of the opportunity over the course of a standard time period (for example, one year).

2. Apply a percentage to the opportunity based on the likelihood of the deal closing (for example, Stage 1, 10 percent chance of close; Stage 2, 25 percent chance of close)

3. Add the adjusted opportunities.

This information is a good foundation. If a technology consulting company is not doing these basics, you need to probe more deeply to see how it does projections. However, even within this framework, there are a lot of chances to play around with the numbers that you need to have an eye on.

How Is Opportunity Size Measured and Adjusted?

One of the first questions to dig deeper is to ask how the company determines *opportunity size*. Opportunity size is an initial guess at how big a project is prior to any detailed estimation being done. It tends to be a "what is the client looking to spend" type number at first but should never be seen as a hard-and-fast number. That said, even at this stage, someone from the delivery organization should have done some sanity checking against the number.

Even more important, though, is to make sure that the number provided at the initial opportunity phase is adjusted as the work moves through the pipeline. New information routinely coming in during the sales process will adjust the number, and if the number isn't adjusted, the overall projection becomes patently useless.

What Adjustments Are Made at Each Pipeline Phase?

No company closes every opportunity that comes into its pipeline. One of the fundamentals of pipeline valuation is coming up with good "likelihood of closure" coefficients for each phase of the sales pipeline. Typically, you want to see a conservative valuation that has a good basis in reality (see Table 5-3).

TABLE 5-3
Sales Pipeline Valuation

Stage	Typical Coefficient
Stage 1: Appointment	0.00 to 0.10. Some firms assume nothing about an initial appointment; some assign a 10% chance of closure. However, given that size of opportunity is so volatile at this stage, it is much safer to go with 0.00.

Stage	Typical Coefficient
Stage 2: First Meeting	0.05 to 0.15. After you have a first meeting, you have a slightly better sense for what the opportunity is, and depending on how well the overall organization qualifies incoming opportunities, often somewhere between a 1-in-7 to a 1-in-20 chance of reaching a deal. Anything higher or lower than that merits asking more about how well the lead qualification process is working.
Stage 3: Technical Meeting	0.15 to 0.25. Slightly better chances than first meeting, as now the client has much more vested into the process because an initial stakeholder has probably gotten others involved.
Stage 4: Proposal	0.25 to 0.65. Some consulting firms proceed with proposals only when they think they have a better than average shot at winning the deal; others will write a proposal even for long-shot deals. How the company values stage 4 opportunities tells you a lot more about how effectively it spends its time in sales.
Stage 5: Contract	0.50 to 0.80. Some firms send over a contract with the hopes that it gets signed; others won't write a contract unless a deal has been verbally accepted. Regardless, by the time you reach the Contract stage, there is usually a pretty good chance something will happen.
Stage 6: Signature	0.75 to 0.90. You have a client signature, and you are getting ready to start. This is often the riskiest time for a deal, with often between 1-in-4 and 1-in-10 chance of its being "killed on arrival."
Stage 7: "Butt-in seat"	1.00. You have a consultant working at the client. At this point in most firms, the opportunity is considered realized. Although it may become larger or smaller, for pipeline valuation purposes, it is usually considered done at this point. The revenue is converted into backlog for management by the delivery organization.

You might not have enough time to dig into each sales process step and ask questions. However, getting a sense for the numbers and asking follow-up questions in cases where the number given is outside a somewhat generous range are good ways to learn about how well the sales organization is run. If the numbers are too high or too low, you probably want to dig deeper and ask what deal qualification process the company uses. If you are given a high set of numbers, but the interviewers can't elaborate on how they qualify deals, that could be a signal that they tend to be overly optimistic about their pipeline. If you are given a low set of numbers, the company might just not be that good at deal qualification. Either way, such a response is a red flag that you should dig deeper and at least make sure that the company has a reasonable explanation.

> *A deal qualification is the process of making sure that the sales staff is not just calling up random companies, but rather makes sure that the target company has a reasonable chance of doing business with you. Many of the biggest mistakes technology consulting companies make is that they have their sales staff spend time chasing deals that they are highly unlikely to win.*

You also should make sure that the sales pipeline is routinely scrubbed; that is, lost opportunities are removed, and the pipeline valuation coefficients are adjusted over time based on actual data (such as what percent of stage 4s over time actually reach stage 7). A well-run technology consulting firm frequently requires its sales staff to scrub its pipeline and has the discipline to adjust projections to make sure they reflect a good estimate of reality. You should be wary of companies that fail to do either of these tasks.

What Is Your Sales Process?

Just as no company today would rationally say it does not have a software development process, it should strike you as very odd if a company does not have a recognizable sales process. For a technology consulting firm, particularly the kind of firm that is doing high value work, you will want to have some sense that the sales process has an emphasis on building relationships with executives who have the authority to spend money. Ask questions like these:

+ How are leads generated? Purely on relationships? Cold calling?
+ What is done to uncover the "pain"—that is, problems that need solved?

- How are leads qualified? How do salespeople know when to end a conversation and stop a pursuit?

- Is there anything you do in your process that nobody else does?

The most significant red flag to look for is lack of a sales process. Although there is some merit to the idea that some organizations just let each individual decide how they sell, that answer is too often code for "we have no idea how we sell." Just like "cowboy-coding" tends to create problems related to lack of repeatability and maintainability, "cowboy-sales" tends to lead to inability of salespeople to work well with others and provide any sense of predictability.

Does the Delivery Organization Work with Sales to Make Sure Estimates Are Realistic?

Even if salespeople had the requisite skills to properly determine the level of effort required to do a technical task, having salespeople estimating work on their own deals is almost always a bad idea. Even though sales has a long-term stake in the idea that long-term relationships are built and that delivery can actually deliver a solution, the pressure to close work and meet a quota is immense. Because the pressure to make short-term numbers frequently overrides long-term concerns, sales tends to underestimate work most of the time. And that is when sales has the skills to do the estimation! Having salespeople without technical skills doing estimation is a guaranteed path to disaster.

Lack of delivery organization involvement in the estimation process is a huge red flag. Simply put, do not work for a technology consulting company that does not have the delivery organization involved in the estimation process.

If the delivery organization—the people responsible for making good on the promises—is not involved in doing estimates, you need to dig deeper and ask why. Given that the disconnect between the people doing the estimation and the people doing the real work is one of the biggest causes of project failure in technology consulting, you need to simply avoid joining any technology consulting company that does not get delivery involved.

Michael Hugos   In my experience I find that delivery people must always be involved with salespeople in creation of project estimates, but that does not mean delivery people have the right to demand more time and bigger budgets. If salespeople feel the customer will not go for longer time frames or bigger development budgets, then development people need to find ways to build what the customer wants (or at least most of what the customer wants) in the shorter time frames and smaller budgets advocated by sales.

What Are the Basics of the Commission Structure for Sales?

Most technology consulting firms compensate the sales organization with relatively low base salary, but with a commission plan that pays generously if the salespeople generate a significant amount of revenue. In fact, in many firms, the best salespeople make more than even the CEO! Of course, how well salespeople do is not your direct concern. What is, however, is making sure that salespeople in any organization you consider joining have a reasonable basis for acting in the best interest of the company.

An organization that pays its salespeople a straight salary, without commission at all, is likely to have a hard time attracting really good people. The reason is that the really good people generate enough business such that working for straight salary will undercompensate them relative to the market. On the other hand, a sales organization that pays straight commission and no base will be unlikely to attract new talent because it frequently takes six months or so to build a book of business, and during that time, you still have to eat! This is why the base plus commission structure is so common, and variation from this structure should be questioned.

If a firm is paying its salespeople a straight salary, you should ask how salespeople will be motivated to sell beyond their quota. There may be good answers to this question, particularly if the salespeople are partners in the company with equity, which means they benefit directly because selling more helps the business. When you dig, the explanation should at least be credible, not asking you to believe that salespeople will just work harder because they are nice people—a somewhat dubious assumption.

On the other hand, if a firm is paying straight commission, you need to ask how salespeople are recruited. Seldom do salespeople arrive at a company with an intact book of business. In almost all cases, there are very enforceable noncompete agreements that stop a salesperson from taking accounts from one company to the next for at least a year, sometimes even longer. Lack of a base is probably a bigger red flag because the realities of consulting indicate that the lack of a base means sales will work for free while building up a book of business and moving initial prospects through the sales pipeline.

Another good question is to ask whether commission is based on revenue or other measures, such as margin. Some firms are starting to look at compensating salespeople by more sophisticated measures than raw revenue. This is particularly true in companies that have had bad experiences with salespeople selling bad deals that generate revenue but little margin.

How Are Leads Generated? What Happens If a Consultant Generates a Lead?

You could have the best funnel, with the best gauges on the funnel that measure what is coming through it. None of that will matter, though, if you do not have a good source of leads that you can put into the funnel in the first place. Making sure that the company has a good source of leads is critical. Without a good source of leads, the rest of this conversation is probably a moot point.

Leads mostly come from two sources: existing executive relationships/ networking (warm leads) and new leads generated through cold calling. Most firms employ both techniques, with an inside sales force that generates leads primarily through calling on target companies on the phone, and the outside sales force working warmer "relationship" leads. Both techniques can work, though there are those who will argue passionately that cold calling is a difficult and time-consuming way to build strategic relationships. What technique is used is less important than the fact that the company should know what it does and how well one or the other works. A good company will know how much of its revenue comes from cold calls versus warm leads and invest in one or the other based on what is working.

It is highly unlikely that you, as a technology consultant, will be doing cold calls. However, you too will build relationships over time, sometimes which result in opportunities. To that end, you should ask what happens when a consultant generates a lead. Ideally, you will share in some of the upside—beyond a small gift card and a thank you. Most good technology consulting firms have programs specifically designed to reward individuals who bring in leads, sometimes even getting a cut of the revenue or profit earned from the lead.

Why Ask All These Sales Questions?

You might be asking yourself why you need to ask these sales-related questions. Remember, you are not just joining a department; by joining a company, you are investing yourself into a business. Because of that, you need to make sure you are joining an organization that has reasonable prospects for success. Half of that success in a technology consulting organization is in generation of sufficient demand for the organization's services. By not asking questions about it and understanding it, you are bypassing one-half of the factors that separate the bad organizations from the successful ones.

⪢

Delivery-Related Questions

A company can't just be about sales. Before you join a technology consulting firm, you should have a good sense that it can deliver on the promises it makes. Good firms have a sane development process, leverage bench time effectively, and measure estimates versus actuals so that future estimates can be more accurate. They know the skills of their people and make sure that clients are not sold something that the firm does not have. The questions in this section ascertain the actual capabilities of the company so that you can have the best chance of success (see Table 5-4). It does not matter how good you are individually if you are given a horrible process, mediocre coworkers, and clients with mismatched expectations.

TABLE 5-4
Questions About Delivery

Question	Why Ask It?
What is your software development process?	If you are joining a technology consultancy that writes custom software, you need to know what the process is and make sure the firm is not stuck in the dark ages.
Where does work usually take place? At the client, at the consulting firm office, or some combination?	This question should tell you how collaborative the work is and how much control the consulting organization has over delivery.
How much travel is required?	There is no right answer, but you need to know one way or the other whether the travel requirements are a match.
Do you do fixed-bid work?	Generally speaking, fixed-bid work and software development for all but the smallest projects are a bad combination. If the company does fixed-bid work, you need to find out how it manages the risks.
What is the typical client employee-to-consultant ratio on projects?	This ratio is a good indicator of how work actually gets done. If most engagements have the client staffing most of the roles, it is a sign that you are either talking to a body shop or, at best, a firm that does not manage its risks well.
Who manages the projects?	This question allows you to get at the true nature of the organization—whether it is a body shop or a real consulting firm. Most real consultancies manage their own projects.
What happens if we need nonstandard development tools?	This question leads into whether the organization invests in software required to help you be successful. Be wary of consultancies that seem reluctant to give you the tools to do your job.
What do you do with bench time?	Is the time invested into something useful to the company or just spent going to the office with nothing to do but play solitaire?
How does the organization learn from delivery mistakes?	Ideally, you should make sure the company encourages post mortems and other opportunities to learn organizationally when mistakes are made. If a person representing an organization says it does not make mistakes, that person is almost certainly lying!

What Is Your Software Development Process?

The proper answer to the question about the software development process is, in all but the most limited circumstances, going to be some variation of Agile delivery, or at least something like Spiral, which has some mechanism for dealing with incorporation of knowledge learned along the way into the end product. Although some organizations are still holding onto more dated Waterfall-style delivery techniques because they promise a certain simplicity about them, the vast majority of evidence shows Agile development processes to be vastly superior to the older Waterfall-style methods they replace (see http://www.infoq.com/news/2008/09/state-of-agile-results). Although a broader Agile versus Waterfall discussion is beyond the scope of this book, it would be dishonest to say, with the evidence that has come in, that all processes are of equal value. You should make sure you are not going to work for a technology consulting firm that lacks the ability to adapt.

That said, the answer that should give you even more pause is lack of any process at all. Without any discernible process, there is no way to track with, consistency the accuracy of estimates, progress against a plan, or any other metric that would allow you to know how a project is doing. Hope is not a strategy for assuring success, and lack of a process really leaves you only with, "We hope things are going well." In the likely event that they don't, it generally means that the newest person (you) will take the blame—something definitely not good for your career.

Where Does the Work Usually Take Place?

Where the work takes place, along with some of the other questions in the delivery section, gets at aspects of how much the technology consulting firm really controls the work. If you are seeking to do technology consulting, and not simply technology *contracting*, there should be at least a mix of projects taking place at a client site and some at the consulting firm's offices.

There can be very good reasons why a project controlled by the consulting firm would still need to be onsite. In most Agile development processes, there exists a need for an onsite customer, or at least a customer-proxy or representative. This person works for the client, understands the business, and in a well-run project, is a member of the team. Some clients are comfortable with such a person working a few days a week at the consulting firm's office. Others have no such comfort. The proportion of work done at the client versus at the office depends on how many have this level of comfort versus how many do not.

That said, the ratio is rarely 0 percent or 100 percent, and thus, answers at either extreme should be viewed with skepticism. All work done in the office usually speaks to a development process that is insufficiently agile. All work done at the client means that you may not be dealing with a consulting firm at all, but rather a contracting company posing as a consulting firm (refer to Chapter 2).

How Much Travel Is Required?

How much travel is required is usually a pretty easy question—often being asked early in the process because travel requirements often are a problem in the recruiting process. Some firms require that you be able to travel 100 percent of the time if needed so that if there is weakness in demand in one region but strength in another, you can be moved around.

Some people enjoy this type of arrangement and the lifestyle of a traveling consultant. Others, not as much. One way isn't better than another, but you need to know what is expected early on and exit the interview process if you are not going to be comfortable with the travel demands.

Some companies have softer travel demands during good times, when work is plentiful, but increased travel demands when times are not as good. Despite what your tolerance for travel is, if you are going to work in technology consulting, it is probably a good idea to accept that a time may come when the travel demands will change, and you will be forced to either leave the company or reconsider what you are willing to do.

Chris Williams   As someone who does a fair amount of recruiting and interviewing, I always find it disappointing when promising candidates get all the way through the process, right up to the offer stage, and then decide they (or their family) can't handle the travel. It's not for everyone, and it's important to know your limitations. If you aren't willing or able to travel, don't gamble on a job that may require it in the hopes that you'll just dodge the bullet for a few years.

Do You Do Fixed-Bid Work?

Whether a company does fixed-bid work is a critical question because the fixed-bid versus time and materials debate continues to rage on. A substantial number of clients demand fixed-bid work, and some firms attempt to fill this niche in the market. However, making a sane software development process like Agile work in the context of a fixed bid is always going to be a difficult proposition. There is no force of nature that can change the fact that you can pick only two of cost, quality, and scope when executing a project. Fixing the bid (cost) forces trade-offs between quality and scope. Because quality is usually sacrosanct (for good reason), scope has to be adjustable if cost is not. Sadly, fixing the bid to most clients usually means requesting to have all three values fixed, which, despite many claims from aspiring firms trying to enter this space, is nearly impossible.

Usually, the consulting firm charges a risk premium, adding 30 percent to the initial cost estimate. Although this amount can be lower for short-term and/or simplistic work or higher for riskier/complex work, adding a premium to cover the risk is the only real, honest way to deal with this problem. If a firm states it does not add such a premium, it thinks it has the ability to predict all future issues, combined with uncanny negotiation power that makes it such that it will win every argument about whether a feature was part of the original scope or whether that feature should be counted as a change request. More likely, the firm simply picks up the additional scope and converts it to unpaid overtime by using tactics like those used by Fear Consulting in Chapter 2. A fate you most certainly want to avoid.

> **Michael Hugos** Learning to do profitable fixed-bid work is the biggest challenge (second only to the mystery of learning to do sales) in the consulting world. Clients are less and less willing to agree to long-term open-ended consulting engagements where the consultant gets paid for every hour worked regardless of value delivered. This arrangement places all the risk on the client and also encourages bad behavior on the part of the consultant. Doing fixed-bid work differentiates your firm from your competitors and can play a big part in making the sale. However, it involves a high level of skill in estimating work, negotiating change orders, creating clear system specifications, and managing projects.

What Is the Typical Client Employee-to-Consultant Ratio on Projects?

If a consulting firm is going to take on responsibility for project outcome, it is going to need to staff the majority of the team. Although this rule does not apply in some special cases, such as mentoring engagements, where your purpose is to transfer knowledge to members of a client team, most of the time, you want to make sure the typical consultant-to-employee ratio is better than 4 to 1. When it is lower than that, it would be appropriate to ask what is done to manage the risk of a nonperforming client employee.

Such arrangements with a 1-to-1 ratio are called *partnering* arrangements with a client in some firms. Although they may be good in theory, these arrangements tend to be losers for the consulting firm because they make the cost differential much more stark. Such arrangements frequently turn into staffing deals, with those consultants who do really well "going native" and getting offers to join the client. Although this is a perfectly good model for a staffing firm, it is not really consulting. At firms that do this a lot, the staff tend to identify more with the client than the consultancy, which further weakens the consultancy.

Who Manages the Projects?

Real technology consulting firms hire project managers to manage the projects. If the company you are interviewing with replies with a more nuanced answer than this, the response should give you a great deal of pause. Some firms claim that the salesperson manages the projects. You should be aware that even in the rare case you find a salesperson who has the requisite skills and knowledge to manage projects, it is not a role that you can do effectively while you also work in sales. Project managers often need to make decisions that reduce the size of a team, whereas salespeople often are reluctant to take any action that would do that because they are usually incented to increase team size. Salespeople generally tend to be eager to please in the short term, whereas project managers need to have a longer-term view. The roles almost never mix well.

Never join a firm that takes on accountability for project outcomes without insisting on owning the project management function.

Especially in cases in which projects are fixed bid, the consulting firm needs to provide the project management. In any case where the consulting firm can be sued for not meeting a contract standard—due to quality, timeliness of delivery, or anything else—having the client also provide project management is a conflict of interest. If the client project manager is unable or, as happens more frequently, unwilling to control scope, the consulting firm takes on the consequences. If nothing else, make sure that when you join a firm the project management and accountability for results reside under the same corporate umbrella.

What Happens if We Need Nonstandard Development Tools?

Although it is not practical or advisable to have no controls at all on how money is spent on software, it should not be too difficult to get any special tools you need to do your job. Most consultancies provide an integrated development environment (IDE), some data manipulation tools, and a laptop that has typical office software (Microsoft Office or an equivalent). Most of the better ones provide that for items below a certain cost threshold (typically around a couple hundred U.S. dollars), you are able to simply pick and choose additional tools with at least reasonable justification. Higher than that, any purchases may be more of a corporate-level decision, but even then a profitable technology consultancy should have no issue spending money on tools as long as they can be cost-justified.

> *Asking the client to pay for your tools is a little like being a mechanic and charging your customers directly for a wrench.*

Not all firms are profitable—even when they say they are. One way you can scout out a company that may be in a bad cash position is to see whether they insist that the client pay directly for any special tools. Although doing so might just point to a painful level of inflexibility on the part of someone running the company, such a condition more likely points to a company that is so cash starved that you have to wonder whether it is making payroll. Most clients do not want to be burdened with those kinds of issues; that is the reason they hire a consulting firm in the first place!

What Do You Do with Bench Time?

Asking the question about bench time is a great opportunity to set yourself apart by demonstrating that time not billing will be put to good use. Ideally, bench time is spent working with the sales team on upcoming proposals. Time not spent working on proposals should be allocated to picking up a new skill that makes you more marketable, working on internal projects that help make the company more efficient, or working on open source software projects.

In less well-run technology consulting companies, bench time is used to "look busy," but rarely does the sales team work with those on the bench to win projects. The best person to ask this kind of question isn't the management, but the peer-level interviewers because they probably have the real scoop on what they actually do when they are on the bench. Although nobody will openly say, "We spend our bench time mostly goofing off on the Internet," an answer that does not seem credible or confident probably means that is precisely what happens.

Some organizations use bench hours to develop internal products for sale. Although such a business model can be tough, a few firms successfully pull it off. To develop a good, profitable software product, you need different sales skills, a tech support department, and a consistent software development team. In a properly run technology consulting firm, the bench is rarely the same people for very long, which makes a cohesive team almost impossible to put together. Thus, rare is the case in which consulting firms have developed good, marketable software for sale. There are exceptions, but those are typically large organizations that treat the software product division as its own division with a core staff and profit and loss responsibility. In those cases, however, you really are not using bench people at all; you really have a software product company that acts as an internal client.

How Does the Organization Learn from Delivery Mistakes?

You should avoid working for firms that (1) can't admit that they make mistakes and (2) when they do, refuse to systematically look at them and figure out how they can do better next time. Post mortems—having meetings to talk about what worked and what did not work—should be regularly conducted after all projects, not just failed ones.

Some firms come right out and say they don't do post mortems. The reason is that everyone points the finger of blame to one another. If the question is answered that way, you should be thankful that the potential employer is being so open and honest about its weakness. Such an answer is interesting not just because the employer probably doesn't learn from its mistakes, but because it tells you that the culture of the company is one that is deeply political and likely not terribly meritocratic.

Others say they do but in reality do not do them or only do them when things go very badly. The best way to find the truth is to ask your peer-level interviewers. Compare the answer given to the same answer given by the senior-level interviewer and make sure that they are consistent. Not all firms are going to be ideal and have post mortems after every project.

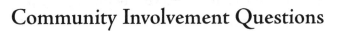

Community Involvement Questions

Both you and the consulting company benefit when its consultants are active members of their broader technical community. You should make sure you are joining a company that will encourage and even invest in your community involvement. Although few openly discourage it, companies that are merely neutral toward the idea tend to be places where development of people is not really a priority. By asking these questions (see Table 5-5), you get a sense for the true level of support that your prospective employer has for technology community involvement.

TABLE 5-5

Questions About Community Involvement

Question	Why Ask It?
Does the company sponsor a blog? Are all consultants allowed to blog on behalf of the company?	Even if you do not intend to blog, you should join a company that trusts its people enough to let them if the interest is there.
How many consultants have written books, authored articles, or regularly speak at conferences?	Saying you support community is one thing. Actually having results is better.
Do you have to take personal time off or vacation days if you want to attend a conference?	Ideally, the company pays for your travel expenses too, but if it makes you take personal time off to do events, this is a sign that the company really could not care less about community involvement.
How does the company invest in advancing the skills of its consultants?	You want to see some sort of investment here, not putting it all on the consultants to self-invest. A weak answer here is a sign that the company does not really see its consultants as assets.

Does the Company Sponsor a Blog?

Some technology consulting companies fear what might happen if management loses control of the marketing message and allows its consultants to write things that have even a remote chance of causing someone to disagree. You should make sure not to work for such a company. Places that operate in the "management knows best" line of thinking tend to be miserable places to work.

Blogging has become nearly an entry-level activity in the overall world of community involvement. Many of the industry's most important conversations take place in the blogosphere. Not allowing people to contribute to the conversation *as a representative of the company* really tells you a lot about its position on employee trust.

Seeing people argue against corporate blogging is quite interesting, especially when they get really upset that it might turn off customers. The fact is, as a technology consultant, you will likely interact with customers on a daily basis. If the company you are interviewing with does not sponsor a blog, ask if there are any particular reasons why. At the very least, you might have an illuminating conversation in which you get a real sense for the degree to which fear permeates the management ranks of the company.

How Many Consultants Have Written Books, Authored Articles, or Regularly Speak at Conferences?

If a technology consulting company is established, does not have excessive turnover, attracts bright individuals, and supports community, there will be tangible results of some type. When you ask about consultants' contributions, you might consider asking how the organization encourages these kinds of achievements. If a company has been around for very long and there is no tangible evidence of involvement, it is probably a sign that the company talks about doing it as a way to recruit, but that is where the community involvement ends.

The other reason you should make sure there are tangible results is that you want to make sure you are surrounding yourself with people who do these activities. If you join a company that lacks a community culture, you are essentially on your own pursuing these activities. Without any sort of peer pressure or others helping you, you are much less likely to follow through.

The best way to improve is to surround yourself with others who are successful. If you have not done any sort of writing or speaking and are interested in not just surviving, but thriving, it is essential that you start to work with such people who can help you cultivate your own skill and alert you to opportunities as they arise.

Do You Have to Take Personal Time Off or Vacation Days If You Want to Attend a Conference?

Not all companies have the financial means to send you to the ends of the earth to go to conferences, though it is certainly nice to find those that do. However, if a company considers such attendance *personal*, this is effectively like saying, "Your learning is your responsibility and yours alone, even if we benefit from it." It is a statement of the company's lack of desire to invest in its consultants.

Of course, there are limits. Sometimes, you have to change when you may or may not attend a conference due to business concerns, such as starting a new project at a new client the week you wanted to go. And if the conference is sufficiently off topic such that there is no discernible business benefit, you will probably be asked to use your own time to attend it. That said, if the policy is that you use your own time-off allowance for events and conferences, even when there is obvious business benefit and such events do not conflict with an important client deliverable, you probably should consider whether you really want to work there.

How Does the Company Invest in Advancing the Skills of Its Consultants?

Most successful technology consulting companies view their consultants as assets. Given that consultants are effectively "money machines" that generate a return in exchange for a regular salary, anything other than consultant as asset would be very bizarre. However, just about anyone will give lip service to the idea that "employees are our greatest asset," but far fewer practice what they preach. When you ask about the company investing in its consultants' skills, ask for specific examples. The reason is that it is not uncommon for recruiters and even company management to overstate the level of skill investment done.

One way to get at this answer is to ask about the book policy. Firms that invest in their people often allow for a book budget of perhaps a half-dozen technology books per year. Others provide accounts to services like Safari, which allow you unlimited access to large technical libraries. If you ask about the book policy and get an answer about an approval process, you have to ask yourself what that says about how much trust the firm has in its own people.

Although the form may vary from company to company—some investing in certification, others in paid training, and still others in events like "lunch and learns"—the point is that it should be doing *something* of significance and, in particular, putting some reasonable level of company resources to the effort. If you receive no evidence of investment, you should very much reconsider investing *your* energy into such a one-sided arrangement.

⮞

Summary

Some employers might scoff at your turning the tables and asking *them* hard questions. Indeed, some people still hold onto the idea that interviews are for the employer to select an employee, and the employee should be happy to have an offer at all. We all have the angel sitting on our shoulder, telling us not to ask hard questions of the nice person at the other end of the desk, for fear of being impolite or making the person less than comfortable.

Do you really want to work for a company that would scoff at the notion of you looking after your interests? Sometimes, perhaps deep in a recession, you may decide to accept a technology consulting position despite multiple red flags. But by the time you have asked these questions, you know what you are dealing with and have demonstrated a lot of business acumen that might just win you some respect.

Of course, once you get in, whether or not the company meets all these criteria, you need to survive in the business. Chapter 6, "Surviving," is dedicated to these strategies to keep you in your job after you have secured it.

CHAPTER SIX

SURVIVING

Keep your sanity and avoid living in fear when tough economic times inevitably occur.

Like clockwork, the economy will go through boom and bust cycles. Many people fondly remember the dot-com bubble—and not so fondly remember the dot-com bust that followed it. In Silicon Valley, you even see bumper stickers such as, "Pray for Another Bubble." Hope is well and good, but it isn't the best career strategy if you want to have some semblance of sanity when the news media is pounding fear into your head via dreary economic prognostication headlines day in and day out.

This chapter provides specific strategies for keeping your position as a technology consultant, even when times are bad. Although there are no guarantees in life—you could perfectly apply all these techniques and still be laid off—it does not hurt to do everything you can to maximize your chances of getting through the downturn with your job and career intact.

⌒

Reality Check: Avoid Fear and Greed

There will be times in your career—particularly as a highly coveted technology professional—when you feel invincible. When times are good, recruiters are calling you every week, and it feels as though the wind is at your back. It is easy to assume the good times will last forever. For a time, in the late 1990s and the first three months of 2000, such thoughts were helped by numerous magazines telling us that there was a new economy, centered on the Internet, created by software developers. This "new economy" would be impervious to the economic cycle, and the world had changed forever.

In 2000, we went from a wild sense of enthusiasm in the first three months of the year, until the dot-com bubble crashed, at which point the enthusiasm quickly turned into a sense of doom (see Figure 6-1).

January 2000

February 2000

April 2000

May 2000

Figure 6-1   From boom to bust in six months.

If you let your sense of how the world was doing be controlled by the cover stories in the business press, you went from a sense of wild enthusiasm—a world where software people would be hailed as masters of the universe—to a sense of total doom—where it would be hard for competent software developers to find work flipping burgers. For most people, the story all seems very overblown, in both directions, thinking about it in hindsight. The world of technology did not become a utopia during the boom, nor did the sun stop coming up in the morning during the bust.

We humans have a tendency to romanticize the good times in the past and demonize the bad times that, as we read from the business press, will occur in the future. The sober reality is that the truth is neither: The good times are probably not as good as we remember, and the bad times will almost certainly not be as bad as we fear.

Surviving in the technology consulting business requires making good career decisions. If you assume that every upcoming bump in the road is going to be the ruin of the company you work for, you will likely put yourself in a worse position by possibly jumping ship and leaving perfectly good consulting companies for jobs that might appear to be stable but really are no more secure, and often substantially less secure, than jobs in consulting. Making good career decisions depends on not overreacting to the news and getting jittery when headlines are making it seem as if the world is in imminent danger of ending. It means not succumbing to the fear and greed that recruiters and others will try to use to take advantage of you.

Survival Strategy #1: Avoid making decisions from a place of fear or greed. You really do have nothing to fear but fear itself.

The consequences of fear, in particular, go beyond leaving a company too early. When software developers are operating from a place of fear, they cease to communicate bad news to the project manager, thinking that being the bearer of bad news will lead to being removed from an engagement. This leads to project managers, who might be operating from fear themselves, not communicating bad news to the project sponsor. This leads to the sponsor miscommunicating to his or her board, or worse, to his or her customers. This, of course, leads to something worth fearing: a client potentially failing because of fear. It should not be a surprise that fear—and the poor decision making that results from fear—kills more technology consulting companies than recessions do.

In this respect, surviving means using your head, not your heart, to evaluate your current and future prospects. When times are good, it means moderating your prospects and being realistic with yourself. And when times are bad, it means working hard and doing things to increase your marketability, but still continuing to think of both the short-term and long-term implications of your actions.

People Who Create Profit Don't Get Fired

It can be said with certainty that if you are a billing consultant on a long-term project, you will probably keep your job … as long as you keep billing. Now, this doesn't mean the converse is true: You are probably going to be fired as soon as you hit the bench. However, it certainly means that recessions are not the best time to start complaining about the lack of a nice window with a view at your client's facility.

In fact, your company can go bankrupt, but if you are still on a billing contract, you will almost certainly have a job with a firm that acquires the "assets," that is, billing engagements, of the bankrupt company. During the dot-com crash, many technology consulting companies that were servicing venture-funded companies either got sold in fire sales or filed Chapter 11, "An Anthology of Sage Advice." Groups within those companies that constituted billing teams of consultants were traded like baseball cards between various private equity groups until a more permanent buyer, usually a larger firm, bought up the billing consultants. Although this is certainly not a terribly fun scenario for the participants, if nothing else, it provided secure employment as long as the billing continued.

Survival Strategy #2: Consultants who create profit don't get fired. Do everything you can to be the go-to person that your client depends on. Getting extended at a client during a recession is never a bad thing.

That all said, such a scenario is really the worst case. Many consultancies go flat during recessions, and some get acquired. But most good ones manage to stick it out and use the recession as a mechanism to "clean house"—that is, allow some attrition from lower performers and upgrade the talent level of the company. Your chances of survival have more to do with the perception you help create; you therefore should do everything you can to be so valuable to your client that you can stay there throughout the recession. Although such conditions are not entirely under your control—clients can go bankrupt, or orders can come from the CEO to get rid of all consultants—doing everything you can to be "sticky" helps create confidence in management that regardless of what client you are working with, you will likely continue to bill and have high utilization. Being a highly utilized consultant, even during the majority of a recession, is a great way to increase the likelihood that you will survive a recession without layoffs whatsoever.

So what are some specific ways to be sticky? Although these approaches might not seem fair, being sticky is more than just doing good technical work. Stickiness has the following dimensions:

- **Trust:** Have the trust of your client. Of all the factors, this is probably the most significant.

- **Identification:** Culturally identify with your client. If you seem like "one of them," the client is more likely to not see you as an outsider and therefore dispensable.

- **Skills:** Have specific skills the client needs. This is about continuing to build skills *relevant to your client*, not hoarding and protecting knowledge to protect your job. Doing the former puts you ahead of over half the people who work in technology and therefore increases your sense of value.

- **Low Maintenance:** Don't be "a problem." Although there are as many valid reasons to complain about things that are not perfect, unless a situation is serious, the less you are seen as high maintenance, the less likely some people will see losing you as a consultant as a way to reduce their own work (the "don't be a pain in the rear" rule).

It is no accident that these are also good things to do simultaneously in reference to the firm you work for. When times are tough, being the person who doesn't act from a place of fear, but rather moves forward, builds skills, anticipates needs, and delivers value is a sure path to survive any economic downturn.

☙

Rainmakers Are Always Welcome

Over your years as a technical consultant, if you are doing a good job, you will develop relationships with clients. While being a salesperson is not technically in your job description, it is quite the understatement that it never hurts when consultants can start to help bring potential leads to the table, providing material that, with the help of the sales team, can result in opportunity not just for yourself, but your colleagues in the company.

Put another way, one of the best ways to be a hero in a consulting company is to bring a good lead to the table that results in billing work during a drought—or at least helping others who do. Being the person who brings the water to the caravan stuck in the desert is one of the most significant accomplishments you can do for yourself and your colleagues. So how do you go about this?

> **Derik Whittaker**   During the dot-com bust, my team was able to work with our client to take on a new project with our firm when we were able to identify a few very significant efficiency issues with one of the client's products. This allowed our firm to provide additional resources to a new, albeit short-term, project which helped the company and made our entire team look good in the eyes of our company.

If you are in the middle of a recession, reaching out to long-lost clients you worked with five years ago might be a valiant effort, but it is probably not going to be terribly effective. To do this really well, you have to think like an account executive, even if you are not. During the good times, you need to establish a Rolodex of people you have enjoyed working for and with and regularly keep in touch with them, checking in once every three months on a friendly basis to see what is up with them personally and professionally. There are two things that are almost always true with people:

- People love to talk about what is going on with their lives.
- People love a free lunch or cup of coffee.

If you have genuine interest in keeping up—or can at least do a very good job of trying—there is a good chance you may be alerted to opportunities for your company without trying too hard. The secret weapon the technical person has over the salesperson is that people know telling a salesperson about an opportunity means a barrage of phone calls. Because the technical person has his or her guard down, you might have a chance to learn details a salesperson from the outside could only dream of.

> **Derik Whittaker**   When you're a consultant, nothing can be more valuable than gaining the trust of your client, especially the decision makers. If you can gain their trust, you may be able to see and hear about new needs of the client by simply having a friendly conversation.

Do you then break this trust and send the salesperson calling the minute you find the opportunity? Of course not. A much better strategy is to dig deeper, see whether your firm can help, and then ask if it is okay for you to get an account executive involved so you can win the company's business. By this point, since this person already likes you (heck, you have been buying lunch for a couple of years), he or she is more than likely to return your favor to at least be on the field competing for the business.

Survival Strategy #3: Keeping in contact with previous bosses, client managers, and colleagues is a good way to build a source of leads that make you very valuable to the consultancy you work for.

By the time things get to this point, you should probably be working with your management team at the consulting company to allocate the account. (Note: Never do this with an active account managed by a current account executive.) By virtue of bringing the relationship, you will likely be part of the pursuit team that will make an attempt to win the business. This activity of building relationships, turning them into leads, and winning business is colloquially known as *making rain*. It is the job of account executives, but given that you, as a consultant, will have a lot of natural contacts through the course of your work, it is certainly viable for you to work these contacts over time and make some rain yourself. Consultants who are seen as potential rainmakers, even when they are on the bench, tend to be seen as valuable resources who more than make up for their own salary costs.

If you decide to go this route, it is important that you honor nonsolicitation agreements you may have signed with previous employers. Nearly all employers, especially in consulting, bar you from developing business with former clients after you leave the firm for a period of a year or, in some cases, up to two years. If you have any questions, you should contact your management and potentially hire your own attorney to review with them any nonsolicitation agreements you have from former employers, and make sure you are clear to contact anyone you have worked with in the past if it was through a previous employer.

One-Trick Pony? Better Be Good at Your Trick!

Nobody would ask that the world famous cellist Yo-Yo Ma join an orchestra so he could play bass. That said, Yo-Yo Ma is truly the best at what he does. Of course, there are quite a few of us who have a high opinion of our own capabilities, thinking we are the Yo-Yo Ma of our chosen speciality. However, unless you are really in the top ten programmers of a given technology with a world-famous reputation, chances are, you will likely need to be what is often called a *multiposition player.*

A multiposition player is the Java specialist who also has a deep understanding of ERP systems. It is the DBA consultant who has developed her skills in business intelligence (BI) and is working to extend those skills to dashboard development because she is frustrated by all the great BI that goes unused and unseen. There are thousands of ways you can specialize in more than one complementary skill in a manner that makes you substantially more marketable.

Taking this step, of course, is a win-win deal for you and the consulting company you work for. It helps you because in the event that despite your efforts, your technology consulting company lacks the cash flow to keep you around, you have a better resume with which to look for work. For purposes of survival, it helps because you are now an easier sell to clients, and thus, it is more likely that the consulting company will be able to place you on a project during a downturn.

> *Survival Strategy #4: Avoid being useful for only one kind of skill.*
> *The more different things you can do technically, the more*
> *likely you will find a spot on a project or with a client.*

The reason for this is, during good times, budgets for projects are larger, and thus, it is easier to have both a DBA and BI expert with separate roles on a large project. When project budgets become smaller, some companies will insist that two complementary part-time roles be combined into one. Thus, the project manager has to become the business analyst/project manager. The BI expert has to become the BI expert/DBA. The developer becomes the developer/build expert, and so forth.

Is this ideal? Not usually. In recessions, there are lower budgets to be had, and frequently, the solution is not perfect (separate roles concentrating on what they do best) but is good enough to get the job done given the available budget. Having the flexibility to move between roles gives you a leg up on people who can do only one thing—particularly those specialists who might have an overly high opinion of their own capabilities and therefore refuse to do anything outside their chosen domain.

When choosing your complementary skill (often called a *minor*), work with your account executives and management to determine what is currently marketable and complementary to your own skill set. Given that they hear from needs frequently and from clients directly, they usually have good guidance about what you should go about learning next so that you can more easily fit into the projects coming up. Ideally, it will be something interesting to you as well, given that people are rarely happy working on technology they hate. But in the worst part of a downturn, having billing work might just be better than nothing at all.

> **Derik Whittaker**   When choosing your minor, make sure it is not only something that is marketable, but also something that you can become passionate about. If you can become passionate about this technology, you will most definitely become better at it, thus making you more valuable to your firm and new clients.

↝

Leave the Drama at the Theater

The art of survival depends on attracting the right kind of attention. Attention for being that person who, somehow, can be placed on any project with an opening. That is great attention. Attention for being the person who, somehow, manages to go beyond his or her role and find leads. That is also great attention. Attention for being the person who is always mad about something, is never satisfied with his or her pay or promotion prospects, and generally always seems to have a problem with coworkers. You might as well paint a target on your back!

This is not to say that you should not bring up problems or that you should just let people walk all over you. The issue is not so much whether there are problems, but how and in what manner they are brought up. Bringing up legitimate issues with a project backed up by verifiable facts is a good thing. In most cases, bringing up an issue in a constructive way will be applauded, not punished. On the other hand, someone who just complains a lot, whose arguments center on what is right for him or her versus the company as a whole, well, that is never going to go over well, but it especially goes over badly when there are ample numbers of people who would be happy to be doing billing work at all!

Survival Strategy #5: Engage in office politics as little as possible.
When doing so, always be seen as the cooler head—a force for
"drama reduction" rather than "drama escalation."

Of course, this survival strategy is easier said than done. The term *office politics* exists for a reason. Even in the best companies, there are those who will use the office to act out their own version of the TV show *Survivor* during harder times, forming alliances, bad-mouthing coworkers, and otherwise creating drama as a way of coping with conditions that are not ideal. Strangely enough, these instigators tend to have the same behaviors in good times too. As tempting as it might be to get into these games, consider the following:

- This person says things behind the back of others. What might he or she be saying about you? (Even if not now, someone who acts like this stands a good chance of turning on you in the future.)

- Is this person creating drama with good intentions? If that were true, would it really be something handled in a manner where you need to be involved? (If the intentions were good, the issues would be going through more discreet channels.)

- What does getting involved in something like this really say about you? (Most office political issues tend toward the relatively petty; you don't want to be seen as someone like that.)

When it comes to these kinds of issues, you want to be seen as the "adult in the room." The person everyone knows is fair-minded (considers both sides), trustworthy (does not spill information back out in a gossipy manner), and fact-based (when judgments are made, the question is, "What are the facts of the case?"). By demonstrating an even-handedness and fairness with how you approach office politics, by being a force for drama reduction rather than drama increase, you become perceived as someone who can keep your cool when dealing with clients that can be difficult. By being the person who is known as the cooler head, you put yourself far past someone who, even if that person has more well-known technical skills than you, is perceived as an engagement risk because of his or her demeanor.

⮐

Being Overpaid Is a Curse

Imagine you are working on your personal budget. If you want to figure out where you are going to save some money, where might you look? Are you going to start with small expenses, or are you going to look at the larger expenses first? Well, when companies do this on an organizational level, they first target the highest expense, namely people.

As strange as it may sound, when you are working for a company, unless you are the CEO, being the highest compensated person in your peer group is a perilous place to be. This concept can seem strange at first blush; most people associate having a very high salary with happiness and security. There is no shortage of articles on the Internet about how to get a raise and so forth. So how can this be a bad thing?

When times are good, being overpaid generally is *not* a bad thing. The downside to having the highest salary in your peer group does not really become evident until you start thinking about layoffs. At this point, you start to really wonder whether you are bringing in enough money to cover your salary, benefits, and other ancillary costs.

Survival Strategy #6: Being overpaid is hazardous to your job security during a recession. If you don't bring in revenues equal to at least 1.4 times your salary, you are probably overpaid. Consider volunteering for a pay cut.

The way technology consulting companies do layoffs is as follows: Generally, the office of the chief financial officer (in a smaller firm, this means *the* chief financial officer) looks at the individual utilization rate and, more importantly, the profit that each consultant has brought to the company over the past 12 or so months. Even if you have been consistently billing, if you are a highly compensated person who finds yourself on the bench during a downturn, and your rates have been slipping as a result of the economic conditions, you need to be aware that you are at risk.

On the other hand, people who are paid less generally have a better means to survive because the firm sees them as more profitable. If you don't stick out as having a cost that is high compared to what consulting revenues you are bringing in, you are much less likely to be let go. Indeed, in technology consulting, like most other business endeavors, there is a trade-off between risk and return. When the downturn hits, taking a lower return (salary) results in less risk of layoff, assuming equivalent skills.

Now, this isn't linear, per se. If you are the highest paid person in your firm, and your billings are not only consistent, but your profit margin is also higher than most others, you are safe despite your higher cost. If you make a substantial salary, you should not just volunteer a pay cut right off the bat. On the other hand, if you can figure out how much you have billed over the past year, and that number is less than your salary times about 1.4 (at least!), you might want to consider the proactive move of offering to reduce your salary.

Yes, you read that right: If you are overpaid, you should offer to reduce your salary. Although some firms will be happy to offer salary reductions as an alternative to layoffs, most are of the opinion that they would rather let someone go than ask someone to take a salary cut of more than a few token percentage points. The reason is that many believe that for reduced pay, someone will, in turn, put in reduced effort. However, if you offer to work for a reduced base salary plus a bonus that gets you even more if you hit a number like 90 percent utilization, for example, you accomplish a couple important goals.

First, you demonstrate some flexibility and understanding of the situation that the consultancy finds itself in. By stepping up to the plate and volunteering, you again seem like the "adult in the room" who is sacrificing himself or herself to make the company successful. Demonstrating you can take the pay cut helps the company understand that you are probably able to operate your household on less money. If you weren't, you probably would not make an offer like that!

Second, if you really are as good as your pre-pay-cut salary indicates, if you can strike a deal that gives you a bonus based on hitting or exceeding your old revenue target, you actually give yourself the opportunity to do better than you would have in the first place! By formalizing the exchange of risk for reward (you had the risk already), you at least give yourself a chance to capitalize on the situation.

⁓

Early to Bed, Early to Rise

It never hurts to be seen as the person who has just a little more work ethic than the next guy when it comes to surviving a downturn. Of course, this won't matter a hill of beans if you are the person who is always in the office but never billing. However, as a deciding factor that can tip the scales, there will always be a tendency to keep the person who seems to be more dedicated to the success of the company.

Is this entirely fair? Of course not. When it comes to surviving rounds of layoffs, from criteria A to Z, fairness would probably be a Z. When you get down to it, perception becomes reality when hard times strike. While it isn't fair, you can use this fact to your advantage as a survival skill. If you are staffed at a client when times are tough, do not be afraid to come in a little early, particularly if you can use the time effectively to get some work done before 8 a.m. when people are not around to bother you. I know many consultants who get more done from 6 a.m. to 8 a.m. than other consultants get done all day! Mostly because the office tends to be a distraction-free environment during those hours.

Now, for some of you, 6 a.m. is the time you tend to get to bed, not go to work. You might think you can apply the same strategy to staying late.

Although that is certainly better than nothing and can potentially result in your getting more work done, management tends to notice the industriousness of early risers more than people who stay late. Part of the reason is probably due to the stereotype that software developers play World of Warcraft and Halo late into the evening, putting them into another cycle of "in at 11, out at 7." Bucking this stereotype can help create the perception that you are more business-focused than technology-focused. Furthermore, because meetings tend to occur during the middle of the day—the period between 10 and 3 when most people are in—you will generally be better prepared if you have had the entire morning to prepare with the most recent information versus preparing the night before and having more outdated information.

Survival Strategy #7: Come in to work one to two hours early, if at all possible. You will get a leg up on the day's events, be there when most of the executives arrive, and be as prepared as possible for any of the day's important meetings, which are typically held in the morning. Don't overdo it though; more than 10 hours a day and you are at risk for burnout.

Does this mean you should work 16 hours per day when your consulting company is only getting paid for 8 of them? Not at all. This really means you should make sure you are putting in 8 full, professional hours, after deducting the time spent checking personal email, viewing sports scores, and catching up on RSS feeds. Most people (maybe not you, but probably) spend a net 2.09 hours per day in nonproductive work (a.k.a. goofing off), so extending yourself is really a mechanism to assure that your clients are, in fact, getting the 8 professional hours they paid for (source: http://news.cnet.com/Stop-reading-this-headline-and-get-back-to-work/2100-1022_3-5783552.html?tag=nefd.ac).

One of the worst things you could do is to throw yourself so into your work that you have no balance in your life. Burning yourself out is the opposite of a survival strategy. When the economy is down, you are going to need the energy to keep going, even when things seem like they are going very badly. Working enough to show you are committed more than average but not so much that you burn yourself out is the key to implementing this strategy.

Billing Work = Good Work
(with Few Exceptions)

Let's assume you work for a reasonably good consulting firm, one that does not send you to coal mines after your previous gig doing COBOL because some client decided it would pay a software developer to mine coal. If the firm you work for is somewhat less than horrific, if it was good to you during good times, you should probably allow the firm some leniency when the client pool starts to thin out and you end up doing some work you would rather not do.

In other words, now is the time to consider "taking one for the team." There are exceptions to this, in decreasing order of importance:

- Someone at the client's office is putting your life in danger.

- You are being asked to shred documents for a company whose name starts with *E* and ends in *ron*.[1]

- You are told that flex time is offered and you need to pick the 20 hours each day you want to work (and oh, you can bill for only 8).

- The commute is in excess of 3 hours each way, and mileage expenses are not covered.

- You are independently wealthy and in a position to say, "Take this job and shove it."

Outside reasons on that scale, it is probably not a good idea to ask to be moved to a different engagement because you don't like the technology, you don't like filling out TPS reports,[2] or you don't like how your coworker smells. Asking to be moved in a declining market means there is a good chance you

---

[1] For those who missed the financial scandals of 2001–02, the answer is Enron.

[2] If you have not seen the movie *Office Space*, (a) shame on you, go see it right now; if you don't, you won't understand half the pop culture references that exist in this business; and (b) *TPS reports* is a general term for useless paperwork that serves no reasonable purpose whatsoever.

will be moved … to a bench where, during recessions, the time period from hitting the bench and getting a pink slip shortens appreciably.

> *Survival Strategy #8: A recession is a very bad time to ask to get put on another client, unless the issues at the client have to do with ethics, morals, or legal concerns.*

If you find yourself in this category of an engagement—the irritating but modestly tolerable—you are best served by doing everything you can to cope during the downturn. The upside to working in such a situation is that there is a good chance—exactly because the place is such a hell-hole—it will have a hard time getting permanent employees, recession or no. If you can stick it out, there is a good chance you might be able to hold your nose there and at least get to the other side of the recession.

Make sure of two things: that the firm you work for knows what the conditions are and that you are happy to work with the client to "take one for the team." By letting the firm know the conditions and that you are happy to live through them for the good of the firm, you position yourself to be rewarded once better work comes along when the economy improves. Of course, you do need to be careful: There is a fine line between informing about conditions and complaining about them. But if you can state in fact-based terms what the challenges are and do so in a way that is more about a warning to others than your own misgivings about it, you can definitely get points for being a trooper willing to go into tough conditions to help the company rather than demerits for being the jerk who complains just because every day isn't sunny.

Jason Bock   When the DotBomb occurred, I ended up on a project that wasn't very technically challenging. I didn't have the maturity to understand that in lean times, I sometimes have to take a gig to keep the money coming in, even if the work isn't what I really wanted to do. I made a bad decision to leave the consulting firm to join another one that I thought would lead to better gigs. In hindsight, it was a shortsighted move, and I ended up back with my current employer, where I've been happy ever since.

Derik Whittaker If you are going to "take one for the team," do yourself a favor—don't complain that you really do not like your engagement. You are doing your company a good thing, and you are helping out a client. If you are really unhappy but know this is a short-term job, suck it up. You will be better for it in the long run.

≈

The Three Words You Want to Hear: You've Been Extended

During good times, you should strive to work for different clients so that you can build out your network and diversify the amount of vertical industry knowledge you bring to the table. However, when bad times hit, you are most interested in being extended at your current client.

Most firms consider the strongest consultant during a recession to be the person who has been at a client forever, who somehow manages to get that client to bring others in when everyone else is sending consultants packing. To get to that position, not only do you want to extend your term as much as possible, but you want to do everything you can to become the trusted advisor to management. You want to be the kind of person about whom, if your name is Sam, people say, "We need three more Sams to get this *critical thing X* done."

Survival Strategy #9: It is always in your interest to get extended on an engagement during a recession. More than ever, during bad times, you should do everything possible to get contracts at current clients extended, even if the client isn't your "favorite" client.

When times are good and the market is constrained by the recruiting pipeline (a seller's market to the consultancy), it is in the mutual interest of the consulting firm and you to get exposure to different clients because it is easy to spread good people around to different clients. On the other hand, when times are bad (it is a buyer's market), that same collusion of interests makes it better for you to stay with a single client. If you are doing your job well, that client probably will value you more than any new client is likely to. To put it another way, all things being equal, the rate at your current client during a recession is likely to be higher than your rate at your next client. The reason is that deals are harder to close, and in many firms (though not all), rate cuts become a tool to secure the subsequent engagement.

So how do you go about getting extended? Coming in early, being extra vigilant about documentation and putting in extra effort to make it effective, going the extra mile in small ways and large ways so that you demonstrate your value—these approaches are all helpful. That all said, the one single best way to become indispensable to the client is to speak and act as if you own the deliverables you are working on. If you can manage to treat each project for the client as though it was your business and your next meal depended on doing the best job you possibly could, chances are you will deliver value at a far higher rate than the median software developer.

Of course, to be extended, you need to be aware of how long your current contract is going to last. Whereas some firms post this information on a staffing sheet, others are less public about this information, and still others don't really know how long a given project will last or when the next round of project funding will come in. That said, it never hurts to ask your project manager, account manager, or other person at the consulting firm when your end date is and what you can do to help tip the scales toward getting extended as that end date draws closer. Most of the time, based on their knowledge of the client relationship, those people will have real good ideas about what can be done to help.

⁓

Don't Live "Three Steps Ahead"

If nothing else, software developers, particularly in the First World, are some of the most well paid people on the planet. Are they on the tier of Hollywood actresses, rap stars, CEOs, and plastic surgeons? Well, no. But they generally are in the top quintile (20 percent) with regard to compensation compared to the general population. Nobody is going to cry too much for the plight of software developers with respect to their paychecks.

Although a primer on personal finance best practices is well beyond the scope of this book, a chapter on surviving could not be considered complete without some words of wisdom about saving for a rainy day. The boom and bust cycles of technology, as pointed out earlier, can play tricks on your mind. For years, it can feel as though you do not need to save money so you can handle the possibility of a layoff. Why bother when you have recruiters calling you once a week, right?

In fact, this feeling makes some feel so invincible that they live "three steps ahead." Also called "fake it until you make it," it is the tendency for some to extrapolate current successes in a manner that makes them feel as though buying a 7-Series BMW for $80,000 is a good idea when they are making only $60,000. In general, it is the act of borrowing against an extrapolated expectation of future success. This is also known as "living above your means."

Sadly, most of the time, what goes up does inevitably come back down. The comedown that occurs when you operate from such a feeling of invincibility is really tough on your mental health. When a recession hits, you discover just how mortal you are with respect to the job market. You can take up each and every survival strategy in this book, but if you work for a company that, for whatever reason, is experiencing sharply declining sales, there is nothing you can do, outside of changing companies, that will make it possible for you to keep a job. Remember, when it comes down to it, "you are what you bill."

As an individual, you can't control the sales force, and you certainly can't control the economy. One truism in life is that it is much easier to control the sail of a ship than it is to control the wind. This is perhaps a more eloquent way of saying *concentrate on what you can control*. One of the things you can control is your personal standard of living.

Does this mean that technology consultants and their families need to live on Ramen noodles their whole life? Of course not. But it does mean that if you can help it, you should always be building a base of capital, otherwise known as *money*. Most personal finance experts recommend having three months' worth of expenses in "safe" savings (no, cattle futures are not safe). My recommendation for consultant software developers is to extend it to 12 months—one full year of expenses.

> *Survival Strategy #10: Live within or, better yet, below your means. All the stuff in the world does not mean a thing if you are in a job you hate. Having low personal expenses and high savings allows you to be more selective about whom you work for and less likely to choose a bad consulting company just because it happens to offer employment.*

So how do you do that? Well, notice I didn't say one year of *income*. If you are doing this right, your expenses should be well below what your income is. If you make $5,000 per month after taxes, strive to have your total of all expenses, *regular and occasional*, average less than $3,500 per month. If you can manage that and save the money as though your career depends on it, you will probably be close to a goal of having a year's worth of expenses saved in around two and one-half years. This does not count investing for retirement or other long-term savings; this is purely for building a hoard of money you can reach at a moment's notice.

So what happens when you have this cash hoard? Well, for one, you become less likely to succumb to fear, which helps with survival skill #1—avoiding fear. It helps you make better decisions because you are making decisions based on what's best for your client and your company, rather than what is least likely to put you in an unemployment line in the short term. Having a cushion allows you to sleep better at night, making you a more effective consultant.

Most importantly, though, having these savings helps you be more selective in what company you join, in the event you ever do become unemployed. People who live three steps ahead end up working for one of the Seven Deadly Firms from Chapter 2. Their choice is either do that or miss their mortgage payment and eventually get foreclosed on (unemployment insurance does not cover a $4,000 monthly mortgage, after all). Then they wonder why they are miserable, working grudgingly in a job they hate because they are slaves to their stuff. The stronger your own personal financial position, the lower your own expenses, the less likely such an awful scenario will come to pass.

> **Michael Hugos**   The greatest opportunities come when the economy gets tough because tough economies weed out so many of the people or firms that would otherwise be competing with you. If you practice living below your means when times are good, you will have the room to maneuver when times get tough. The more maneuver room you have in tough economic times, the better the chances you will find (and be able to capitalize on) opportunities that lead to real wealth and not just the overpriced appearance of wealth.

∽

Summary: What's The Worst That Can Happen?

Of course, you could implement all ten of these strategies and still find yourself out of work. There are plenty of reasons why layoffs occur that have nothing to do with you. You could just find yourself on the bench at the wrong time, when management is looking to cut costs. Indeed, a certain amount of luck is involved in surviving downturns, which is why I stress not only factors on the job, but factors that transcend your job, such as how you manage your finances.

So what options do you have if you find yourself laid off? Well, the good news is that during recessions, the time is often ripe for finding contract work. During a recession large companies often get mandated headcount reductions from their CFO ("cut 10 percent of all full time employees, and I don't care how"). This does not mean the company stops doing business; it just means that there are going to be fewer employees. This scenario usually comes about the same time as the demand to "remove all contractors" comes about. However, the latter tends to be short-lived because individual directors tend to have budgets too, and most of them have some reasons to need technology projects done. So while full-time employees (FTEs) remain under tight control, there tend to be fewer controls around hiring individual contractors for short- to medium-term needs. In fact, economists usually look for this uptick in temporary help as a leading indicator that the economy is starting to improve because it happens well before companies start hiring salaried employees again.

And if that contracting work does not materialize? Well, there are always routes such as taking out a student loan to work on an MBA or some other advanced degree. Or, especially if you took the advice to have 12 months' worth of savings or more ready and available, perhaps you can use the downtime to consider starting your startup or micro-ISV (Independent Software Vendor). The key is not to let yourself get into too much despair in this situation and do nothing while your skills rot. If nothing else, do something you should have been doing anyway, and do open source work. At least then you put some code out there, you stay sharp, and you prepare yourself for whatever interviews you can manage to get.

Michael Hugos Unless you are born into a rich family and endowed with a large trust fund, you will have to work for a living, and layoffs are an inevitable part of working. Layoffs have never been easy for me, and they do test my self-confidence. Sometimes I've been laid off because I personally screwed up, and I've had to get over my pride and learn from my mistakes. But often layoffs have nothing to do with me or with anything I could have or should have done. So I've had to get over blaming myself for being laid off and get on with preparing myself for the next thing I want to do with my career.

Chris Williams When I found myself in this situation, I was fortunate enough to be able to do exactly that. I actually took out two loans, one for school and one to live on for a few months. Even though it didn't feel like it at the time and I ate a LOT of Ramen, it ended up being a good thing and a pivotal moment in my career.

CHAPTER SEVEN

THRIVING

To get past survival and focus on thriving is your real chance to turn your occupation from a means of making a living to a means for making things better for not just you, but your fellow man as well.

If you are a software developer, even if it isn't true for you now, there was probably a time when you were so into what you were working on that it seemed as though the workday was simply ending way too early. Unless that was the day your network administrator allowed you to install an XBox on the company network so you could play Halo at work, chances are those days when you were really into what you were doing were probably some of your most productive.

Thriving in this business depends on, among other factors described in this chapter, being engaged in your occupation, to the point that putting in the extra effort becomes almost effortless. This chapter is about specific techniques to get the most from your career:

- Putting yourself in a position to thrive
- Staying "in the zone"—enjoying what you do
- Doing meaningful work

181

- Making sure you are always advancing and improving your capabilities

- Learning to think in terms of "win-win" when interacting with others

- Building your brand so that you can drastically increase the quality and quantity of opportunities at your disposal

Of course, getting in the zone is considered *self-actualization* in the context of Maslow's hierarchy of needs. To thrive in technology consulting or, for that matter, any career, you need to take care of the fundamentals. The preceding chapter covered some of the things you need to do to put yourself in a position to thrive. This chapter focuses on completing those preconditions and positioning yourself so you can achieve real career satisfaction as a technology consultant, regardless of where your career path takes you.

∾

In a Position to Thrive

Yes, it is true that weeds can grow everywhere, even in the cracks of a concrete jungle. However, nobody would really call survival in such an environment *thriving*. Similarly, although you might manage to stay afloat and not get fired, to thrive, you have to position yourself such that your basic needs are basically being met. This allows you to focus on higher-order issues, like "Am I delivering a software solution that helps my fellow man?"

Put another way, before you can thrive, worries about survival have to be out of the way (see Figure 7-1). If nothing else, thriving means you need to be able to take professional risks, so you can do work that you believe in and feel like waking up in the morning. Whether pushing back on a timeline given to you by management so you can do quality work or perhaps leaving a job if you are working for a company that does not meet your ethical standards, being in a position to take such risks means that the downside risk can't include homelessness or starvation. Not being able to take these risks or, for that matter, not being in a position to take them in a bold and confident manner, seriously impairs your ability to thrive as a consultant.

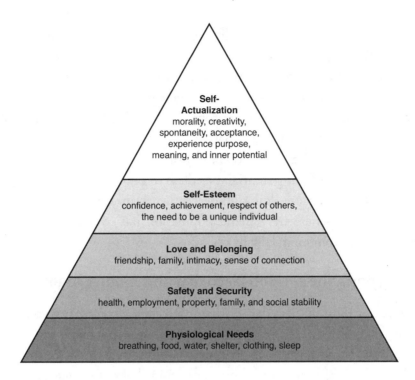

Figure 7-1 Maslow's hierarchy of needs.

> **Derik Whittaker** Being willing to be fired because you stand up for what you believe is right (pushing back timelines, ensuring quality, and so on) is a powerful thing. Being confident in your skills and your abilities (without being arrogant or an egomaniac) can pay huge dividends.

Thriving is really another word for reaching your potential, actualizing your own capabilities. To understand this concept, imagine trying to run a business in a country like Zimbabwe in 2009—a place where you worry about where the next meal is coming from, worry whether the pile of money you have today is going to be enough to buy so much as a cup of coffee tomorrow, and where law and rule are generally arbitrary. In such a place, the rules of business, if there are any at all, are constantly in flux.

In such a place, when (and if, sadly) you wake up in the morning, the first thing you think about isn't which Dependency Injection framework you should use; it is more likely something along the lines of "from whom are you going to acquire enough potable water to make it through the day?" And even in the event that the situation improves and availability of potable water becomes less of an issue, the need to worry about health care and safety—not to mention things further up the hierarchy of needs—will impede your really being able to achieve your potential. Needless to say, there are not many software consultants who are doing innovative work in Zimbabwe or, for that matter, any place where the general population has to worry about where water is coming from on a daily basis.

Food, Shelter, Job Security, and Code Quality

For the reasons just discussed, to thrive as a software consultant, you need to focus on making sure your needs further down the hierarchy are met. Chances are, if you have a job in the software development business, you probably at least have access to food, water, and shelter (as long as you don't live in Silicon Valley, where even after the real estate bubble has crashed, a tiny house costs more than $1 million).

The next level, however, is less certain. If your health is in question, or if your employer operates a culture of fear where you always feel as though you are going to lose your job, you might feel as though your safety and security are very much at risk. When you lack safety and security, your decision making suffers—as you start to optimize for short-term results rather than long-term good. If you are worried that you might not survive the short term, you really have no need for the long term, right? Having a short-term orientation tends to result in your writing lower-quality code; it is faster to write something that appears to work, even if it completely ignores good design principles and is impossible to maintain. If chances are that you are not going to be around next year, why bother with quality?

Love, Belonging, and Having Purpose

The middle level, love and belonging, has to do with having sense of connection with something other than yourself as a condition for thriving. Without this chances are, you are going to have a crisis of meaning in your career ascent. A lack of purpose—the belonging part at this level—generally leads to narcissism, which as covered in Chapter 9, "Avoiding Career-Limiting Moves," is a condition that acts as the cause of many career-limiting moves that get made. Although many narcissists may look as though they are thriving from the outside, if you get to know such people, you will rarely observe any real joy in their lives. This situation is certainly hard to call thriving.

Does this mean that you need a meaningful personal relationship to thrive as a software development consultant? Absolutely not! The real meaning at this level is to belong to something larger than yourself and, ideally, more than just a company. It could be a cause, movement, association, religious group, or any other entity that has goals beyond just making money. But whatever it is, having such an association is critical because it gives you an identity beyond just yourself, your job, or your work.

From Self-Esteem to Self-Actualization

The fourth level, self-esteem, is critical because without confidence that you can, in fact, make a difference, you are not going to be able to gain the trust of others. Without your own confidence, you will tend to spend your whole career seeking the approval of others. This need holds you back from thriving because it presents a factor in decision making that often has nothing to do with the decision. People who lack this ability tend to seek status and fame at the cost of integrity—or worse, start to defraud themselves or their company in search of status.

Getting to a place where you honestly feel that you don't have anything to prove to anyone is critical to truly thriving. To get there is hard. Most people, once they start to find success, go through a period in which, to put it kindly, they start accepting invitations to high-school reunions. Most of us (myself included) have a strong desire to show people from the past—an employer who fired you, the girl who got away ... whomever it may be—that you have "made it."[1] Although such expressions can be cathartic, they also indicate that you need to come to terms with your past, so you can act outside those influences and in a manner more aligned with whatever higher purpose you have.

⮡

Enjoying What You Do

Let's assume that for the purpose of this section, you have done all the work required to be positioned for thriving. Safety isn't a concern, food and shelter are taken care of, and you have a sense of purpose driving your activities. The only problem is that when you think of the idea of sitting down and writing some code, you simply can't get excited about it. As much as you believe in the idea—maybe you work for a company writing systems that reduce the cost of distributing antimalarial drugs and you are really into the cause—the idea of actually *coding the darn thing* makes you want to call in sick.

Getting excited about getting up at 6 a.m. is a lot easier when you enjoy what you do. Although I previously covered the idea of coming in early as part of what it takes to survive the economic downturns, doing so from a place other than fear is critical. Lots of people who hate writing software somehow survive in this business. There are scores of others who, while not hating it, are indifferent to it, seeing work as primarily a means to make a living.

People in either of these two groups are probably not likely to have a spark of creativity on the drive home, turn on the computer at home, and start an open source project. People in these groups are also not likely to write, blog, or really do much of anything else other than what might be needed to get by and collect a paycheck. And they certainly are unlikely to spend a lot of time

---

[1] If you are a former employer of mine receiving a copy of this book via FedEx, this sentence probably explains why.

going to user groups or other industry events unless sent by their company, and even then, participation tends to be passive.

If you hate computers but decided to pick up this book because some career counselor told you that you could make a lot of money writing computer programs, despite your disinterest in the subject, the following message applies to you:

> *Your career counselor has no idea what he or she is talking about and is likely full of it.*

Chris Williams   Honestly, most career counselors are. Mine suggested I should consider a career as an electrician because that's what was considered a good job at the time. My skills and interests never entered into the discussion.

Yes, it's true. You will never thrive doing something you hate. Chances are, you won't really survive that long either—though many try. If you hate programming computers, there is no book, article, magic codex, or other technology short of a brain transplant that will change that fact. If you truly hate programming or technology work, please put down this book and find a different occupation that is more aligned with your interests.

Dealing with Burnout

Now, let's assume going forward you don't simply hate programming. There are many other good reasons why you might have lost the love for the craft, but you might be able to get it back. Maybe you got into computer programming with visions of writing video games or something else of meaning to you, but somehow ended up writing bank software for a company like the fictional Initech from the movie *Office Space*. You might have once loved programming, but the last 5, 10, or 35 years have certainly changed that for you.

Unless cynicism has completely taken over, this problem is completely solvable. Most of the time, when I see someone in this situation, there are two main causes. The first, raw burnout, is the kind solved with some time away from the day-to-day work of programming. Whenever someone has been doing an activity constantly for a long period of time—even if the activity is extremely rewarding under most circumstances—the curse of boredom and familiarity sets in and causes loss of enthusiasm.

One of the simpler ways to solve this problem is to simply take a *real* vacation. When I talk about a real vacation, I mean something other than the typical fare that, as often as not, becomes not a vacation at all, but simply a different stressful activity that has its own burnout factor involved. In this context, I am talking about doing something for a couple of weeks that involves immersion outside your normal routine. If you like to go fishing, take two weeks and go fishing in a remote location away from all phone and Internet access. If you like road trips, get out there and drive for a couple of weeks. Whatever it is, it needs to get you away from coding, work, and anything else that gets in the way of spending time *thinking* about day-to-day work activities.

> *The cure for burnout: Take a two-week vacation from work where you actually don't work (no Blackberry, no email). If that does not change your thinking, try to change something with your work situation so you can get away from coding for a longer period.*

If that doesn't work, you might need to go to greater lengths to mix things up a bit. If possible, look to do something other than software development for a couple of months. Work with your company to see if there is a way to do something else other than code. Perhaps it is a good time to consider working in a close-by, noncoding role, such as quality assurance, business analysis, or project management. Pick something you like but different enough from your current role that it gives you a break that allows you to come back to coding without the cloud of burnout over your head.

Derik Whittaker   We all go through ruts where we do not want to code a particular project. When I find myself in this scenario, I try to find another project (open source or personal) that makes me passionate. I find that when I do this, I become passionate about all my projects gain. Just need to restoke the fire sometimes.

If none of those things resolve the situation, the problem could just be the company you work for. The context in which you think about work might be the problem. If you have not changed jobs for a couple of years and are not currently in the middle of a consulting assignment, it might not be a bad idea to change jobs. A lot of people tend to confuse a lack of identification with their company's mission with burnout. In such a situation, getting out and finding an organization with a mission whose goals are more aligned with your own may not be a bad idea if, after a couple of weeks completely away, you still can't get excited about coding.

Bringing Back the Fun

Of course, there is only going to be so much fun in corporate software development, whether you work as a consultant or as a full-time employee for a company. One way you can start to bring back the fun element is to start doing projects in your spare time that you personally care more about.

Assuming you have a computer at home, you can download many free and cheap tools that give you a development environment for home use. You can use free tools such as the Express Edition of Visual Studio, Eclipse, and many others to set up a development environment. From here, you can start to look at open source projects of interest and find something to tinker with that you care about. Sourceforge.net and codeplex.com are good places to start. Both sites give you access to the source code of thousands of open source projects that you can start tinkering with right away.

After learning the ins and outs of the source code to a few projects, you might start adding features to the project. Of course, you need to contact the project organizer and see whether you can submit your work (both sites have a means to do this). But even this activity helps you thrive because it grows your network.

Think of this as a fun way to get back the passion factor in your career while giving you something you can put on your resume. It is a nice way of pushing yourself to do something over which you might have a bigger sense of ownership—at least more ownership than the fourteenth bug you fixed in the Initech bank balance reconciliation system.

Jason Bock   I know people who have worked in environments where managers yelled at employees, working conditions were less than mediocre, and generally the lay of the land did not allow anyone to thrive. Life is too short to let yourself spend a goodly percentage of it at a place that is mentally beating you down. If you're in such a place, you may have to spend the time offline to bring that passion back. Thankfully, there's so much out there to learn about that it shouldn't take long!

The Payoff

When you like what you do and have outside projects over which you have a sense of ownership, you will start to find that in all your work, you have trained yourself to always have a sense of ownership. The sense of ownership is a precondition to real engagement with your work, which in turn is a precondition to really thriving and being successful as a technology consultant.

When you hate what you do, time goes by slowly, and your career is torture. When you love what you do, time flies, and the work day ends too soon. You find yourself going to community events, commenting on blogs, reading books, and in general, being engaged with your profession. Not because you have to, but because you legitimately *want* to do these things and (don't tell your employer this!) would do it for free if you were not being paid. You can be assured that your value as a happy consultant, engaged in his or her profession, who goes to community events and learns new material without having to be constantly sent to training, is vastly higher than the burnout who crawls into his cubicle at 10:30, avoids work for the next two hours, and spits out just enough grudging, uninspired lines of code to keep his job. And although not all employers will immediately recognize this value and give you a raise as a result, it *is* value you will realize throughout your career based on the quality of contacts you get from being an active and engaged person in your profession.

Michael Hugos   As the saying goes, "If you love what you do, you never work a day in your life." Because consulting is such a demanding and competitive business, you cannot succeed unless you do what you love. You will have to work free at times to keep up and learn new skills and make new connections. If your consulting career feels like work and not fun, it's a clear sign you need to discover what you really love. I've learned more than once that I need to do what I love first and then figure out how to make money at it, not the other way around.

How to Do Work That Matters

Doing work that matters is a tough subject, in the sense that there will be times in all our careers when we have to do work that does not matter a lot in the grand scheme of things because of various circumstances. Rest assured, for every advanced green energy power distribution system that saves the planet you may get to write in your career, you will probably also have to write a system that is, in essence, the 167th interface to the company payroll system. Hey, look on the bright side. At least the latter might help you get paid *this* month!

Jason Bock   There is a limit to the "getting paid" philosophy, though, and that's when it collides with your moral framework. Yes, even as a consultant, you still have morals (whatever they may be for you), and although it's very rare to end up at a client that pushes a product that you may have strong objections about being a part of creating (either directly or indirectly), it can happen (it almost happened to me). Nothing can kill the desire to thrive faster than to end up working at a client that you feel directly clashes with your morals and ethics.

Meaningful Work in Ordinary Places

Let's face it; a lot of work in this business is oriented toward pushing and pulling stuff about someone else's money into and out of databases. If you take the position that "work that matters" is always going to mean "changes the world in a manner such that utopia will imminently be upon us," you are likely going to be very disappointed.

If you can lower your sights from that lofty ideal and focus on doing meaningful work that can help a business save money or capitalize on a market opportunity, you can find meaning in more ordinary work. When a company is able to save money and be more competitive or find a new market, either productivity is increased or opportunity is or both. When this happens, the ultimate end effect is usually more capital available for investment. Unless the company is in a monopoly position, simply refunding all profits to shareholders, advancing the productivity agenda of a company will mean more investment in technology.

> *In most companies, there are endless opportunities to leverage technology to make the company more productive and/or able to penetrate new markets. Finding and executing these opportunities are great ways to give meaning to your work.*

A key to advancing into the higher-level career paths available to software development consultants is to learn how your client's business works so that you can recognize those opportunities to do meaningful work. Advancement in most of the career paths for software development consultants—advancement to positions like engagement manager, account executive, and especially, to a vibrant career as an independent—depends on developing a skill for *finding and executing* opportunities where meaningful work can be delivered.

When starting down this path, try shooting initially toward the center of the graph depicted in Figure 7-2; these solutions go beyond what a commodity-level software developer can produce but are not so outlandish that the company will think you are nuts for even suggesting the idea. After you have established a level of credibility and trust with your client, you can start moving toward solutions that are closer to the right sector of the graph, where the most meaningful work resides.

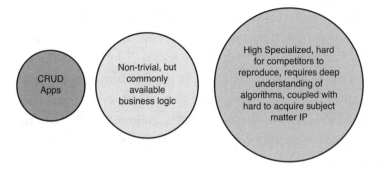

Figure 7-2   Business value continuum.

Although not all improvement opportunities you find will be executed, chances are, if you become the kind of person who has an eye for finding opportunity, you will develop the skills for building a business case to support the projects needed to act on them.

> **Jason Bock**   Clients that have "mediocre" work may be in that mode because they really don't know that it can be better. It may take some hard discussions, but it can also end up becoming a "win" for you to help the client see the benefits of a new architecture and then take on the challenge of getting that into place.

Software Developer/Inventor

Of course, you don't have to let the fact that most work in this business is of the more ordinary "help a company make more money" variety stop you from keeping your eye out for those opportunities that not only have a company-wide impact, but an industrywide one. That said, the chances of your scoring this kind of opportunity are somewhat related to your skills at networking and, in particular, being a student of the ideas your predecessors have brought to the table. Seldom is the most important work built in a vacuum; most of the time, the really interesting stuff integrates innovative ideas of others in new and interesting ways.

For example, the best spam filters are based on the application of Bayesian networks with email to determine whether incoming messages are junk. This is just one example of a technique that was well-known to researchers for a long time, waiting for someone to apply the technique in an actual shipping product (it now is the technique most really good spam filters use).

The good news is that there are many, many opportunities in corporate development where combining the more advanced tools of computer science, math, and statistics (for example, Monte-Carlo simulation, Regression Analysis, Bayesian classifiers) with advanced industry knowledge can result in opportunities to invent important advances that have broad impact. Even if you are not the person who comes up with the invention yourself, it is not a bad idea, in the interest of thriving, to try to position yourself around people who are thinking "big."

Ordinary Work Can Matter, Too

What if your consultancy does simple work—nothing that is going to change the world or even have a long-lasting impact for the client. One of the neat things about consulting is the fact that, at least to the consulting company, any kind of work that solves a client problem is meaningful, insomuch as a job well done provides the consulting firm with revenue that helps build a business. Especially if the broader goals of the consulting firm are in line with your own goals, any kind of billing work that helps the company financially contributes.

The real point, of course, is to do two things: expand the pool of things you would define as "work that has meaning," but at the same time, when you have work in that pool, pursue that work with an enthusiasm and urgency that conveys a sense to others that "everything you touch, you own." Do that, and it will be hard *not* to thrive.

Keep Moving: Constantly Learning

Indeed, the cliché is that in software, you have to be constantly working to keep up and that those who do not will fall by the wayside, ever doomed to jobs writing reports against a corporate database using antiquated technologies. Although the cliché is half true, newer, better technologies are always being invented, keeping up isn't nearly as hard as some make it out to be, losing ground does not make you doomed forever, and the fact that things "move so fast" can be as much of an advantage as it is a disadvantage. There are few other businesses in which seniority and years of experience matter less relative to actual demonstrable expertise in a technology that renders something older as pretty much obsolete.

Thriving in this business utterly depends on your ability not just to keep learning new technology, but to take learning to a more holistic level, learning about processes that enable software to be built, and ultimately, learning enough about how businesses work so that you can recognize where technology can be effective (see Figure 7-3). The technologist who couldn't care less about process will spend a lot of time working on the "shiny new thing" without thinking about how to effectively make it work in a real live company. The technologist who focuses only on business domain knowledge tends to lose sight of the realities of technology and processes that make improvements possible. The process specialist who loses connection with technology, of course, becomes the nightmare with a GANTT chart who has no idea how long something should take and is therefore easily fooled by people who will ask for the impossible on an estimate.

Jason Bock If you start hearing yourself saying, "That's the way I've done it for years," you may not be that far off from uttering statements like, "Get off my lawn!" Repeating successful practices is a good thing, but not at the expense of at least hearing out different alternatives. Keep challenging your entrenched notions of success.

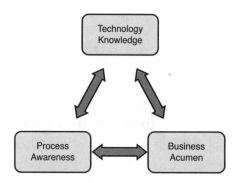

Figure 7-3 Consultants are constantly learning.

Areas of Focus for Technology

Should you try to learn every new technology that comes out? Of course not! You need to be strategic in what you decide to spend time learning; there simply are not enough hours in a day to learn everything. A good place to start is to assess what part of consulting you enjoy the most. If your love is programming, you probably should spend your time focusing on learning the ins and outs of programming languages you find people talking about a lot. If your love is product configuration, focus on learning products in which there is a good deal of client interest (if you work in consulting and you don't know, your general manager or firm owner probably has some guidance for you).

In 2009, if you are a programmer, it is a good thing to focus on learning dynamic languages (Ruby, JavaScript, Python), functional programming (F#, Scala, Erlang), or some of the newer features of the more mainstream languages like Java, VB, and C#. It is probably also a good idea to learn some of the newer UI frameworks, such as Flex, ASP.NET MVC, and Silverlight, at least to a level where you can work effectively with a UI designer. Although there are many subdisciplines in these areas, you should not specialize in anything that is so specific that a vendor can make you irrelevant by simply canceling a product.

Derik Whittaker I have found that although I cannot learn about all possible technologies, having a level of awareness of them helps. You can gain this awareness by simply reading information that details the technology at a high level. Doing this will add another tool to your tool belt and will pay dividends in the future.

On the product side, there are many more options; the product stacks of Microsoft, IBM, SAP, and Oracle are good places to start. Thriving in this area depends on being tied to a thriving product. Choosing what to learn is always going to be a combination of what your interests are (databases, portals, middleware), what your previous knowledge base is (that is, if you have worked with a particular vendor, it is best to stay there unless you have a compelling reason to change), and where market share is going.

Areas of Focus for Process

On the software development process side, in 2009, Agile development is very much relevant. And even if you do not agree with all the tenets of Agile, there is a good chance you will end up working on an engagement that purports to be done using Agile development techniques. Therefore, it is a good idea to be familiar with the process, study it for yourself, and give it a chance.

Also worth mentioning are processes such as Lean, based on the work of Tom and Mary Poppendieck; Cleanroom; Iterative; Scrum; XP; and RUP; not to mention the old, traditional Waterfall method. This last method should probably be studied for the same reason that someone who wants to understand human languages should study Latin, namely to provide a base of understanding for more modern methodologies.

Learning a methodology is very different from learning a technology in a couple of different ways. A technology is typically something you can learn by yourself to a certain degree—reading on your own, writing "hello world," and getting to the apprentice level by working on smaller problems. A methodology, by contrast, isn't really learned by anything other than experience. You should read about as many as possible to gain awareness and knowledge of what to expect. But prior to rendering a decision about a methodology, it is best to experience it through practice. Whereas technologies can be experienced solo, processes are inherently about group interaction and therefore are really quite impossible to learn about until you see for yourself how the group dynamics work.

Areas of Focus for Business Acumen

Technology and process alone, sadly, do nothing for the world without a context in which they are used. That context, unless you work for the government, is usually the world of business. Keeping abreast of the ultimate reasons why we use technology in the first place and being in a position to offer up ways for technology to further help are key to thriving as a technology consultant.

There is no human alive who can possibly learn each and every detail about every business. For that reason, some consultants find a niche developing deep knowledge in vertical markets, such as financial services, insurance, health care, manufacturing, supply chain, and others, where technology is known to frequently give some companies advantages over others. One of the nice things about consulting is that early in your career you can get exposed to a variety of different businesses, allowing you to decide which vertical is most suited to you and your interests. Later in your career, you can then choose to specialize in a *vertical*—that is, a specific area of business.

There are a couple of specific ways you can go about picking up business acumen, despite the daunting nature of it. Some consultants choose getting an MBA as an effective way of picking up business acumen. If the cost makes sense for you, that particular method can certainly be beneficial, though given the expense, make sure that it is worthwhile! Others are effective learning the business aspects on the job and supplanting that knowledge with a lot of self-study, through resources that range from Peter Drucker's famous book, *Management*, to picking up a subscription to *Harvard Business Review*. Regardless of specific method, having an understanding of basic business and economic principles will generally serve a budding software development consultant well.

One fact many software developers will find after a certain amount of experience and self-study is that much of business is really common sense. Of the three areas of focus, it is the broadest—with a lot to learn from a jargon standpoint. But once you pick up the basics, it is one of the more rewarding skills. Learning the language of the people who ultimately pay you—the language of business—is a key to not just surviving, but thriving as a technology consultant.

Learning to Think "Win-Win"

When you go to a store and make a purchase, who is worse off after the transaction? Is it the store, you, or both? The answer, of course, is neither; both sides win. The store sells an item to you for a profit, and you get something, presumably that makes your life better, in exchange for money. A key to thriving in your career as a technology consultant is to internalize this idea of "win-win" in your relations with others in the business world.

Why is this thinking so important? Many people get caught up in thinking of the business world as a place with finite resources, which leads to a mode of thinking along the lines of "if the other guy wins, I have to lose." Such thinking is typically the source of most bad things that can happen internally within a company: from company politics where people fight over "scarce" promotions by undercutting each other to various constituencies fighting over some limited budget.

Embracing a win-win philosophy means instead of fighting over a fixed set of resources, you constantly focus your efforts on "growing the pie" for everyone in the firm. It means instead of looking at competitors as a threat, finding ways to partner with them when appropriate. More generally, it means taking an approach to this business that focuses on simultaneously improving your position and that of those you serve.

When you have such a philosophy, even during the bottom of a recession, you have a sense for fundamentals of why companies need to spend money on technology. Remember, technology in general—information technology in particular—is a key area that allows a company to literally do more with less in a way that does not mean either making huge capital investments overseas or increasing the hours that its people must work. You can push down the cost of labor only so much, and frankly, most big organizations have done this already, leading to only marginal improvements being possible. When you get to the bottom of a recession and can't save money on people anymore by simply cutting them, you need technology and innovation to get further gains in productivity.

Good technology consultants understand this fact and use this as their means of keeping sanity during bad markets. In good markets, because the money is flowing, getting productivity ideas funded tends to be relatively easier than in bad markets, where such funding is scarcer. In bad markets, it is true, you have to do more work to get people to buy into an idea, and the idea has to pay off faster. This does not change the fundamentals of whether technology investment is a good or bad idea; it just means you have to work harder and be more persuasive.

Consider the airline industry, for example. In this industry many companies probably have on their Outlook calendars recurring appointments with bankruptcy attorneys. You can imagine the following conversation with an airline executive:

[*Airline Executive*]: So, is there really any business value in making applications pretty? I am an important executive, and I don't want to waste money on fluffy crap.

[*Me*]: Do you fly on a private jet, or are you still flying on your own airline?

[*Airline Executive*]: Sadly, in this environment, we are flying commercial, so I settle for First Class.

[*Me*]: Whew! Okay then, maybe you can relate. Have you ever had to change a flight?

[Airline Executive]: Yeah, sure have. Once I was on the way to Washington, DC, to get another bailout, and I had to change the flight. Man, what a nightmare!

[Me]: Wow, well, don't you wonder sometimes if that ticket agent behind the counter is really changing your ticket? Doesn't it seem as if she is doing enough typing back there to write an entire master's thesis?

[Airline Executive]: Sure does! There is a lot of work required to change from the 6 a.m. to the 8 a.m. flight to Reagan National!

[Me]: Well, think about it. You can go online or, for that matter, to the kiosk six feet away from the agent and accomplish the same thing with four clicks and two keystrokes.

[Airline Executive]: Wow! You're right!

[Me]: In fact, think of all the money you could save if the user experience on your systems that your agents have to use didn't suck so much.

[Airline Executive]: No wonder we are constantly going bankrupt. Can I have your card?

How can a technology company and an airline work together to make both sides better off? If you can move to think in terms of win-win even in an industry like airlines, which is perennially in a recession of one type or another, you will find yourself a more effective advocate for what your consulting company does—namely, offer solutions to tough problems.

Of course, you may not be in a position right now to influence such things in your consulting career. However, training your brain to think not in terms of "what can this person/client/company do for me," but rather "how can we help each other achieve complementary goals" is critical to your not only thriving now, but especially thriving as you progress along your career path. Even if you don't end up heading down the sales or independent path, generally speaking, people who think in terms of win-win are much easier to work with than people who are always thinking of their own success in terms of someone else's lack thereof. The whole "don't be a jerk"[2] factor involved in win-win thinking will definitely help you in your career, regardless of what you decide to do.

Building Your Brand

Although you can survive in this business for an entire career being an anonymous, heads-down type person, really thriving requires actual work building a brand so that you distinguish yourself in some manner. Building a brand—broadly defined as a perception others have about you that speaks well of your skills and capabilities—is a good way to make sure that your career really takes off.

The usual advice here, of course, applies. If possible and you are at good writing or if you are good in front of an audience, you should consider pursuing activities like writing technical articles or speaking at conferences. Those kinds of activities help build your brand, while at the same time give you many opportunities to develop skills that are useful in other contexts. Speaking isn't just for conferences and user groups; the same skills become useful when presenting at board meetings or sales calls. Writing is also useful in a lot of areas for your career, be it writing a whitepaper, writing a proposal, or even writing good documentation.

> **Derik Whittaker**   Building your brand is not too hard, but keep in mind it does take time. You cannot simply flip a switch and expect to be famous. You must work at it. It takes effort but is well worthwhile in the long run.

---

[2] See *The No Asshole Rule*, by Bob Sutton, for more detail on this topic.

Where to Start

The tips from the preceding section, while certainly fun, are not the entire basis for building your brand. In fact, it is best to think of those things as the icing on the cake of an already good brand built through

- Delivery of great solutions to multiple clients and/or customers
- Development of open source tools that are broadly applicable to the development world
- Development of a reputation for being a person who reliably and steadily delivers value for his or her firm

In other words, before you can build an external brand, focus on building a great internal brand first. In your early career, that means being a good student of what others are doing right—either within your own company or on the outside. Of course, it helps to find a good company where you surround yourself with others who, ideally, are smarter than you are and can "raise you up."

If you find yourself as the smartest person in your company early in your career, you either need to move on (because you need to go somewhere with a higher bar), or you need to be more honest with yourself (maybe you are not as smart as you think).

After a couple of years of working around people who have already built their own brands and building a good reputation for yourself in your day job as a software developer, you will start to have more opportunities to express your own capabilities in a more visible way. Starting out, this might be in opportunities like "tech nights," "lunch and learns," or "brown-bags," where you get a chance to demonstrate and speak about a new technology or technique to some coworkers in a relatively friendly audience.

Another good way to get started is to volunteer to write a whitepaper for your firm. Most consulting firms appreciate having their consultants provide good written material that is of interest to either other technologists (which helps in recruiting) or clients (which helps in sales). As long as the writing activity does not interfere with your normal billable work, being active like this is a good way to build a good internal reputation as an expert.

From Internal Branding to External Branding

At some point, after doing a few sessions, writing a few whitepapers, you are going to get some feedback. If you don't get feedback, make sure to ask for some, and especially ask for constructive criticism, which will help you become better at what you do. The latter is the most important because as you move from an internal audience to an external one, the feedback you receive will go from mostly positive, unless you are truly awful, to possibly somewhat negative, unless you are truly exceptional. This transition can be tough for your ego unless you learn how to handle constructive criticism and, for that matter, even nonconstructive criticism! In other words, the more your audience grows, the more likely it is that you will start to run into people who will disagree, challenge, and even heckle. The better prepared you are, the better off you will be.

On the speaking side, good places to start when you transition to external branding are local user groups, particularly more specialized ones in areas where you have expertise. Remember though, if you are going to take this step, it is incumbent on you to become comfortable enough at public speaking such that you do not freeze on stage. People invest time and energy to go to user groups, and not taking the time to learn how to really be effective at one does both the user group and you a disservice. In the event you get an opportunity to speak, it behooves you to practice the talk a few times and make sure all your demos work!

On the writing side, start by looking to submit content for some of the second-tier journals, as well as writing regularly in a blog. The traffic at first will be minimal, if that; building readership takes time. It takes a combination of writing about things people will care about, bringing a perspective that makes your content worth reading, and lastly being persistent enough not to give up after a couple of articles. That said, bloggers who stick with it, putting up good, useful, and occasionally mildly controversial content over a long period of time tend to build up readership. If for no other reason, it is a human tendency to quit activities that don't yield an immediate payoff.

Lastly, it is worth mentioning here that mentoring more junior developers is not a bad way to help make the transition and build your external brand. Working hard to be a good mentor is a great way to build a good base of support within your company and to become comfortable with the responsibilities of guiding others. The last part is critical because when you are guiding others, you have to take the responsibility seriously. Giving bad advice can be worse than not giving advice at all. So if you choose to go down this path, it is incumbent on you to make sure you are giving advice in areas where you are qualified.

Building the External Brand

When you start to have an external brand, it is probably time to consider engaging in activities that have an even broader impact. Good ideas at this stage are to consider authoring books, submitting responses to speaker requests at national conferences, and seeking to publish for top-tier journals. At this stage, there is no particular method that will make you successful, though generally, the importance of networking skill, perfecting your skill at speaking, and learning to write effectively are all very important.

One point to remember when you get to this level, and especially when you start to see some success, is that it is still important to focus on your day job. Unless you are one of the very small handful of people in this business who are paid to be an evangelist or guru and speak at conferences full time, chances are, you are going to still need to bill at clients and otherwise provide direct value to your consulting firm. If you are independent, this is doubly true because the reality is that you would have to probably write four successful books and talk at 20 national conferences a year to generate income equal to that of a typical software developer. Until that day comes, it is critical that you make time to still serve your clients well.

Michael Hugos   I've come to realize that building my brand is the essence of what I do in my career. That means discovering the things I love and working at them. They have to be things I love because I have to devote myself to them for a long time and get good at them to create a distinctive brand that differentiates me from all the other people who do what I do. I've also learned I have to develop my own opinions and my own methods for getting things done, and that means breaking with conventional wisdom at times. Brands are built on new ideas that deliver real-world results, and it takes time and courage to find these ideas and try them out.

Summary

If nothing else, thriving takes a lot of work. It is not easy to do, especially during economic times that are not positive. Although this chapter covered many techniques that help, the one unifying theme is to, as much as possible, try to have a positive attitude about what you are doing, going about your work with a predisposition toward making the most of your opportunities.

Staying engaged—that is, operating with focus, enthusiasm, proactivity, and persistence—is the real key to thriving in any activity; technology consulting included. When you effectively apply these traits to your own work, your company, and your broader industry, it is very hard not to be successful.

That said, it is also important to realize that few careers are a straight moonshot up. You will have ups and downs, and you will not always be able to be focused and engaged. Sometimes the most important thing in your life, frankly, will not be your career at all. The point here isn't to assert that every day must be spent advancing your brand or anything like that. There will be lulls, periods of decline, and periods of reflection. As long as you balance those with periods of true thriving and advancement, chances are you will get a lot more out of your career.

CHAPTER EIGHT

YOUR CAREER PATH

In the typical career path of a technology consultant, there are many twists and turns.

Life sure would be easier if the next goal for your career was one, nice, obvious linear path. Sadly, nothing is that easy in the world of technology consulting. You can take solace, though. There are few career paths in which it is really that simple; you certainly are not in the only such occupation. Although many occupations seem to have a clear career path (law associate to partner, for example), even then, modern life conspires to make things more complicated than what most people plan.

The first curve in the otherwise linear path comes in the form of the economic cycle. As covered in Chapter 6, "Surviving," sometimes you have to change plans and adapt to situations. Maybe asking for a promotion to an overhead management position isn't the best idea during a recession—both because it is likely to be denied (no money for overhead) and because even if your wish is somehow granted, it puts you in a riskier position. Or you might decide to take a year or two off to help raise a young child or to do relief work. Or you could simply decide after a couple years that technology just isn't your thing and you want to switch to an entirely different career track. The first rule of career paths is that there isn't just one and that by not being flexible about how you pursue your goals, you greatly limit your options.

This all said, some consultants tend to find themselves on a few typical career paths at some point in their careers. Understanding where each of these paths leads and techniques on how to navigate them can help you, at least, have an answer to that HR interview question, "What do you want to be doing in five years?" It would have to be better than the one I have been known to give, namely, "Well, I would like to be a rich venture capitalist with CEOs begging me for money and flying me around on their private jets."

> **Michael Hugos**   Thriving in my career has involved a sequence that moved between consulting and corporate positions. Consulting positions have always offered me more opportunities to learn new skills and more opportunities to take on new responsibilities. A couple of times I parlayed my consulting experience into corporate management positions that gave me a prestigious title and a deeper understanding of the world my corporate clients live in. When I returned to consulting from those corporate positions, I found I was a better consultant because I was better able to communicate with and relate to my corporate clients.

Path #1: Rise to Management

When you get your first job in the consulting business, there is a tendency to use your boss as a role model for what you want to advance to. It is therefore not that farfetched to consider a rise to management as, at least, a possible career path. Being the boss has a lot of benefits, but elements of the job are thankless. However, if you are doing a good job, advancing through the various ranks within consulting that most firms provide, you could find yourself with this opportunity.

Of course, just as there are lots of types of managers in this business, as covered in Chapter 3, "How Technology Consulting Firms Work," there are also many different subtypes of management. Although there are many possible permutations, one frequently seen in multiple firms is shown in Table 8-1.

TABLE 8-1

Common Management Career Paths

Title	Scope	Billing Responsibility
Team Lead/Principal	Within a single project, responsible for leading the efforts of a small group of 1–3 people.	Full. Typically has the same billing target as any consultant would.
Project Manager (PM)/Solution Architect	Typically responsible for a single project at a time, managing a small team of up to 4–6 people.	Mostly Full. In most firms, this person is still dedicated to a client with full billing responsibility. Might bill across more than one client, rarely.
Engagement Manager (EM)	Under most circumstances, responsible for multiple projects for a single client. Manages the client relationship. Typically manages 7–20 people.	Possibly Partial. Some firms charge for engagement management, some don't; for others, it depends on the client relationship.
Consulting Manager (CM)	Manages a portion of the efforts of an entire office or company, in larger companies. If there are more than a few large engagements, a consulting manager typically has a responsibility span across them. Sometimes acts as an engagement manager for smaller engagements. Typically responsible for a headcount of 10–40 people.	Light. Typically fills in when there isn't an available PM, EM, architect, and so on, but has more internal responsibility.
General Manager GM)/Director	Is effectively the CEO of an entire office or region. Typically responsible for a headcount of 20–100 people.	Seldom. Adds value purely through others, except under extenuating circumstances.
Senior Management/ COO/CTO/CEO	Responsible for the entire company's operations. Focus is strategic unless someone below needs tactical assistance on a specific issue.	Almost Never. Senior management billing (in a company >250 people) is a sign that the company might be in deep, deep trouble.

Rising to Team Lead/Principal

As you become a better consultant, within two to five years (fewer in the best boom markets, more in the worst), you will probably get an opportunity to lead a team in a role like team lead or principal. At this initial level of management, you still lead by example because you almost certainly have hands-on responsibility as well as direct billing responsibility at the same level as any other consultant.

Getting to this level usually depends on being a dependable individual contributor who is also seen as having good "soft skills"; that is, a consultant who

- Management feels can be put in front of client management without fear of putting the engagement at risk
- Is recognized as a leader among his or her peers
- Demonstrates a high level of interpersonal maturity and a low level of drama
- Is effective at proactively networking with others and building relationships

Having these skills well developed will almost guarantee you a ticket into a role as a lead, provided the other conditions you don't control exist, such as room for a person at a higher level on the organization chart of a given project (see Figure 8-1). You can be thankful that in consulting your ability to be a lead depends more on your own skills than an org chart. An effective lead developer can be put into an engagement as a lead and have people hired around him or her, assuming the role can be sold to a new client who happens to have a project.

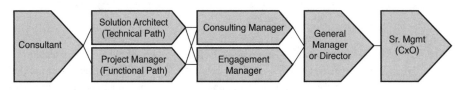

Figure 8-1 Typical management career paths.

Rising to Project Manager or Solution Architect

One possible step, though possibly optional depending on the case, is spending some time as a project manager. A parallel path is that of a solution architect, who is usually seen as an equal to the project manager (though the hybrid, technical project manager is sometimes attempted, with varying levels of success). Although both of these roles have elements of individual contribution to them (one makes plans, the other conceives of solutions and sets architectures for them), when done properly, these roles start to introduce much more in the way of leadership elements.

Getting to either of these roles typically involves demonstrating the same skills as those that got you to team lead—only to a greater degree. Added to the core set is also a sense that you have what it takes to own an entire solution, whether you are a PM or solution architect. Both roles require people who can demonstrate "soup-to-nuts" follow-through capability on projects.

Project Manager: More than the GANTT Chart Secretary

If you are doing your job correctly as a project manager, you are spending most of your time in relationship-building mode. This job is *not* just about gathering status, updating a project plan, and writing a report once a week. If it were, even in teams executing a daily scrum, it would require less than one hour for the morning scrum, one hour to collect status data at the end of the week, and one hour to perhaps write a report. One PM would manage a project in eight or fewer hours per week and could spend the other 32 playing golf.

Of course, there is much more to project management than that. A good project manager (or, as I prefer to say, project *leader*) facilitates keeping the right kind of collaboration going on a team—resolving conflicts in the team and managing the outside forces so that team members can concentrate on their job, chiefly developing software. A good project manager negotiates the politics outside the team to create a mostly politics-free environment inside the team. Although the project manager may not know the technical detail that the team does, nor will he or she know the domain detail that either a business analyst or onsite customer will, this person knows enough to make good decisions about how to allocate resources and funding for the project.

In other words, if herding cats is your calling, being a project manager is a great place to aspire to once you have spent some time as a lead. Of course, that type of work does not appeal to most software developers; most would rather leave the PM path to aspiring business analysts. The more alluring path for most people who really enjoy software is that of the solution architect.

What Solution Architects Really Do

You might have heard this old joke about architects: The term *architect* is Latin for "does not write code." Sadly, this joke is still true in some organizations. Whether that should be the case is another matter.

> **Jason Bock**   I rarely see architects who do not code. In fact, I'd say architects are pretty useless unless they're actually coding. They may not do the bulk of the work, but if they can't actually implement the solution they're proposing, then something's wrong. The best architects are the ones who can still "walk the walk."

Solution architects are responsible for making sure the solution is cohesive, is of the appropriate level of quality, and generally passes muster with the client. The word *solution* precedes *architect* because a solution architect is responsible for the quality and usefulness of the entire solution.

Does this mean that you sit in an office, writing UML diagrams that some developer in a cube farm—either in the next room or in a far off country—writes to spec? Well, in most cases, no. It means that in the same way a project manager leads on business and outside political concerns, your job as a solution architect is to be persuasive about design matters. Often, you need to demonstrate by example what the right practices and patterns are. The actual heads-down work you do will vary according to the project. Sometimes you will work with the rest of the development team on the more novel parts of the design, helping the team get past roadblocks. In others, you might be the integrationist, who makes sure that individually or pair-developed components fit together properly in a solution and do so in a way that is maintainable.

In other words, as a solution architect, you are the person to whom the finger of blame will be pointed if the solution has too many bugs or has maintenance problems later. Although you might not be the programmer who did the actual work, you were probably supposed to do code reviews and other architectural guidance so those problems did not happen.

Rising to Engagement Manager

Moving up to the role of engagement manager, also called client partner in some organizations, requires a very different orientation from the previous roles in this progression. Engagement managers put a much stronger emphasis on finding ways for technology to add value for a client and then getting buy-in from that client's highest-level decision makers to execute on those initiatives. In other words, engagement managers exist to find ways for the client and consulting firm to further find situations in an existing client where said client can exchange money for services in a way that benefits both sides.

Engagement managers do oversight over project managers, often acting as an escalation resource when problems occur and in some cases doing project management if no project manager is available. Their real job, however, is to build relationships and be the value detectives who help save the client money or capitalize on new opportunities. As with most promotions, getting to this level is not simply a matter of being promoted to it. The promotion happens after you have been working for a client for some time and have demonstrated relationship-building and expansion skills. Engagement managers are usually not named; rather, they are ratified after having worked in the role on a de facto basis.

So how do you go about taking the step to engagement manager? If you are interested, you should probably spend less time in your code editor and a lot more time getting to understand the pain of your primary client contacts—that is, what keeps them up at night. Then try to see what you can do over and above your current responsibility to solve that problem. When you figure that out, network with others in the organization: Buy a lunch or five if you have to and find out what worries them. After a series of conversations, you will probably start to discover ways that your firm can help beyond what you are doing already. Voila, you are doing engagement management. At this point, or possibly even before (assuming you are making good progress), you should keep your own firm apprised of the contacts you are making. When you have a bona fide opportunity, involve either a current EM, the account executive who sold the account, or someone higher up in management.

Rising to Consulting Manager

Of all the roles in the management path, a consulting manager is the most variable in terms of the responsibilities on a firm-to-firm basis. For a particular client, you generally report to the EM, PM, or architect. Outside the scope of the project, however, you generally report to a general manager, director, or consulting manager.

Getting into this role, unlike the engagement manager role, is more about the internal focus on making your colleagues better, regardless of what client they are with. All the management skills that get you into management apply, but in particular, the no-drama, "adult-in-the-room" qualities are particularly meaningful in this role. The reason is that being a CM mostly involves a good deal of conflict management (when consultants disagree or get into political problems), delivery of bad news (when raises are not good or layoffs occur), as well as the ability to manage projects, be a software architect, help in the sales process, and generally support the overall efforts of the office.

If you want to move on to general manager/director or higher, you should find the common path to that role. In some companies, general managers are pulled from the ranks of engagement managers. In others, they come from consulting management. An organization that values relationship building with clients more will probably tend toward promoting EMs, whereas one that values care and feeding of consultants more will tend toward promoting CMs. Although both roles value sales and delivery, some value one slightly more than the other, and knowing which side yours is on should affect how you position yourself if you are seeking further advancement.

Rising to General Manager/Director

At this point in your career, typically 10–20 years in, with increasing responsibility, and a few promotions under your belt, you might consider running your own division, practice, or region. Generally, what occurs when you get this itch is you either decide to start your own firm (see the section, "Path #4: Rise to Entrepreneur"), or you get your own company to take the leap and let you take the reins of your own piece of the business.

If you want to get to this level, the recipe is pretty simple: Deliver great results for a long period of time (generally over a couple years or more) as an EM or CM. You should spend some time getting to know some of the other EMs and CMs from around the office, not just to understand your competition, but to earn a position of respect by being helpful. You also should try to build a base of support from the rest of the office, consultants, sales, and sales support, recruiting, and everyone else. Running for GM, as with most higher offices, is as much a political decision as anything. You want to make yourself into the obvious choice because of your support base.

Most important, though, you need to demonstrate to your most senior management that you understand the business of consulting. At this level, you are essentially running a business within the larger organization, often one of substantial size (>$10M revenue). Demonstrating that you can make difficult decisions, such as who to let go during a downturn, when to exit from a bad client engagement, and so forth, not only positions you for the job, but ultimately positions you for success. At this level, failure isn't just personal or even local. It can bring down an office and possibly set back the careers of dozens of people in the process. Not the kind of thing you want to do if you don't like pressure!

Rise to Senior Management

If you work primarily in smaller consulting firms, you can probably safely skip the next two paragraphs because senior management in said cases is the same thing as "owner" and likely means that it is not a position you can be promoted into. In fact, if you are even being considered for this level, it is highly likely that you have been running a successful business-within-a-business as a GM or director for some time and, for some strange reason, still want to move up further.

If you are interested in moving to a position in senior management— COO, CTO, CEO—and you are currently not a general manager or higher, I can say with near certainty that the fastest and most profitable path would be to skip ahead to Path #4: Rise to Entrepreneur. Simply put, unless you work for one of the largest firms, such as EDS, IBM Global Services, or Accenture, these jobs are usually going to go to people connected to the founders or investors.

Moving to this position isn't impossible, however—merely very unlikely. To position yourself for this move from GM or director, you need to run a business that generates consistent, increasing returns regardless of economic conditions. When people think of you, they need to think, "Safe bet. Need everyone to do what he or she is doing; make him or her the chief operating officer." It is also a waiting game because most firms already have a chief operating officer (or Senior VP or someone else with that role). This means that you could wait for years, even decades, for the role to open up. Getting this position is really the intersection of preparation *and* being in the right place at the right time, which is much harder to plan for! If you want to plan for this kind of position, Path #4 is probably more of a direct path there.

Reasons to Pursue the Management Track

Management tends to be about proving you can be responsible for generating sustainable profit from successively larger groups of people. Done well, this can be a position where you leverage the responsibility and trust that others have in you to provide good individual results for you and your client and to leverage your leadership skills so that you can inspire others to do those same things, increasing the "multiplier" on your efforts. Although an individual can create great software, the fact remains that to develop most broad-reaching solutions that provide real competitive advantage for companies, you will need a cast of different people with combinations of skills that make those results possible.

If you are the type of person who can inspire others to do great work, if you are good at sharing credit, and if you are not afraid to hire people who are smarter than you are, chances are you will do well in a management track.

Of course, if you want to progress far, you can get only so far by managing. Whereas managers can do a fine job of making sure employees show up on time, file the right reports, and generally put in eight hours, a leader must ensure that people are inspired to go beyond "just good enough to not get fired." The difference is that a leader doesn't just report progress and give orders to people. A leader gets people engaged and ready to achieve the goals of the project. A leader inspires people to do the right thing, to put in extra effort. A leader communicates effectively how the shared effort is a win-win-win deal—for the client, for the leader, and for the people involved on the project. A manager gives orders and then writes a status report. A leader inspires people so that they self-manage. A leader creates the conditions that allow the status report to communicate a reality that is the best possible result for the client given the circumstances.

Being a leader can be gratifying. And not just for your ego, but in the broader picture. When you lead, you funnel the creative contributions of large groups of people to achieve significant things. That's not a bad outcome if you have those ambitions.

Reasons to Avoid the Management Track

In consulting, management typically does not pay much more than you can make being a billing consultant. You might get an additional $10,000 to $20,000 per year, at best, and if that is the only reason you want to do it, you will almost certainly fail. In fact, for the money, the additional responsibility is almost never worthwhile.

Additional responsibility? Oh yes, when you are just an individual contributor, you can pretty much control the level of your performance. On the other hand, when you are the boss, you are completely dependent on others performing on your behalf. The effect is that you suddenly feel as though you are putting together a paper airplane using mittens: Most of the control you have is indirect. For a programmer who is used to having direct control of his or her subject—namely, the computer program being worked on—management can be a very frustrating experience. This makes the initial experience in management miserable. If you are not strongly motivated to learn how to create results through other people, through use of charisma, persuasion, and general influencing skills, chances are, you are not a good candidate for management.

Do you like office politics? Well, if you do, you will love management. Your job isn't just to survive them; your job is to manage them. In fact, to be good at management in all but the smallest companies, you need to be able to use politics as a tool to accomplish things—if not internally, certainly at the client organizations you work in. In management, skill at politics is part of the job. If you are the type of person who changes jobs because of political situations, management is probably not the best path for advancement. There will be others that, for you, would be more enjoyable, fulfilling, and successful.

Path #2: Rise to Sales

Although the path from the junior ranks of entry-level consultant to becoming the CEO of a multibillion dollar enterprise can be excruciatingly long for the upwardly mobile, there are faster ways to riches. In fact, if you want money more than anything, you should really consider a career in technology services sales, particularly if you are that unusual (at least according to the stereotype) technology professional who happens to also really enjoy the art of the hunt.

It is definitely true that this career path can be, and typically is, a lot shorter and simplistic than the management career path. In fact, it tends to look something like what's shown in Figure 8-2.

The career path for those in the demand generation business (the fancier term for *sales*), unlike management-oriented career paths, is not typically a straight line up in terms of compensation. In fact, when you move from the consulting side of the business to the sales side of the business, you will almost certainly take a substantial decline in income as you switch roles.

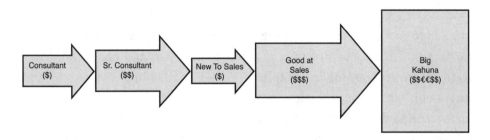

Figure 8-2 The sales career path.

Why is this? Well, when you make the move to sales, you move from a role in which "you are what you bill" to a role that is more akin to "you are what you sell." Generally, you only directly bill an amount related to the number of hours you work; hence, there is an upper bound on revenue you can directly generate. When you move to sales, the upside increases: If you are good, you are not only billing for your hours, but are generating demand for many others as well. Because you are getting a cut from each deal, that is, a commission, you drastically increase the amount of income you can earn. For this reason, the best salespeople, the big producers who generate $10 million of revenue per year or more for their consulting firms, can have incomes that exceed even the CEO's! It is not unheard of for an eight-figure producer to make $500,000 per year or more. If you are interested in financial upside, the sales path is only exceeded, perhaps, by that of the entrepreneur path.

Of course, all things with a large upside tend to have more risks. The downside, in this case, is that you might just not be very good at selling software services. It is a very different world than that of software development. In software development, every day is filled with small accomplishments: The code compiles, the bug is fixed, the tests pass, the user story is complete, and so on.

There is no other engineering discipline in which the feedback loop from thought to accomplishment is as fast.

On the other hand, in sales, days or even weeks can go by without any sense of real accomplishment whatsoever. In fact, in sales, the situation is often the opposite, often a long series of events, some well outside your control, some not, where you are constantly working without seeing the light at the end of the tunnel. The business of sales is a people business, and people tend to be irrational creatures, unlike compliant CPUs that, when reduced to their instruction set, do exactly what you tell them to do. The developer-turned-salesperson finds that buyers often make purchasing decisions based on illogical concerns, such as which salesperson is more fun to play golf with or who provides better box seats at a baseball game. And people are notoriously unreliable when they are buyers, canceling meetings at the last minute, failing to call back when they promise they would, and so forth.

Worse for people coming in from a relatively high-paying field like consulting, the fact that a starting salesperson tends to make a low base salary usually means that the consultant has to take a substantial income hit to get started. A senior consultant who makes around $100,000 per year might choose to go to sales, where the base is closer to $60,000 per year. So combined with the demoralization that is moving from an accomplishment treadmill to an environment where you might wait several months before your first real accomplishment, you also take an income hit. Right when you need to upgrade your wardrobe too! Programmer clothes will not work in sales, where presentation is everything.

Working in sales requires perseverance through all these obstacles, working through a hundred no answers to get to a single yes. It requires a lot of small talk with people you may or may not like, a desire to take networking to the level of your highest order skill, and it requires a hardened shell against rejection. You need thick enough skin not to take things personally when they don't go your way. This path is very difficult for most software developers to go through, which is why a huge number of people have not made the transition.

If the preceding job description does not scare you out of a sales track, you probably need to demonstrate your mettle as a consultant, probably taking in a promotion or two before getting ready to make the move. Generally speaking, the skills that make you a good *consultant* (that is, the people skills) are the skills that help you operate in a sales role. After you establish some credibility with your firm, you can start asking to help in the sales process, especially if you are on the bench. If you get the call to help, of course, don't be surprised when the salespeople give you the tasks they don't want to do. The sales process is not all eating lunch at Spago's! As long as you are doing good work for your current client (if you have one), doing some after-hours sales help, or at least offering it, is almost always appreciated and a good way to start the move.

The process to get the rest of the way there depends on the specific firm. Some companies, as they expand, open new roles for account executives. These are opportune times to ask to apply for the position, as long as you are not booked on a long engagement. In some companies, if you demonstrate competence in a sales support role, they might open up a position for you under the assumption that if you are good, the role will pay for itself very quickly. Either way, the least likely way you will get a chance to move into this kind of role is a lateral move to another company because most companies either want to hire people who have a demonstrated history of producing or make internal transfers.

Reasons to Pursue the Sales Track

More than almost any other career path save entrepreneurship (which you can think of as "sales on steroids"), sales is a position in which you never ask for a raise. If you want a raise, the answer is "call more prospects, get more clients." When you get into sales, your career becomes less about maneuvering for the next promotion and more about maneuvering to get into the next client. Although the wins come much less frequently than the small wins you experience as a software developer, when they do come, you get quite an awesome feeling of accomplishment!

The occupation of sales is oriented toward the "hunter" personality. If you enjoy the chase, you enjoy the feeling of creating demand that keeps other software developers employed, and you are willing to go through sometimes very difficult obstacles to get there, sales may be the right career track for you. It is slightly less risky than all-out entrepreneurship but riskier than the traditional management path, at least in the short run as you get started.

On the other hand, when you have a large book of business built with a diverse set of companies, you actually can reduce your career risk. When recession hits, the last person to be let go is a salesperson who is producing results and making progress toward getting more clients. And as long as all your income is not coming from one or two large clients, you get the benefits of diversification, in that one company can stop and you still will have an income base from which to work. If you have the personality and skills to get to this level where the risks start to level off and even decline, you should seriously consider this career path.

Reasons to Avoid the Sales Track

If you simply see big dollar and euro signs but don't actually like people very much, you almost certainly will fail in the sales part of the business. As a consultant, you can go a long time before your job becomes "people-intensive" beyond once or twice per day interaction with others. (Be cautioned, at all higher levels, people intensity increases.) As a salesperson, you are literally in the people business. If you don't like them, you will not be very convincing, you will not enjoy your job, and even in the event you somehow overcome those obstacles and are successful, you will make yourself miserable in the process.

Furthermore, for some people, having variable income is going to be an issue. If you are a primary breadwinner with a family that depends on each and every dollar of income that you make, taking a 40 percent cut in pay to get started in the sales business is probably not going to work. If you are in this category, you should probably avoid this situation until your finances allow you to take a 40 percent pay cut and still be able to operate your household. Most people in sales either (1) have messy finances and very bad credit or (2) arrange their lives so that they may have high variable costs (green fees can be expensive!) but low fixed costs (so they can weather storms in demand). Either that, or they keep a war chest around that allows them to live on something other than income for a while.

Lastly, if you absolutely can't stand golf, you probably should avoid this line of work. Golf is to salespeople what *World of Warcraft* and *Star Wars* are to software developers. Part of the culture of sales is closing the deal on the golf course. If you are unable to at least pretend to enjoy the sport, you will likely be at a disadvantage to those who are! Although some salespeople have excelled in the absence of golf, they are the exception, not the rule!

Path #3: Rise to Evangelist/Guru

For those who do not want to sell their souls and become managers or salespeople but lack the desire to take the high risks of starting their own business, the path to evangelist or guru can be attractive. This is the path of the blogger, the frequent user group speaker, the writer of journal articles, the book author, leading to a position where you go around the world talking about what you know. All this happens while your knowledge of current technology fades because all you do is speak at events and write blog posts. Or so it can seem during your day-to-day life as a technology evangelist.

One of the first things to understand about this path is it can generate fame (at least among other developers), but it rarely generates fortune directly. Sure, you might pick up a speaking fee here and there for a national conference, perhaps a few hundred dollars here and there for writing articles, but the reality is that few people get to the level in this career path such that mere existence as an evangelist is enough to replace anywhere near the income you make from employment.

Derik Whittaker   If you want to rise to this level, you need to understand that with this knowledge comes responsibility. Other developers will be looking to you to guide them. If you are not willing to be a voice for your community or make the effort, you should not strive to be an evangelist.

When you look at this path, however, you have to look past the direct income benefits. Over time, becoming a source of community authority is a great way to give yourself employment stability in consulting (that is, you become sought after for advice). You also can provide a base from which to launch or accelerate your rise through other career paths.

Moreover, though, whether you actually become an industry-recognizable name or perhaps an authority on a topic within a local niche, this path is a great way to take your energy and enthusiasm for this business and help others in your technical community. Learning about a concept in detail, developing good examples, and going out and teaching others are good both for you, because you raise your profile in a good way, and others, because they actually learn something.

Unlike other paths, the path to guru is more parallel than serial. There are as many ways from A to B as there are imaginations. For some, the process starts by simply being a good and frequent blogger about a relevant technology. Having good, consistent material on a blog and making sure you get that content in front of people who can use it can be a very effective way of making a name for yourself.

For others, working forums like stackoverflow.com and being consistently good at providing content are effective ways to become known as "one of the top 10 experts at X." Still others get there by doing important work on open source projects that provide meaningful functionality that is broadly applicable to others. The list can go on and on, but the most important components are as follows:

- Produce good technical content, written or otherwise.
- Communicate that content to as broad an audience as possible.

Mastery of those elements, mixed with some skill at effective self-promotion—that is, being smart about when and where you should do promotion and not going too far—is a good start toward becoming an authority on one or more topics. And this is what leads to becoming the sought-after author/speaker/guru.

Reasons to Pursue the Evangelism/Guru Track

When I talk to people who have successfully gone this route to evangelist/ guru, they almost always say that they never purposefully went down this path. Rather, they just did what they loved to do, and their enthusiasm over what they did carried themselves to the position. This idea gets at the heart of the best reason to do this, which is an incessant desire to get your ideas out and try to use them to help others through teaching and mentoring. When the effort comes from a place of trying to be helpful, you come across as more genuine, more helpful, and less in the role for the status that might come your way.

Of course, because this is a book about taking purposeful effort to being in the driver's seat of your career, you might consciously decide to go down this path. This is not a bad thing at all. If you are the kind of person who has skills at writing, speaking, teaching, or mentoring, this career path is probably a good way to leverage those skills into some measure of job security through the networking and other opportunities that occur after you start to get a name for yourself.

Reasons to Avoid the Evangelism/Guru Track

Although just about any consultant will benefit from doing some community activity, this path is certainly not for everybody. If you don't like getting in front of crowds or don't really like writing, this path may seem like torture— a constant stream of speaking attempts that seem forced and fail to effectively communicate an idea. To make this a career track rather than something you do from time to time, you need to master the techniques of effective public speaking. Even if you intend to just write, most writers participate in speaking engagements to help sell their blogs, books, or magazine columns.

If you just want the fame and don't want the real work that comes with it, including establishing and maintaining credibility by being on top of your business, this isn't going to be a path where you can really be effective.

Path #4: Rise to Entrepreneur

Some people don't like having a quota, don't really enjoy public speaking, and don't really have enough respect for authority ... or at least temporary tolerance for authority required to make it in corporate life. Are such people doomed to live in a dumpster? Are they forever going to be miserable, moving from short job to short job whenever their whims or, more likely, their fights with "The Man" end up limiting their upward potential in someone else's company? Not always. Whereas some in this category end up either learning to live with authority or learning to live in their parents' basements, others decide to start their own consulting companies and become entrepreneurs.

Without question, of the four paths presented, the path of the entrepreneur has the most upside. It also happens to be the one with the risk, at least initially. When you go independent, meaning you decide that you no longer work for a firm other than "You, Inc.," you might feel as though you have decided to take a walk down the street naked. No longer does money magically appear in your checking account twice per month. You no longer have attachment to a corporate identity other than your own. You suddenly don't have a boss, in the traditional sense, outside those pesky customers pushing you around. You are, literally, on your own, dependent on your own skills to sell your services to paying customers.

Your first job in getting to this position is to make sure you find some billing work. Yes, as an independent, you are the sales, marketing, IT, and recruiting department, all rolled into one—at least until you are so fortunate as to have enough people working for you that you can afford to hire others to do that work. Because your first job, before all the others, is salesperson (no work without sales), if you want to pursue this path, you need to build a network with people who buy software services and be in a position to sell them on yours. All the things you need to do in the path to sales apply to this path as well.

Of course, when you find billing work, you then need to execute on it. Although this is not entirely unlike what you might do in a current position as a developer, as an independent, you need to be cognizant that you have a much bigger stake in getting extended. Or, short of that, you need to be aware of balancing your work with new business development, as well as administrative concerns like accounting.

In fact, you might find that you suddenly have a newfound appreciation for the CFO at the consultancy you left before going independent. For one, even getting good clients to pay on time can be painful. Even with bigger clients, sometimes, it is just policy that you put "Net 60" on the invoice, which means your check goes in the mail on the 59th day after the client received the invoice. As your own shop, you are responsible for all the negotiation that account executives and other folks do in a large firm to get paid on time!

Indeed, if you intend to go independent, it would not be a bad idea to educate yourself on small business operations, corporate structures, general liability insurance, tax law, and so forth, so that you have a better understanding of what is entailed when you decide to start a business. Although how to start an independent consultancy is well beyond the scope of this book, you would really do yourself a huge favor by learning everything you can before you start. A good place for this in the United States is the Small Business Administration Web site (http://www.sba.gov/), which can give you some good starting points for what you should consider.

If you decide to go this route, you should generally have a much larger cash cushion than you would otherwise. I recommend 12 months' worth of expenses in the bank for all consultants to deal with the inherent layoff risks in consulting. If you're an independent, I recommend increasing this amount even further: two years' worth of expenses ideally. The reasoning is twofold. For one, you could have long periods when there is no work at all, and you still need to eat. But the second reason is that you want to be able to expand.

Now, consider you are an independent looking to expand. You find a project where you might be a lead developer, and you want to hire two other developers. Initially, I advise not to hire them as employees because then there is an expectation that you can support a bench. When you are this small, this prospect is just not realistic. Thus, you are best off to bring on others on an hourly contract basis.

Now, just because people are on an hourly contract basis does not mean that they get paid on your schedule. To the contrary, most of the time, unless you are dealing with other independents, the hourly contractors you hire are going to expect payment as if they were salaried employees. Thus, you need to have cash reserves so that you can make a payroll. You might not get paid for 60 days, but the employees get paid right away. If they have to wait longer, they are likely other independents and thus will require higher rates (because of the higher risk), reducing the margin you are able to make or possibly eroding it altogether.

Margin ... ah, the "mother's milk" of any business. As you expand, your profits—your margin—make it possible for you to take on larger and larger projects, which have more upfront costs but have more rewards when executed in a manner that allows you to get paid. In fact, having sufficient profits is the only way that you will expand from a one-person shop to a real company that can pay for marketing, publicity, a real office, and real employees. Without these things, you are at a competitive disadvantage. Achieving the real upside of independent consulting—growing a company into something that generates profits at sufficient scale such that you can spend your time working *on* the business rather than *in* the business—is completely dependent on retaining earnings to pay for measured expansion.

Reasons to Pursue the Entrepreneur Track

If you have the skills, a lot of patience, no fear, and a good deal of self-discipline, entrepreneurship might be a track you can be successful at. Some folks literally become addicted to the game of business, and for these serial entrepreneurs, this might be the *only* possible path they can take. Such people just don't fit in within anyone else's corporate environment, and it is either this or not working in software at all.

The rewards are great; but without hesitation, I can say all things considered, it is the riskiest and potentially most difficult track of all, requiring not only good sales and management skills, but a ton of discipline and delayed gratification to really be successful.

Reasons to Avoid the Entrepreneur Track

If you do not understand the risk of becoming an entrepreneur, don't like sales, or live paycheck to paycheck, this is certainly not the path you should take. This is also not a path for those who don't have an identity outside corporate life; if you need a company name to feel important, this path is going to seem miserable for a long time. It will almost certainly be many years before your independent operation really matters to anyone beyond yourself and those close to you.

Entrepreneurship is also not a good option for those who are not effective without some sort of structure imposed on them from others. When you are independent, especially between projects, you have to be a true self-starter. Someone who needs to take direction from others to be effective will simply not work out well in an environment where income depends on getting up in the morning and calling on clients without some guaranteed reward for activity.

〰

Summary: Paths and Direction

No chapter on career paths would be complete if it were not noted that you will, as a consultant, likely have at least some setbacks from time to time. Adversity comes in a lot of forms, from layoffs to changes in plan after, say, pursuing the entrepreneur path and perhaps failing a couple of times. Career paths are frequently exercises in "two steps forward, one step back." If nothing else, it is important to be flexible and note that certain principal behaviors—like always growing your network, doing great work, acting with integrity, and keeping financially solvent—will support you regardless of the path you are on.

Also, it is important to consider that you can stop the climb. There is no rule that says you must go beyond simply being a good consultant and being happy with that! In fact, a great number of people simply love to code, love to work on networks, or love to do work at a given level without worrying about management, public speaking, or running a business. Frankly, that is just fine too. You might find that you happen to simply enjoy consulting, and by all means, if you like what you are doing, you are best served by continuing to do it if it is benefiting you and your clients.

Of course, you can take (or avoid taking) certain actions that can help make sure you keep moving forward on your chosen path, rather than experiencing downward mobility. These are the subjects of the next chapter.

AVOIDING CAREER-LIMITING MOVES

Proven steps to avoid the pitfalls that can cause you a case of "unplanned downward mobility."

Although consulting companies can do a lot of things that make no sense and cause them to fail to reach their potential, the same is true for individual consultants. As discussed previously, nothing will make the management of a consulting firm madder than having someone pulled from a project for reasons that might have been within a consultant's control. The purpose of this chapter is to point out main paths to avoidable failure for you as a consultant. Although it should be noted that these paths, which descend from the infamous "Seven Deadly Sins," are probably good things to avoid anyway, in the consulting business, there are lots of specific patterns of failure in these categories.

These patterns of failure are common enough that I have designed a scheme to visualize these failure modes. I call this model, somewhat tongue-in-cheek, the Consultant Career-Limiting Move Model (CCLM) (see Figure 9-1).

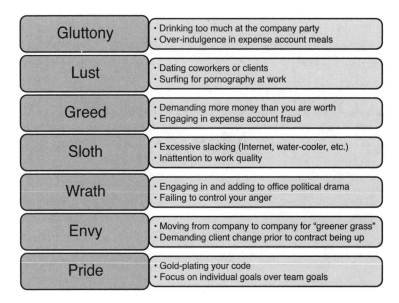

Figure 9-1 A conceptual model for career-limiting moves consultants make.

Of course, note that everyone is going to make mistakes from time to time. However, you can avoid most workplace problems—and in particular, workplace problems that software development consultants will find themselves running into—if you can avoid actions that fall in one of these seven categories, presented in no particular order of importance in the following sections.

⮑

Career-Limiting Move Category #1: Gluttony

The sin of gluttony is oriented around excessive consumption, desire, and generally a lack of moderation. Although historically linked to such behaviors as overeating or generally withholding from the needy, there are several ways in which gluttony can be a career stopper as well.

Whenever you think you are overdoing it, you might be engaging in this category of career-limiting move. You could start out doing something high-minded and noble, like open source work, but take it too far and do that to the exclusion of your primary responsibilities. And unless your client *is* the open source project, your primary responsibility is your client.

This section covers two ways consultants typically overdo things in a manner that can definitely hurt their careers, from the more minor overextravagant but technically within limits treatment of client expense accounts to the more embarrassing and definitely harmful overindulgence at the company party or other work event.

Eating Steak Every Night Is Harmful to Your Health

Your doctor will tell you that eating steak every night is a bad idea. I will leave judgment on the health of such a regimen to the medical experts. However, I do make the observation that those who push the edge with expense account limits are playing Russian roulette with their careers.

First, let's assume you are a consultant on a project that requires regular travel; you get on an airplane early Monday morning and perhaps return Friday afternoon. In such cases, there is a good chance your meals are covered by the client, and in the off-chance they aren't (maybe the consulting firm signed a bad deal), your firm will generally cover them. One of the nice perks of traveling is that although you may not see your family for days on end, at least dinner is covered.

Whereas most people do not take advantage of this situation, some people take it too far, looking up the limit for how much is allowed on expenses every day and making sure that they come in as close to that number as possible. They treat this expense like the highway speed limit—never under and always just enough over not to draw unwanted attention. In most cases, there is a significant lag between when the expenses occur, when they are reported, and when someone might start complaining that some vendors are abusing the rules (or at least pushing the limits). Because of this, something that might have started as a one-time thing develops into a habit that becomes a sticking point on a contract/extension renegotiation.

This problem is easily solved. When you are on the road, be mindful of your client and your company. In general, spend money as if it were your own. The more you take this attitude, the more likely you will never have any problems with people questioning your expenses and, thus, your becoming labeled as a wasteful glutton who pushes the limits. Although nobody will ever pat you on the back for staying within expense limits, chances are at least you will never get the dreaded call from your boss asking why you think eating at Morton's Steakhouse every night demonstrates to the client that "yes, we do spend your money carefully."

Boozing It Up at the Company Party

It is well known that alcohol, when consumed beyond a drink or two, impairs judgment. When you are at a social event with your boss and coworkers, you should avoid any situation in which exhibiting good judgment will be a challenge.

This advice is hard for a lot of people to swallow. Most people, after work or, moreover, after a hard year of work, long for an opportunity to let loose a bit and enjoy time with coworkers at a company event. Given that programmers, at least stereotypically, are awkward in social situations, it is very common for them to drink heavily and, as a result of the liquid courage, go overboard on these occasions.

What happens in such cases can be benign, but it can also be deeply career-limiting. Many of us have heard the story about the guy who gets drunk at the company party and tells off his boss, returning to work the next Monday only to find he has been fired, without even remembering how it happened. Such situations happen occasionally but are certainly not the most common problem. Much more common is that you do or say something that just makes you look very dumb in front of your coworkers and bosses. Under the effects of the alcohol, you lose control of that part of your brain that regulates the urge not to disparage your client in a petty way, make lurid comments about someone, or generally say things that under no circumstances would you say to the CEO while sober.

When promotion time comes along, the antics at the party stick out, and you are not seen as manager or promotion material. It may not be in the official explanation, but considering that the company party might be one of the higher exposure moments you have to upper management, demonstrating your lack of control there is certainly a good way to limit your promotion potential. Think about it: If your main exposure to someone is at a party where that person ended up running naked through a hotel lobby on a dare, you might not entrust a division of a company to him or her either!

Depending on your personality, even worse things can happen, however. Some people are known to combine the sin of lust and sin of gluttony at the holiday party, using the occasion to engage in an ill-advised hookup with a coworker or, worse, boss. A lack of judgment drawn from gluttony plus a dosage of lust makes for a very bad combination that can, at the very least, result in an awkward situation, if not an outright hostile environment in the workplace that causes legal problems for you or your company.

The best advice is not to drink at all during the company party. Get a nice glass of club soda, and if anyone asks what you are drinking, say it's a gin and tonic. Or just say you're driving. Because chances are, you might be anyway, and driving home drunk isn't a good way to demonstrate your responsibility either.

> **Jason Bock**   I wouldn't go as far as Aaron suggests (that is, no drinking). Just do it in moderation and be responsible at company outings if you want an alcoholic drink. The key is to not end up being that person who everyone is gossiping about come Monday morning. You might not get fired, but you could end up with a questionable reputation.

Career-Limiting Move Category #2: Lust

The next career-limiting move category, lust, is generally defined as excessive thoughts or actions of a sexual nature. Although we can thank our own existence to the idea that there exists sexual attraction, giving into it excessively—at least as it relates to your workplace—can cause you all sorts of grief in your career.

Some people say that the best place to meet your future mate is your workplace. However, given the risks both from an office politics and a personal sanity perspective, it is almost certainly best to check those ideas at the office door. In this general category, two general cases come to mind, one having to do with direct relations between people in a place of business (workplace dating) and the second, and surprisingly common, problem people have with abuse of clients' computer facilities to gain access to pornography.

Dating Clients or Coworkers

It is not uncommon for someone to go to Las Vegas, gamble for a while, and come back with more money. However, attested to by the presence of very large and fancy casinos built with money that used to belong to gamblers, the odds favor the fact that more often than not, taking your mortgage payment to Vegas is probably a bad move. The same could be said for dating coworkers.

Remembering this idea is useful because, especially if you happen to be single (or worse) and you find a coworker attractive, a lot of people manage to forget the finer points of "career risk management." So to help solve this dilemma, the initial piece of advice in this category is to state the following:

> *In no uncertain terms should you ever date or become romantically involved with a coworker. And for the sake of everything good and right, never, ever, ever become romantically involved, nor even give the appearance that you could possibly be romantically involved with a client.*

Why such a strong warning? Well, relationships at work can be stressful enough. You do not want to be seen as someone who might be basing decisions on anything other than what is in your client's and your firm's best interests. Say you are dating a coworker who is also an engineer on the team. Although it may be fun at first, over time, the following questions start to arise:

- Will you or the person you are dating be able to provide honest peer reviews, be it of source code, documentation, or other deliverables?

- If the coworker is a tester and you are a developer, will the tester be easier on your bugs or not report them officially?

- Do you report to the coworker, or does the coworker report to you? There are some obvious problems if that is the situation— notably favoritism, ethics, and even possibly legal complications.

You likely could conceive of a couple of exceptions to this rule (there are always exceptions), such as the idea that maybe the person technically works for the same company but is so far away from you politically that it doesn't matter. Chances are, however, if you met this person at the company, this probably isn't really true! Besides, if the relationship doesn't work out, having to think about going to work to see your ex can't be too thrilling for you, even in the best of circumstances.

Of course, dating a client is even more fraught with peril. There are the same independence problems that can occur in this case as the coworker case just described. Worse yet, though, if or when the relationship falls apart, not only do you have an unfortunate reality of going to work with your ex, but now you have created a risk for your company in that the ex may influence decision makers not to do work with your firm. Besides the fact that nearly every consulting firm with a remotely competent legal or HR department likely prohibits this kind of relationship in no uncertain terms, it should be obvious that dating a coworker is literally "flirting with disaster."

> **Jason Bock**   Again, I wouldn't be so black-and-white as Aaron suggests. Different situations call for different choices; saying that you shouldn't date someone "in no uncertain terms" is a little restrictive. There are potential risks in becoming romantically involved with someone where you work, so just handle it with maturity. After all, if you really like someone, why prevent yourself from being involved with him or her?

Porn at Work: Bad Idea

Of course, the bad judgment train as it relates to the sin of lust does not end with mere dating issues. The Internet provides many of those prone to problems with pornography the opportunity to get into trouble. In my life as a consultant, I have heard stories of people getting assigned to work at places like a national business office for a major church, and on the second day, the network administrator sending reports from the office proxy server that showed the new consultant in question was surfing for hard-core pornography. During the first two hours on the job for the client!

If this kind of expression is an interest of yours, it is almost certainly a good idea to keep it off-campus, off work computers, and strictly personal. This nuance is especially important because when a consultant has a laptop for use at home or on the road, it may not be unusual to have personal and business worlds mix. There are more than a few consultants who, on a business trip, do some work in the hotel room but later mix in a bit of their personal "interests." Without realizing they are on the company's or client's VPN, after doing the work, they leave a trail on the company's or client's servers. In the days or weeks that follow, some call comes in from HR, and in an act of risk reduction (as in "he was surfing for WHAT on the client's network?"), the consultant finds himself or herself sans employment.

The effects of mixing these two things—your work life and your libido—are almost always like mixing gasoline and matches. For the sake of your career, if you want to have one as a consultant (or frankly, have any sort of professional career at all), it is best to do everything possible to avoid mixing the two.

∽

Career-Limiting Move Category #3: Greed

The third original sin, greed, has been the doom of many careers, both inside software development as well as out. Greed can drive you to rationalize taking actions that, under normal circumstances, you would never even think of doing. But greed can work in more subtle ways too, undermining your career in ways that are hard to detect. There is a saying that "money is the root of all evil," and although that may not entirely be true, it certainly is at the core of many bad career decisions that many people make over the years.

This section covers both main kinds of greed: the kind of overt greed that leads you to do things that are unethical or even illegal and the more subtle kind of greed that causes you to sell out long-term growth for short-term dollars. Surprisingly, most developers who succumb to this sin do not commit the illegal, seldom commit the unethical, but frequently commit the greed that takes the form of "stealing from oneself."

Expensing Dates and Other Very Bad Ideas

The first category of greed is the more direct kind: committing fraud against your company. From taking dates out to dinner and expensing it, to padding your hours, there are all sorts of ways to get into trouble when greed is motivating you.

To commit fraud, you need three things: motive, rationalization, and opportunity (see Figure 9-2). Motive is the need for money. It would be safe to say that most people have a need for some extra money, given that generally speaking, most people tend to think that if they had only a little more, they would be happier. Most people have some motive there. However, there are some who, for various reasons—whether high debt, substance abuse, and so on—have more need than others. Others still are, frankly, just plain greedy, which causes them to really, really want more than they have.

The second of the three preconditions for fraud, rationalization, comes along when excuses start being made for taking up a fraudulent action, such as "I earned this" or "well, the CEO flies a private jet, so I am entitled to pad my hours." When a motive is established, the greedy quickly start to figure out a way to rationalize the actions that lead to fraud.

The third leg of this, of course, is opportunity. In consulting, consultants have many opportunities to commit fraud. Traveling consultants can easily do low-level expense account fraud by taking actions such as having a group dinner, collecting cash from colleagues in what was supposed to be a split check, and then running the entire dinner through an expense report. Claiming mileage not driven, forging taxi receipts (usually handwritten), and claiming personal expenses as general business expenses are the most notable for this level of fraud.

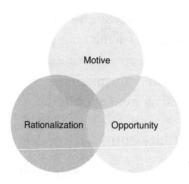

Figure 9-2 The Fraud Triangle.

That said, there are other forms that consultants have been known to avail themselves to. If a firm pays for hours billed over 40 in a week (as some do), the temptation to pad hours becomes very strong because the padded hours over 40 are paid out as a bonus. This kind of fraud can be harder to detect because a software developer's time isn't usually regimented such that the difference between 40 hours of effort and 45 is that big. However, it seldom stays that low-level. As greed kicks in, 45 becomes 50 becomes 60, and the client starts to ask some serious questions. At this point the fraudster has defrauded not only the consultancy, but the client as well. Needless to say, getting caught in such a scheme is one of the most career-limiting moves you can make.

The broader point, however, is that opportunity will always exist for consultants to commit fraud. The best defense as it relates to this career-limiting move is to control your greed in the first place. If you keep your greed under control, you will not be as likely to develop the motive and rationalization to avail yourself to the pervasive opportunities you will tend to have to engage in fraud.

Pricing Yourself Out of the Market

Greed can damage your career even if you do not commit fraud against others. This sin is more damaging when you overprice your own value in the marketplace, in essence, committing fraud against yourself. We can look at this kind of fraud in two broad categories of career-limiting moves: switching jobs for raises too frequently and prematurely going independent.

Switching Jobs Frequently for Raises

Although it is certainly not a career-limiting move to "grab the brass ring" offered by another firm when the opportunity presents itself, doing so too frequently tends to push your salary to the top range, if not well past what you are really worth in the marketplace. This is especially true in consulting, where especially smaller firms, or even smaller offices of larger firms, survive in a feast-or-famine mindset. What can happen is that a small firm, say, 20 people, lands a project that requires 10 people. The company realizes it either has to go to the open contractor market for people, which can be expensive, or it can hire employees. Although the margins are higher for the latter, even at inflated salaries, offers for $150,000 per year for software developers start flying in a market where normal salaries are, for sake of this example, $100,000 per year.

Of course, what is really going on here is that you have inadvertently taken a body shop position for $75 per hour; the only way you are really making $150,000 per year is if the project lasts a year or the sales team manages to land a project and get you renewed. The problem is that, as covered in the section on Body Shop Consulting in Chapter 2, "The Seven Deadly Firms," demand in the body shop for a specific skill set is highly variable, and chances are you will not have a bench to land on when your project is done. The higher salary is just an illusion.

Greed is usually the motivator in a case like this. It works by masking your understanding and estimation of risk, tricking you into accepting a far riskier position without a consummate reward. It is also a motivator in the garden variety switching-jobs-too-often problem, where you may simply get to the logical maximum range of your value and find yourself continually vulnerable, owning to always being the highest compensated person on the team. People are often shocked when they realize that whenever hard times come along, the bosses do, in fact, rank the people who work for them by capability (best to worst) and cost (lowest to highest). Anyone who appears in the top half of both of these lists, fair or not, is at risk during a layoff. You never want to be one of the top five most expensive people in the office and also happen to be sitting on the bench during the eighth month of a recession. By keeping your salary in check and always outperforming your salary, you can avoid this problem entirely.

> **Jason Bock**   There's nothing wrong with wanting more money. But the longer I've been in the business, the more I've realized that trying to get a high salary is not the key motivational factor in staying with a company. Working with smart people and savvy sales personnel that get great projects along with good policies on training are also advantages.

Prematurely Going Independent

Lastly, the greed factor can also come into play when someone goes independent prior to actually having a business plan, means of acquiring clients, or the self-discipline required. Going independent too early—pre clients, pre plan—usually happens as a result of a body shop or agency offering an attractive hourly rate to someone in a salaried position. The person gets the offer, quits a current consulting position (possibly leaving the firm in a lurch), and alienates a good portion of his or her network in the process.

Going independent is perfectly acceptable, but if more money is the sole reason, you should probably take a hard look at the reasons you want to do it. Not that making more money is a bad thing. If you can handle the risks, going independent is actually a good way to make a higher return on your own intellectual capital. The problem is that having this as the sole reason might indicate you are looking at the possibilities without properly considering the risks because you are overly focused on the rewards. Not soberly thinking through the reasons for going independent can cause you to have serious gaps in your resume, limiting your options in the future if you decide to re-enter salaried consulting. Any company that hires salaried consultants will be rightfully concerned that you might decide to go independent again and possibly leave *it* in the lurch.

Career-Limiting Move Category #4: Sloth

While the category of greed is the hunting ground of the overambitious, the sin of sloth is more tied to either lack of ambition or perhaps a lack of will to expend effort that meets your ambition. Generally speaking, sloth is what happens when you stop caring about your work product, stop caring about the fact that others are paying you to produce a work product, or more commonly, a combination of both these factors.

As far as it relates to your job, there are two main types of sloth we cover here: the kind related to work you are actually doing and the kind related to work you are neglecting to do at all. In either case, what happens inevitably is that your work suffers, your client receives less value per dollar paid, and eventually your career comes to a halt. This situation does not always happen immediately. Sloth happens a little at a time in most cases, like a frog boiling in a pot. The situation becomes marginally worse over time, until one morning you realize that you have not done a single useful thing for your client in six weeks and wonder why you are being kicked off the engagement.

Loafing in All Its Forms

Let's look at a riddle. There are four people at an intersection: a software developer who uses the Internet occasionally to look up something of personal interest during business hours, Santa Claus, the Easter Bunny, and a software developer who has never, ever used business facilities for personal use. In the middle of the intersection, there is a $100 bill (see Figure 9-3). In this scenario, who will be the first to jump in and grab the $100 bill?

Figure 9-3   Who will get the $100?

The answer, of course, is the occasional loafer because the other three exist only in fairy tales, children's stories, and the annals of the Internet usage policy of more than a few employee handbooks.

When the Internet was introduced to the workplace, little did most of corporate America realize it was putting a device that combined the worst elements of television and videogames right on the desktop of all its workers. When we look back, it is clear that many corporate bosses were not aware what the Internet could actually do because had they known what they were letting loose, the Internet certainly would have not become a staple of the common knowledge worker's workday. Because of this happy accident, software developers simultaneously gained the power to be much more productive—by having access to all the resources of the Internet to help solve programming problems—and the power to sit in a chair and do nothing but rearrange a fantasy football league while appearing to work.

Whether you call this a sin of greed—giving yourself what Scott Adams of "Dilbert" fame calls a "virtual raise" by lowering the work performed per hour, thereby raising the amount paid per unit of actual work—or a sin of sloth is a matter of personal perspective and motivation. Because most of the time loafing is related to laziness, not greed, I categorize it in the sloth category.

And because loafing is so pervasive, in most workplaces there is some tolerance of this sin. Before we had the Internet for loafing, we had a water cooler where we could exchange office gossip, newspapers we could bring to work and read, and numerous other distractions we could engage in rather than doing work. Loafing takes numerous forms, but the central feature is that it is the product of apathy—not caring about what you do—providing the motivation and rationalization for laziness.

To be fair, software developers work in a job that tends to involve shorter sprints of creativity separated by longer periods of reflection. Given a workplace that commonly operates in the Taylorian ideal of "if you have time to lean, you have time to clean," a lot of normal, healthy activity can look exactly like loafing to an onlooker.

For this reason, it is important to not let surfing get out of hand. You will probably do some, but doing so much that you go for many days at a time without producing anything of value is going to do damage to your career in all but the most tolerant or indifferent workplaces. In fact, if you can go six weeks, produce nothing, and still have a job, you probably are not working in the kind of company that has much of a future anyway.

If You Must Surf

Of course, some of you are going to protest, under the precept that you live a life where you are on 24/7, accessible to your client, and you should not feel guilty about checking the sports scores between recompiles. There are a couple of ways you can keep your limited loafing out of the purview of all but the most dedicated and micromanaging of taskmasters.

One recommended way to surf in a workplace otherwise unfriendly to surfing is to have a mobile device where you can get personal email and at least some of the sites that you use for mental breaks between working on code modules. The beauty of iPhones and other similar devices is that they have a "nearly good as PC" browsing capability without having to use your client's network. Both your consulting company and your client management will appreciate the fact that, when the report of your Internet activity is pulled, the only hits to the Web are questions to vendor forums asking how to solve specific problems or other work-related queries.

Investing in a mobile broadband Internet capability for your personal laptop might not be a bad idea also. Such a device can provide an outside connection that bypasses any corporate firewalls. It works similarly to a cell phone; if you have a cell phone, you can get Internet access completely independent from your company network. Of course, this applies only in a case in which you are not using your laptop on the client's network, where such outside connections can be considered a security risk and therefore get you into a great deal of trouble. Only do this technique if you have a laptop with you completely segregated from the client's infrastructure. Consider the cost of such a countermeasure—$100 per month, give or take—as an insurance policy against the career risk that can occur if you can't control your impulse to check your share prices or fantasy football stats.

Of course, some organizations do not allow outside devices on the premises, thwarting even these measures. That said, places like that are the minority. In most places, having means of independent surfing for those times where you must do it is a great form of career insurance.

Writing Bad, Unmaintainable, and Other Forms of Low-Quality Code

Even if you never surf the Internet at all, there are ways to commit sloth against your client. In fact, this form of sloth is probably as, if not more, common than the loafing variety. One fact of life in the software business is that we often talk about but seldom really do code reviews. If we moved that practice from software development into another business, say, home construction, let's imagine what would happen.

You might wonder how people in Hollywood can produce movies that have such quickly created buildings that look so realistic. What is going on is that the buildings, because they don't really have to be occupied, are really either façades without any real structure, or they are strictly designed for short-term use. They are not built to standards that require them to, say, be designed to withstand a minor earthquake. This allows the buildings to be built at lower cost, which allows the movie producer to have enough money left over to pay Jim Carrey $25 million.

Of course, if the buildings were not destroyed after the movie was completed, and the buildings were allowed to be occupied, the costs related to building maintenance would be very high because they are always breaking, and the buildings would always be in danger of collapsing under their own weight. Sadly, in the software development business, this is a pervasive problem we experience. In some companies, over 80 percent of the software development budget is dedicated to maintenance of old code, a state of affairs that cripples the firms' ability to write new systems that could make them more competitive.

This condition exists because we seldom do the code reviews we know we are supposed to do. And if we do them, we don't really do much with the results, often because either we are afraid of confrontation, or we know that we might miss a deadline if we have to raise quality, or frankly, we are too polite to call out a developer on laziness.

Specific developers get away with sloth only because the entire industry, for the most part, is arranged in a manner such that bad, unmaintainable code is the norm. The reason for this is partly due to the fact that competitive bidding for projects is sometimes based on who comes in at the lowest cost, without specifying a required level of quality. However, times are changing; there is an active movement in many software development communities toward improving code quality and helping organizations understand the long-term costs of unmaintainable code. Furthermore, tools like FxCop (which automatically enforces code standards) and others are making it at least a little easier to measure code quality. As the quality movement in the software business gains further momentum, the sin of sloth in writing low-quality code will become more exposed. It is becoming a career-limiting move to be known as the person who "cowboy codes" his or her way through problems, leaving a mess for the successor to clean up.

Jason Bock   If there's one thing that angers me more than anything else during development, it's developers who produce absolute crap. There are too many tools, frameworks, and principles out there now to ensure that everyone is producing high-quality code. There is no excuse for writing terrible code anymore, especially if you're the consultant coming in as the expert. Show leadership by writing code that's easily to read, heavily tested, and thoroughly reviewed and scrutinized.

☙

Career-Limiting Move Category #5: Wrath

Sloth is a sin that has roots in a lack of any discernible passion for your job. Wrath, on the other hand, is often related to having too much passion, mixed with a healthy dose of pride, contributing to the isolation and alienation that occurs when you decide everyone else is a moron. You know you are committing wrath when your passion leads you to yelling at your coworkers when they don't meet your ideals.

More generally, wrath puts you front and center in the drama that occurs in the office. Quick to anger, always paranoid, the wrathful tend to think that others are constantly out to get them. Always having fantasies of revenge and retribution, people who engage in wrath become dramatic self-fulfilling prophecies, adding to the level of distraction at the office in ways that, when you really get down to it, have nothing to do with the client's or the consulting firm's interests.

Being the Office Drama Queen or King

It is important to note that there are seldom workplaces where office politics do not exist. One of the important points to realize about all these sins is that we all commit them at some level; there is not one of us who has never had a bad day when sloth, greed, or one of the other sins did not emerge. However, if you constantly find yourself at the center of various plots, schemes, and attempts at extraction of revenge as it relates to your client or consulting office environment, there is a good chance that you may, in fact, be the office drama queen or king.

The sad possibility exists that in an argument, you can be right and wrong at the same time. An important skill in career management is to learn to judiciously pick your political battles. Getting mad whenever someone crosses you, comes short of your expectations, or somehow wrongs you is a recipe for becoming the office drama queen/king. Even if you are right every single time (which is not likely), if you are always picking fights, you will become known as someone who is plain difficult to work with and likely be shown the door pretty quickly.

An important skill to avoid career-limiting moves of wrath is to carefully pick where you make your stand politically. One rule of thumb is to operate as though you have a bank of political capital. You accumulate that bank by doing good work for your company, though the balance will vary by individual (keep this in mind when you are picking your battles). You then spend credibility when you push back on others if they suggest doing something that, in your opinion, is not in the best interests of the company. When you realize that you have only a limited balance of credibility to spend pushing back, you are more likely to save it for when it is important, such as when someone suggests doing something illegal or unethical. If you have spent all your political capital previously on more petty issues, you might not have enough for when you really need it.

Spending more political capital than you have makes you an easy target for being perceived as being wrathful, angry, and uncooperative. Even if you generally aren't, you should be very careful not to give others a reason to believe that you are. That said, chances are if you are always finding yourself at the center of political drama, there might be some truth to the point your political opponents are making that you are an angry, uncooperative person.

Lack of Anger Management

Whereas overengagement in political battles can be harmful to your career, being known as the person who is constantly yelling, intimidating, or outright throwing chairs at coworkers is not a way to go particularly far in a software consulting career—or for that matter, in any job that isn't head of a Wall Street trading desk or CEO of Apple Computer. This is especially true in consulting, where you are expected to be able to work in a large variety of corporate environments with lots of different people who come from lots of different backgrounds.

If you are prone to coming to blows over minor points of disagreement, there isn't much advice I can give you short of seeing a counselor and getting some anger management classes or perhaps going a step further and seeing a doctor so you can be diagnosed for psychological conditions such as bipolar disorder. Regardless of how you handle the issue, being able to control your emotions in general and your anger in particular is a critical factor in not constantly picking fights, which become a virtual train of career-limiting moves. Unless, of course, you seek to work at a Wall Street trading desk, where your skills in throwing chairs at fellow traders might be in the written job description.

Anger and Your Network

Being an angry, wrathful person tends to cause problems beyond your work life, spreading to your personal life and ability to grow a network. People who engage in this sin tend to have problems at home that lend to instability, inability to form trusted relationships with coworkers, and more generally, isolation. As we have covered in many places in this book, having a vibrant network of people who can speak well of your skills and capabilities is a critical success factor for your career. If you get angry easily, you are unlikely to have the kinds of good connections required to keep you afloat should you need to find a position at some point. Getting control of anger is a key factor in not only staying in the job you have, but being able to land your next job as well!

Career-Limiting Move Category #6: Envy

A sin closely related to that of greed, envy is a broader sin that relates to operating out of a place where you constantly want what someone else has, be it money, a position, a client engagement where the "grass is greener," or an appearance of respect. If you are constantly comparing your position to others in the company or in your industry, and finding yourself obsessed with the idea that "if only if I had what they had, I would be happy and fulfilled," you are probably committing the sin of envy.

Envy is the driver behind a lot of very bad career decisions. It can affect you in two ways. If you do nothing in response to your envy, you tend to find yourself unhappy and with low self-esteem because you are always comparing your career situation with some ideal that may but more likely may not be attainable. However, even worse is making rash, career-limiting moves out of envy. Two such moves covered here are the common case of demanding to be pulled off boring clients to work with ones that sound cooler and constantly moving between consulting companies seeking that ever greener pasture.

"Can You Move Me off This Engagement?" Is Nearly Always a Bad Move

We have discussed at various points throughout this book the implications of asking to be moved off an engagement early. Let's go through the best-case scenario. In most consulting projects, the client wants to know about personnel moves. By demanding to be moved off a client, you create the need for a conversation with the client explaining why you are moving off. This creates an engagement risk because it puts front and center the questions, "Why does this firm not keep its people happy? I pay high rates for consultants, so why do I need to be affected by their personnel issue?" Of course, the problem might not be just the consulting firm's personnel issue; it might be that the project really isn't that interesting, and the workplace might not be really that good.

You could be absolutely right. However, being right still can mean you are creating a risk to the engagement by causing your firm to be perceived in less than a positive light. In the best case—where the client allows a backfill (someone to replace you)—the client will probably vet that person more and make things at least a little more difficult for the engagement manager. In a (but not *the*) worst case, your departure won't be backfilled, and your account executive or engagement manager will lose revenue. This, of course, is no way to make this person feel good about bringing you onto future engagements.

However, that is not even the *worst* case. An even worse case is that you can create an opportunity for the competitor, who can promise to send the client happy and compliant consultants who are in for the long haul and unlikely to leave. The competitor may be lying through his or her teeth, but the point is that the action allows for the competitive opportunity, which raises the chance of the entire client going away from *your* firm. Nothing is worse for your career at a given company than being known as the person who causes a big client to go away.

There are some good reasons to ask to be moved off an engagement, such as concern for safety. Someone at the client's office threatening to physically harm you, sexual harassment, workplace bullying that causes you to lose sleep and do ineffective work, or a commute that is so long that you are having family problems are good examples. Being asked to perform illegal or unethical acts is also a good reason.

That all said, before taking the step of asking to be moved off the engagement—an action you should rarely initiate and only under very extenuating circumstances—make sure you examine your motives. If you simply don't like the client and go looking for an excuse, such as taking a coworker's action of giving you a less than perfect code review as an act of workplace bullying, then you are probably being driven by envy for an engagement with greener pastures. Prior to taking such an action, it is important that you take an honest self-assessment of your reasons for wanting to move off the engagement. If you end up with a large group of factors that have to do with "how much better things would be if only…," most of which don't involve your safety or your health, chances are, envy, pride, or both are really driving your decision. Therefore, it is probably a bad one.

> **Jason Bock** I would say there is one other legitimate reason to ask for a move: tenure. One of the advantages a consultant has (or should have) is a diverse set of experiences. Being able to say, "I've done that five times at five different clients, and it's always made the code base better," gives you a position of authority that you don't get if you say, "I've been at the same client for three years, and it's worked there." Generally, if I've been at a client for longer than a year, I'll try to gracefully exit the gig if possible.

The "Nomadic Developer" Does Not Mean "New Company Every Nine Months"

Despite the title of this book, I do *not* recommend changing consulting companies more frequently than around once every two years—at least if you want a sustained career as an *employee* of a consulting firm. (Obviously, different rules apply to independent consultants, who, unless they suffer from schizophrenia, can't get a job with a different "self.")

In consulting, it is very easy to suffer from "grass-is-greenerism" when looking at other companies. Generally speaking, your current engagement has its frustrations, its politics, and a range of people, from those you like very much to people for whom you might celebrate if you saw their picture on the back of a milk carton. On the other hand, when you look at other firms, you see their marketing materials, recruiters, and a general image designed to make you think happy thoughts. These facts come together to make you think, "Gee, life would sure be better over there!" This, of course, is never the case, which leads to some consultants never finding a real home because they are always going from company to company.

To understand why being too nomadic is a career-limiting move, let's look at this issue from the perspective of the consulting company. Leaving aside the issue that the firm could invest in you and you could walk in 18 months, leading to a loss of investment, the real "rubber meets the road" issue for consulting firms is that hiring a constant flight risk creates the same kinds of problems addressed in the previous section: people who cause engagement risks by leaving mid-engagement. Having an employment record with known companies that hire permanent consultants where the average tenure is less than a typical consulting contract is going to be an obvious red flag to any hiring manager.

This is not to say that changing companies is a bad thing to do; in fact, I recommend keeping an open mind about opportunities. There could be chances to truly advance your career in ways that a current company, however bad or good, is simply unable to provide. However, you need to make sure you are doing it for the right reasons and with checked expectations.

More specifically, consider the risk that any new employer is as likely to have more dysfunctional people in it as it is to have fewer dysfunctional people. You can certainly ask a lot of questions, such as those offered in Chapter 5, "What You Need to Ask Before You Join a Technology Consulting Firm," to vet the culture of the company. However, no set of questions is a guarantee that your next position will be a utopia compared to your current one.

The point is to change companies unemotionally, without envy, and with the right set of expectations. When you let envy take over and let it drive your career decisions, you tend to take a lot of career risks that, when you look objectively, do not lead to consummate career rewards.

Career-Limiting Move Category #7: Pride

We all should be allowed, at some level, to be proud of good work that we do. A job well done—be it a system that has demonstrated amazing business value to a client or software that lots of consumers find useful—is worthy of a certain level of pride from the people who were instrumental in making it happen. In small doses, pride is not such a bad thing at all. The problem for developers is letting pride drive our day-to-day decision making. When overdone, committing the sin of pride can, and often does, lead to the making of career-limiting moves.

Pride is a sin with roots in overappreciation of your own attributes and underappreciation of the work of others. It is one of those things that developers, sadly, are quite famous for. Pride is the motivating factor in the maxim that "everyone else's code is crap compared to mine." This sin is expressed with great frequency in the world of software consulting, where as a hazard of the job we are asked to (1) have a lot of confidence when coming into new clients and (2) fix the client's problems. Development of too much pride is a job hazard in the world of consulting, and keeping it in check is a critical skill in avoiding career-limiting moves.

Like a lot of things in life, the line between a healthy amount of pride and too much pride is not always a bright line. As with many of these sins, to really know when making a decision, you need to be honest with yourself about what is driving that decision.

"Gold-Plating" Your Code

A frequent trap in which pride leads to bad decisions occurs when a developer decides to "go freelance" and starts adding features to a product that nobody really asked for. This practice, known as *gold-plating*, is the injection of developer priorities, which stem from developer pride, into the group priorities. These additions might align, but more often do not.

When you find yourself saying "Wouldn't it be cool if..." and then spending the next eight billable hours implementing some off-the-plan feature, you are probably gold-plating. Good ideas for the product are appreciated in certain forums. If you are driving home from the client and suddenly have an innovative idea, by all means, sketch it out on a napkin or something. Think it through and present it to your engagement manager or your client. In most circumstances, good new ideas are entirely appreciated.

While sometimes it is better to leverage the idea that you should ask for forgiveness rather than permission, you have to remember that your prerogative to use a play from that playbook comes only after attaining a position of trust with a client. When you are new, and you do not have a complete sense of the players and politics involved, you should buck the advice and ask for permission first. One of the reasons consultants are sometimes brought in is that some internal developer went rogue, developed a new feature set instead of the one the main stakeholders were asking for, and caused the system to go over budget. Consultants might have been brought in to clean up the mess and refocus the effort. Duplicating the gold-plating, in such a case, is a good way to introduce a new engagement risk and undercut the basis for your being there in the first place.

The tricky part here is to differentiate between gold-plating and simply doing quality work. It is not uncommon for developers working on time-constrained projects that are in "death march" mode to be asked to cut corners and to have efforts not to cut corners—such as insisting on spending time updating unit tests—to be accused of gold-plating. In such situations, it is important to be really introspective and ask yourself honestly whether what you are doing is within the charter of the project and you have support for the activity. Or are you doing it as a matter of personal pride? Knowing whether to push back on a request to cut corners is tricky, but if you determine the motive is right after an honest evaluation, it is best to either refuse to cut the corner and be ready to accept the consequences or to cut the corner but carefully document the request (ask for it in writing, if pushed). Chances are, if you are addressing a quality issue, someone up the chain will want to know about it at some point.

"It's All About Me"

Generally, pride expresses itself in selfish actions and behavior—taking actions that raise your profile at the expense of your peers, purposefully "throwing someone under the bus" after making an honest mistake. It can take more subtle forms as well, such as expanding on the "Not Invented Here" syndrome to a more insidious "Not Invented by Me" syndrome. Although in the short term, these kinds of actions may feel good, longer-term, the career-limiting effect is that you end up with few real allies in your corporate life and a network that is very broad but not very deep in terms of people's eagerness to vouch for you.

The logical opposite of pride, humility, is a state of mind that, once developed, will serve you well as a means to avoid getting in trouble with pride, greed, and numerous other sins. When you express humility, knowing your own limitations, you disarm the people you are talking with. It makes you more accessible, less of a threat, and frankly, more likeable. When you embrace humility, you demonstrate a maturity that you understand that making drastic changes to the way a system works at the end of a project will probably have no more chance of success with you than it had for most others who have tried. In consulting, these are all very valuable attributes to have.

Does this mean you should not reach for the stars and be proud of your work? Of course not. By all means, have very ambitious goals for your career! However, be mindful and humble about your own limitations so that you can be effective in choosing the particular path you take to get to those stars and in the process not alienate all those who help you get there.

> **Michael Hugos**   I've been on the guru path for a while, and the two greatest dangers on this path are envy and pride. Gurus need a healthy ego to survive, but they can't let envy prevent them from admiring and complimenting other gurus, and they can't let pride prevent them from admitting their mistakes and adopting better ideas from others when they come along. Greed is another danger because gurus have to do what they do because they love it and not be distracted by money.

Summary

I could not write this chapter without having had experience with most of these sins. We all get greedy, prideful, envious, wrathful, lazy, gluttonous, and thankfully for the future of the human race, lustful at times. And making a career-limiting move once or twice is not going to doom you to the poorhouse. What is important in using this chapter to help your career as a consultant, however, is to always consider what is motivating your actions. You also need to think about your motivations through this prism before you make your big decisions—when to change jobs, whether to drink at the company party, when you push back in the code review, and so forth.

Now that we have spent several chapters talking about how to be successful in consulting, the next chapter covers reasons—beyond perhaps tendency to engage in these sins on a frequent and repeated basis—why you might consider avoiding a career in consulting.

Is Consulting Right for You?

Technology consulting isn't a good fit for everyone. Is it for you?

In the previous chapters, I made the case for being a technology consultant. However, it is important to understand that not everyone is a good fit for technology consulting. There are many good reasons for this, and this chapter focuses on the five main reasons you may want to consider not being a technology consultant, namely

- Lack of risk tolerance
- Incompatible personality
- Incompatible lifestyle and/or responsibilities
- Single product focus—desire to work on one product over a long period of time
- Desire to do it "for the money"

These enumerated factors, although not exhaustive, are typical reasons why consultants either burn out quickly or never really manage to get their careers into a trajectory that allows them to have success.

Indeed, whereas trying something out and discovering it isn't for you may not be as career limiting as, say, surfing for pornography at work or serving time for fraud, choosing to become a consultant when the career isn't a good fit can be quite a mistake. Going down this path when it isn't a good fit presents risks of continually being frustrated, weary, and possibly left unemployed at inopportune times. Although not career ending or, for that matter, even limiting, there is a serious risk of its wasting time and giving you a lot of avoidable grief if you are ill-suited to consulting.

⁓

Sign #1: Lack of Risk Tolerance

Talking about lack of risk tolerance might strike you as odd when I have made the case in this book that in technology consulting, your actual level of risk is lower than working in an IT position. Although I believe this to be true, based on the kinds of networks you build over time supporting you regardless of company, the *apparent* risk, based on the clarity in which your position is directly related to revenue, will feel high at times.

The "Corporate Bench"

You might be surprised to learn that in IT jobs at non-IT companies, there are periods when you are at great risk of job loss. Especially, but not exclusively, during budget time during a recession, because most companies look at software developers as a cost, software developers, middle managers, project managers, and many others who have advanced in their career and look expensive on the budget spreadsheet are at acute risk of being laid off.

I call this situation the "Corporate Bench" because what happens, prior to the big layoff, is that many low-impact projects are created for IT staff only to give people something to do while the decisions are being made. These projects feel like work, and therefore they feel productive. However, the bottom-line impact in many cases is simply not there to make the CFO overlook the position when cost-cutting time comes around.

Let's face it: For good reasons, nobody does profit cutting. In most cases, working for a company in an IT department, you are considered a cost center (note that many believe this designation to be a mistake). When it's time to cut costs, that means cut those who work in the cost center. This especially means people with titles that, if there are no new projects and everything is in maintenance mode, are probably not really needed.

Why Technology Consulting Feels Riskier

What's the difference in technology consulting? Frankly, it's more honest. When you are not billing, you know you are not generating revenue. Because the question as to whether you are earning your keep in technology consulting is more cut and dry, there is little choice in this business but to realize that if you are not billing, selling, or owning, you probably are not contributing. Working in IT masks the risk because you may be on the bench for months or years and not even know it because nobody will tell you that you are vulnerable (see Table 10-1). In consulting, you know that when you hit the bench, the clock starts ticking. In IT, you probably don't even know where the clock is!

TABLE 10-1
IT Risks Versus Consulting Risks

IT	Consulting
Illusion of no risk—the "permanent job" fallacy.	Risks are more transparent.
Lack of transparency allows you to pretend the risk does not exist.	Transparency forces you to live with the reality.

Chris Williams   Early in my career, I took a job at a company working on "internal projects." I was one of the only developers who wasn't required to have billable hours, and I was (foolishly) proud of that fact. Looking back, it comes as no surprise that when heads started rolling, mine was one of the first on the block. That was a real eye-opener.

Of course, on a case-by-case basis, some consultancies are far riskier propositions than certain IT departments, so this rule is more of a guideline. Consider technology consulting firms with weak demand-generation capability—for example, a sales department that isn't getting out and meeting customers, or worse, cutting bad deals. Staying at a consultancy like that is probably riskier than almost any other situation you could ever work in. By contrast, in some IT departments all jobs are probably pretty much secure. The guy who runs servers for Google is probably in a pretty secure position!

Why Avoid Technology Consulting Then?

Why should the risk-averse avoid consulting? The answer really has to do with the fact that there are many people for whom blissful ignorance of their risk is probably a better choice. If the thought of hitting the bench and having daily, visceral fear that you might be let go is going to prevent you from sleeping at night, working in an IT department or for a software company might be a better career choice.

As covered in Chapter 7, "Thriving," to really be effective, you have to feel somewhat secure in your job to be able to do your best work. Of course, almost nobody is truly 100 percent secure. That said, if you are constantly feeling at risk—be it lack of self-confidence or, more likely, lack of confidence in the ability of your company to keep you busy—you will be miserable, and you probably won't succeed. Rest assured, nobody does good work for very long when suffering from insomnia.

Refuge for the Risk-Intolerant?

Of course, if you happen to be risk-intolerant, and you have just read this section and decided that maybe neither consulting nor IT departments are the right place for you, should you avoid technology altogether? Of course not. On the risk continuum, for software developers, the least risky position is to be a software product developer for a successful company that sells software. Although this position is not completely without risk, you could be on a team that makes a less than successful product and again find yourself out of work. On balance, this position combines the aspects of being in a revenue-generating capacity but provides a business model that has less of a "feast or famine" revenue profile.

The downside to this plan is that there are, sadly, far fewer jobs as software product developers than there are jobs in IT and technology consulting. For every software company with a product that is selling well, there are probably 10 consulting companies and 50 IT departments in companies writing software. And just like everything else, there are proportionally as many poorly run software companies with bad products and miserable owners who hate software developers as there are consulting companies that fit the mold of the Seven Deadly Firms from Chapter 2. That said, if you love software but simply hate risk, this is probably the best option for you.

⌇

Sign #2: Incompatible Personality

There is a mostly negative stereotype of a software developer who is a cave-dwelling creature that doesn't like people, doesn't shower or shave, smells kind of funny, and is otherwise socially not the most desirable person to be around. This stereotype is so common that in the 1990s *Saturday Night Live* used to do skits in which the "IT Guy" would go around helping people in a rude and gruff manner and after helping them, respond to their lack of thankfulness by saying sarcastically, "You're welcome." Indeed, this stereotype is so common that a national television show was able to do a skit about it, and lots of people—outside programmers—were able to get a good laugh from it.

Is this stereotype true? Well, there is probably a certain segment in any given occupation that could be characterized a certain way. Given that effective software development demands people who can shut out others for long periods of time to solve complex problems, it should not surprise anyone that this profession may attract more than a few people who generally do not have strong extrovert personalities.

Don't Like People? Then You Probably Won't Like Consulting

One of the main differences between a typical programmer and a good consultant candidate is that the latter doesn't mind networking and other "people" aspects of the job. To consult isn't just to code; it involves getting into a position to advise, which requires building trust. In the best of all worlds, gaining trust would simply be a matter of doing good work for a period of time. Sadly, as imperfect people, we do not always appreciate the work that someone quietly does, but rather we notice the more visible. Good consultants make an effort to assure that their work has visibility, and that requires learning how to promote the work of your team as well as your own so that others see the value in it.

If you find that in your day-to-day activities as a "consultant," you never interact with people, chances are, you are acting in contractor role, not a consulting role.

If this aspect feels too much like brown-nosing or self-promotion for you to feel comfortable, chances are others will grab that spotlight from you with their successes; thus, someone other than you will be "building trust." You may survive for a good deal of time working in a consulting company, but don't be fooled: Consulting is an act between people. If you rarely or never interact with people, and interaction with people is on a "definitely only when required" basis, you probably aren't really consulting.

Answering yes to one or more of the following statements means your personality might be incompatible with consulting:

- If I can't wear shorts, sneakers, and sweats while I code, I can't do good work.
- The only small talk I want to engage in is related to the computer language, not conversational techniques.
- More often than not, I find other people annoying. I really only want to work with people who are mostly like me.

- I don't really care about business results that much; just let me code.

- When I find a code base that someone else worked on, it is almost always inferior to the work I would do.

- Writing documentation is always a waste of time. If the code was hard to write, it should be hard to understand.

- If someone can't figure out how to use an application I wrote, that person is probably too stupid to use a computer.

The key to knowing whether you are a fit is to be honest with yourself and decide whether, despite perhaps some inherent introvert tendencies, those traits got you into software in the first place. If you are willing and able to decide that interaction with the broader marketplace around you isn't just the job of other people, you might have better luck in this business.

Introversion Isn't Universally Bad

For some people, no matter how hard they try, they are going to be awkward in social situations, including those in the workplace. This does not mean you are doomed and unemployable as a software developer. If the trends tell us anything, there are plenty of people who meet that profile who make a fine living in software. The place for people like that is, again, probably in IT or, better yet, in the contracting marketplace. Contractors, who get paid to code by the hour on contracts working on projects designed by other people, can do very well. Although contracting isn't *consulting*, with the right agency to help find projects, it is a great way for a risk-tolerant developer who simply wants to code for money to make a nice living.

Sign #3: Incompatible Lifestyle and/or Responsibilities

The day-to-day realities of consulting, while they can be rewarding, almost certainly go beyond what most think of as a typical 9-to-5 existence. The thriving consultant probably spends at least 40 hours in a week billing for a client but then spends some measure of time doing the following:

- Working for the consulting company, attending company events, helping on presales efforts

- Working on side projects, doing open source work, authoring articles

- Spending significant time learning new technologies

- Commuting to clients that may or may not be particularly close to home

Needless to say, depending on the situation, the burden above 40 hours can be heavy. Especially during recessions when there are fewer opportunities and more need to distinguish yourself with side work, chances are, you will spend 50 to 60 hours on career-related activities in a given week (see Figure 10-1).

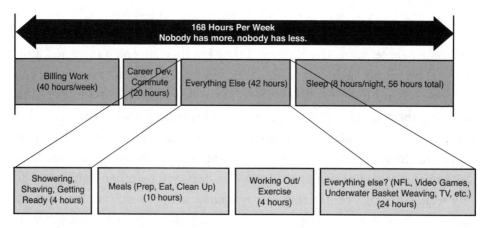

Figure 10-1 Breakdown of the consulting week.

Chris Williams You may be tempted to short yourself in one or more of the "Everything Else" categories (living on fast food, no exercise, and little sleep.) It may feel as though you're getting ahead for a little while (believe me, I've tried it), but eventually you'll crash mentally or physically, and it won't be pretty.

Be aware that some people somehow manage to coach little league, hold the PTA presidency, and do numerous other things, all while still having avid hobbies on the side. I am not saying it is impossible, but a word of caution should apply: If you have a lot of nonwork, noncareer activities you want to be involved in, you need to think long and hard before you pursue a career in technology consulting. Although some manage to do it all, I personally am not convinced they are not secretly abusing methamphetamines (or at least a lot of coffee!) to give themselves 22 waking hours each day.

Travel Required?

In consulting, it is not a guarantee you will *have* to travel. However, if you ever want to work for one of the bigger consulting firms, where the job security is better, you will be working for a firm that probably operates in more than one city. If your firm operates in more than one city, chances are, you will be at least asked to travel occasionally.

You can survive in consulting if you refuse to travel. However, doing so, at least in most firms, puts you on a much slower track than those who are willing to travel, at least in the earlier career stages. The reality, as hard as it may seem, is that you are as valuable as you are marketable for the firm you work for. Being capable of travel opens up a level of flexibility in what you are able to do for your firm, therefore putting you on a faster path. If you can't travel, you have been on the bench for two months, and others who can travel are getting projects (albeit elsewhere) and you are not, you will certainly feel the heat!

The requirement to travel is, like most things, situational. In some cases you might work for a consultancy that is mostly local, a consultancy that sells work that is mostly remote, and so forth. And if you find such a situation, by all means embrace it. However, at least in 2009, this is not the norm, though we would very much like it to be.

But What if I Have a Life?

There is room to have a life, depending on how you define "life." Let's put it bluntly: If you have hobbies that take a *ton* of time, whether it is something noble like working for a charity part-time 30 hours a week in the evenings or something even more noble like running a guild full-time in World of Warcraft, you may need to sacrifice part of that activity if you really want to thrive in consulting.

Of course, the alternative is to become very proficient at time management! Most people waste a lot of time (I write this, of course, after checking Twitter for 10 minutes, checking Facebook for another 10 minutes, checking my Google Reader...you get the idea). If you want to have time for work 60 hours per week; kids 30 hours per week; your hobby 30 hours per week; and time on top of that to occasionally eat, sleep, work out, and so on, you will not have another 30 hours per week to surf for funny YouTube videos.

But What If I Don't Have a Choice?

It is one thing if your life choices are not compatible; at least you can change that if you want to have a consulting career. There are others, however, for whom spending 40 hours per week parenting or taking care of an elderly or sick parent or spouse is not optional. Is a consulting career still possible in such a situation?

Yes, but having this career will be tougher for you than others who do not have that level of responsibility. The problem for someone with this level of responsibility is that you are operating in a marketplace where your peers have, on average, probably less responsibility than you. As a result, in situations in which you are competing for the best assignments, the sad truth in most cases is that there is a good chance, at least in some firms, that you might be at a disadvantage.

How do you get around this problem? Sadly, there is no real easy answer to that. The choices really are to balance the responsibilities, settle for operating from a position of disadvantage, and try to compensate in other ways (for example, compensate for lack of schedule flexibility with outstanding talent) or possibly try some means of being in technology that is less time-intensive than consulting. There is no easy answer, but for those who really want to make it work, there are ways to do it.

⁓

Sign #4: Desire for Single Product Focus

Some people, perhaps by instinct, perhaps by disposition, have a desire to work on a single product flowing through their veins. If you are one of these people, there are very good reasons why the consulting business really isn't for you.

If this description fits you, there simply are much better career alternatives you probably should pursue. The role of consulting in your career, if any, is simply to provide a means of acquiring cash so you have some "runway" (also known as "living expenses") that you need to launch a product on your own. If you can manage to find a place in a software company that shares your mission, has management you like, and has a product you believe in, you will almost certainly be happier working in a software product company.

Unlike some of the other signs, if this is really the situation you are in, you should keep in mind that in the rare event, as a consultant, you are working on packaged software. It is very infrequent that a consultant will be named a product designer, architect, or even lead developer of a software product. It might happen occasionally, but to plan on it would be really hoping to get very lucky on each and every engagement.

Even if you score such an engagement, chances are, the subsequent one is going to be writing software for an IT department somewhere with an internal corporate audience. The nature of consulting is that you are writing software for consumers who work within large companies, for audiences that are typically fairly small. Consulting, simply put, is not the place to go if your career goal is to have every project on which you work be something that will be used by thousands or millions of users. Even if it does happen occasionally, such cases are the exception, not the rule.

⁓

Sign #5: Doing It for the Money

Consulting does, at least for those who position themselves well, offer ample opportunities to make a reasonable amount of money. Even in bad times, a good, seasoned consultant drawing a salary can make $100,000 per year in the United States in most markets. An independent consultant who manages to land a gig where he or she can bring on two or three colleagues might do two or three times that! Although this isn't prefinancial crisis Wall Street money, it is certainly better than a sharp stick in the eye.

Chapter 9, "Avoiding Career-Limiting Moves," covered how greed can do damage to your career in consulting. The advice, however, in this context is that there are places where greed is a great motivator. If you really want to make money, I would submit that training in investment banking, stock trading, sales, or other more mercenary areas might be a better fit. As you saw earlier, when greed governs engineering decisions, the results can be disastrous.

> *If you simply want to make a load of money, there are far better occupations for doing that. Being a software developer without enjoying software development is almost certainly a recipe for acute and frequent job dissatisfaction!*

Besides the tendency that strict money motivation leads to risky career behavior, if you don't have a strong desire to write code and work for clients, this business can be a nauseating experience. The payoff for most of the important career activities in consulting is brutally a long time coming. You can do something extraordinary, like write a popular open source framework, and not reap the rewards of that effort until years down the road. With such a lag between work and payoff, most people who are strictly motivated by "filthy lucre" will not make it through that gap in time between action and result.

⁓

Summary

Don't get me wrong: Technology consulting is a great occupation. For people who enjoy software development, are flexible enough to deal with some curveballs in terms of schedule, are able to handle the risks, enjoy working on diverse projects, and enjoy or at least tolerate working with other people, the occupation is ideal. If those things are going to be issues for you, it may not be a bad idea to look at some of the alternatives presented here or at least think very strongly about what you want to do before proceeding down this path.

CHAPTER ELEVEN

AN ANTHOLOGY
OF SAGE ADVICE

Sage advice from some of the world's leading technology luminaries.

Although advice from one person can be great, as with most things, it is better to get advice from a collection of people who have different perspectives on careers, technology, and consulting. The purpose of this chapter is to provide you with some advice from luminaries who have seen some level of success, as well as learned from their failures.

The group of individuals in this chapter spans many disciplines, career stages, and technologies. Some are independent consultants, some work as salaried consultants, whereas others have since left consulting but still have valuable things to say about the profession.

Although each has experienced a great deal of success, it is important to remember that the path to success certainly comes through failure. In fact, one of the reasons I decided to write a book on this topic is to map out for others how to avoid many of the mistakes I have made myself. Someone who says he or she has never failed at anything is either lying or really hasn't done anything.

"Most success springs from an obstacle or failure. I became a cartoonist largely because I failed in my goal of becoming a successful executive."—
Scott Adams, Creator of the "Dilbert" comic strip

Of course, unless you are failing every single time, if you can manage to learn from failure and integrate the lessons into your routine going forward, it is likely that you will be on a trajectory to success. Each person in this chapter has had experiences to demonstrate that fact, which is the real purpose here—giving you a sense for the various paths you can take to get "there," wherever "there" happens to be for you.

⁓

Adaptation and Resistance

By Jason Bock, Principal Consultant, Magenic

Let me start out by giving you a brief description of my work history: I am a Principal Consultant for Magenic (http://www.magenic.com), a Microsoft MVP (C#), and an INETA (http://www.ineta.org) speaker. I worked on a number of business applications using a diverse set of substrates and languages, such as C#, .NET, and Java. I am the author of *Applied .NET Attributes, CIL Programming: Under the Hood of .NET, .NET Security,* and *Visual Basic 6 Win32 API Tutorial.* I have written numerous articles on software development issues and have presented at several conferences and user groups. I also run the Twin Cities Code Camp (http://www.twincitiescodecamp.com) and the Twin Cities Languages User Group (http://www.twincitieslanguagesusergroup.com). I have a master's degree in electrical engineering from Marquette University. Visit my Web site at http://www.jasonbock.net.

Throughout all the years that I've been a consultant, there are two qualities that I've seen in those that I consider successful that get them to that spot: They change with the times (adaptation), but they know when to put a line in the sand (resistance).

Being a consultant, it's a given that you have to embrace diversity. I've been with three different consulting firms in my life, which spans 12 years of my professional career. In that time, I've consulted at over 20 different companies. Those gigs have ranged from one day to 18 months. The technology has widely varied as well, from maintaining an ASP site written in Visual J++ to writing an iPhone application. There's no question that technologies thrive on change, and consultants have to be at the forefront of it to be successful.

However, even with the inherit aspect of change in a consultant's career, I think it's in the nature for people to want repeatability. It takes energy and commitment to accept the challenge of switching gears quite rapidly from one gig to another. Even at a company like Magenic (who has been my employer for the last eight years) where we focus exclusively on Microsoft-based technologies, we still go to clients that use non-Microsoft databases or operating systems. For us to be a successful consulting company, we have to embrace that diversity. If a company would force clients to have a homogenous environment across the board, they wouldn't be around for long.

That's not to say that you'll never get a wide variety of technical experiences working as a full-time employee at a corporation. However, it's been my experience that FTEs usually end up developing and maintaining an application or system for years on end. There's nothing wrong with this—as I said before, I believe humans tend toward repeatability in many aspects of their lives. Even as a consultant, I try to repeat whatever successes I've had before and try to avoid the mistakes I've made in the past. But at the end of the day, my job requires me to be willing to change, and that's not for everyone. If you want to be a consultant, you have to be honest with yourself and determine if you're okay with moving among different technologies and environments.

You also have to be willing to adapt from a personality perspective. That doesn't mean you have to change who you are. But some people don't fully appreciate how much you have to change according to the client's culture and employee personalities. It's not just about being technically proficient; it's also about communicating effectively to potentially hostile personnel.

I got a quick introduction to this early on in my consulting career. My first gig as a consultant was based around writing a timesheet application. This meant we needed to push a file to the payroll system, which also meant we needed to have numerous meetings with the payroll department. Whenever our business owner would come to the meetings, he'd always clash with the head of payroll. She did not suffer fools lightly, and when he would tend to speak rather loudly about how he was right (or how he thought he was right), she would quickly correct him in a rather terse manner. The thing I picked up on is that she responded well to people around her if they were honest, even if that meant they were honest about their failures. While I never had to speak in the first handful of meetings, as the project progressed I eventually became a focus of her questions. I didn't try to sugar-coat issues or respond in a defensive fashion. I made my answers as quick and as honest as possible. For whatever reason, she liked my demeanor, and it became a running joke in our group that I had to attend every payroll meeting from that point on because she seemed to be easier to talk to when I was in the meeting!

However, even though I think adaptation is a key quality to have as a consultant, I also believe that resistance is needed as well. Sometimes consultants can stray too far into being adaptable that they end up saying the "yes" word too much. They'll agree with the client that their architecture plans are okay even though they know they're suspect. They'll agree to development practices that they've seen fail badly at other clients. The reason they do this is to keep things smooth—in their minds a happy client is a paying client. But if this is taken too far, there can be serious damage at the end.

This almost happened on that timesheet application I mentioned before. We were moving at a breakneck pace, with little to no testing of any kind and no real business requirements to speak of. It all came to a head when I got married and went on my honeymoon. The client insisted on putting major changes in the Thursday before I left, and even though we tried to do more regression testing than we ever had, somehow a 1-line bug made it through. When the users tried to submit the payroll file, it didn't work. Fortunately, the web developer was able to figure out what the problem was late Monday night, but the damage was done.

The problem was we weren't putting our feet down and saying, "Enough!" We weren't serving the client effectively by doing everything they wanted with little to no questioning. After the dust settled when I got back from my honeymoon, we all agreed that we needed at least two months to iron out a lot of details and ensure that everyone was on the same page with respect to new features. At the end of two months, we ran through our new regression test policies and rolled out a new version. After that release, we noticed that our users were happier, and the bug counts dropped significantly. Furthermore, we knew when we messed up our code before we released it to our users because the regression testing process showed these errors.

By saying "yes" to everything the client asked for, we were running ragged with no clear goals in place, both from business and technical standpoints. By saying "no," we were able to turn things around and build trust with that client.

So to me, it's all about accepting change and knowing when to stop it. It's never been easy for me to do right all the time—I still end up saying things at the client that I saw in retrospect could've been phrased better, or I make boneheaded technical mistakes. But I wouldn't have it any other way either. Being a consultant has pushed me beyond my comfort zones, and as a result I feel it's made me stronger in many different areas.

On Being Independent

By David Chappell, Chappell & Associates

I've spent more than 20 years—almost my entire working life—as an independent. For all of that time, my goal has been to help people understand, use, and make better decisions about new technologies. I do that mostly through speaking and writing, although I do some consulting, too. For the work I do, being on my own is just perfect.

How Did I Become a Consultant?

Even though my undergrad degree is in economics, I spent college focused on becoming a musician. When I got there, I didn't much like it. Playing music is a great avocation, but it's a lousy profession. I next got a job as an economist, which proved to be equally boring. When my employer asked me one Friday whether I could write code, I said, "Sure," and then took a book home over the weekend. I returned to work on Monday morning as a fledgling software developer. Like so many of us, I quickly became obsessed, eventually going back to school to get an MS in computer science.

I never much liked having a regular job. While I did work as a developer for a couple of years after graduate school, I took the chance to go out on my own as soon as possible. I gave training seminars for quite a while, wrote a few books, and eventually found myself in my current role of independent speaker, writer, and analyst. It's a good fit for me.

Being Independent: The Basics

If you have a technical job today—software developer, application architect, or whatever—your primary focus is probably on technology. You might imagine that if you become an independent, you'd still have a primarily technical focus. The big difference, you hope, is that you'd have a much better boss.

This is not correct. The reality is that the company you currently work for does all kinds of things that let you focus solely on technology. It finds customers for what you create, it keeps the business going when you're on vacation, and much more. If you become an independent, all of these things fall to you. You might begin as an independent contractor with a company that finds work for you, such as a training company—this is what I initially did—but even then, things like paid vacations disappear. To be successful over the long term, you'll need to learn how to find work yourself. In other words, you've got to learn how to sell.

If this idea troubles you, you're not meant for the independent life. There's no shame in this, so don't feel bad. If the idea doesn't bother you, but you're not sure how to do it, well, that's how pretty much every technical person feels at first. It took me years to get comfortable with the sales aspects of my job, and the learning process was sometimes painful. Even now, I wouldn't count this as one of the things I do especially well. But you don't have to be great at sales, just good enough to keep yourself in work.

Some kinds of independent work, such as the writing and speaking that I mostly do, are inherently public. Potential clients can directly see what you do. This makes it easier for them to figure out whether they'd like to work with you. Other kinds of work, including designing and writing software, aren't usually so public. People who might like to hire you often can't see the quality of your work in a direct way. This makes marketing those skills harder.

Unlike with more public work, which is essentially self-marketing, you'll need to devote significant time to selling yourself outside of actually doing the work. This is perhaps one reason why so many independents who work in technology gravitate toward the more public kinds of work—it's easier to sell.

Another important aspect of leaving traditional employment is deciding what you really want to do. Is your goal primarily to work on your own? Or do you want to start a company, one with employees who carry out business processes independently from you? There's a lot to be said for creating a new company: You can (eventually) take vacations and maybe even sell it at some point. But it's much more difficult than having a career as an independent, and it takes a quite different skill set. While it's certainly possible to change course midstream, it's always useful to have a clear sense of which route you're on. I'm full of respect for people who choose the build-a-company path, but staying independent has been right for me so far.

Whatever path you choose, expect the separation between yourself and your business to become much blurrier. I guarantee that you'll feel differently about your work when all of the benefit—and all of the downside—flows to you rather than your employer. You also need to amp up your reliability. If you don't like being available on email pretty much all of the time, you probably won't do well as an independent. On my honeymoon in Bali, I checked my email every single day, and I was happy to do it. (Having a spouse that's okay with this is important, too.)

One of the great truths of being an independent is that everybody follows a unique course. Each of us has different interests and different skills, and each of us starts in a different place. Forging a career as an independent means figuring out what your idiosyncratic strengths are and then following through on the path those strengths put you on. There's no one right way.

Being Independent: Staying in Business

I often hear technical people express disdain for the human interactions that determine so much of career success. "Politics," they say, "I hate politics." If you feel this way, once again, you're not cut out to be an independent. In fact, you might as well resign yourself to a limited career, whatever job you're in.

Working well with other people—the essence of "politics"—is essential for success in nearly every role. Like it or not, this is especially true of being an independent consultant.

The truth is that being good at the work you're hoping to do is just the ante for getting into the game. People who are technically strong are a dime a dozen. Much less common are people who are technically strong, are good to work with, and can effectively sell those attributes.

Another important aspect of remaining successful is keeping current. Much of the time, clients hire you because you have specialized knowledge. In fact, plenty of people I know (including me) went out on their own because at some point, the specialized knowledge in their heads let them make much more money as an independent. No matter how hot your specialization is when you start, however, I guarantee you that the value of that knowledge will decline. If you're lucky, that declining value won't start for a couple of years, but it's absolutely certain to happen. When I first went out on my own, I was a specialist in something called Open Systems Interconnection (OSI). It was a hot technology at the time, and it let me get a good start. But within just a few years, OSI was completely dead. If I hadn't moved on, I couldn't have survived as an independent.

The challenge is to get yourself up to speed in new and in-demand areas while still making a living with your existing knowledge. One way to do this is to regularly devote some unpaid time to learning new things. Doing this is essential, but it's seldom enough. You also have to find a way to get clients to pay you to learn new things. You might, for example, look for work in emerging areas that are conceptually next door to whatever it is you're already doing. Maybe you're a specialist in large databases, and you run across an organization that's looking at the emerging options for cloud storage. You don't know much about these, but neither does anybody else, and your background makes you a natural fit to move into this new area. (I'm not suggesting that you hoodwink clients into paying for your on-the-job training, but rather that you look for win-win situations—they certainly exist.) Doing this successfully comes back to sales: You need to learn how to get customers to offer you this work. But whatever you do, don't think that the specialized knowledge and skills you start with will see you through an entire career. Plan to change.

Ultimately, sustaining a career as an independent in technology is much like sustaining a successful career in any other area. You need to do some things really well, but you have to do everything at least passably well. And you need to differentiate yourself, which like every business means one of two things: doing different things from your competitors or doing the same things in different ways. Whatever approach you choose, the goal is always to provide a unique competitive advantage, a compelling reason for clients to choose you.

I have moments when I think everybody should be self-employed. It keeps you solidly in touch with what's really valuable, both to your customers and to yourself. And the freedom that comes with being on your own is a wonderful thing. I wholeheartedly recommend it.

⤳

Becoming an Independent Consultant

By Bruce Eckel, President, MindView Inc.

The first issue to clear up is the meaning of "consultant." This term has been overused to the point of obscurity. Once, it had a fairly clear definition, but like so many job descriptions, it became a term of status, and companies started using it to reward employees and to make themselves look good.

The term now has a spectrum of meanings. At one extreme, "consultant" means, basically, a temporary employee who does programming. Theoretically, the company that provides such a consultant has filtered this person and continually trains them. That's certainly the image they project because such an image allows them to charge a lot. But in fact, the accountants running a body shop inevitably discover that the more bodies they keep working, the more money they make, and more importantly, that it takes awhile for clients to discover that the quality of the people has gone down as the consulting company has staffed up. This kind of company produces the Dilbert definition of consultant (CONfuse and inSULT).

Not every company that provides such "consultants" falls into the same category, of course. There are companies who have different goals than just "maximize profits." These companies don't hire someone unless they meet their standards—watching and waiting, instead, for the right person to appear.

If you assume we are not talking about a body-shop/temp agency style of consultant, but rather one that brings special value to a company, then we can look at a range of different services that such a consultant provides.

At one end, a consultant can offer a specialized or expert programming ability that the company doesn't have or can't afford to keep on staff. Such a consultant comes in and programs a solution for the company, then leaves. This is the "I'll do it for you" category.

At the opposite end is a consultant who analyzes what a company has been doing or plans to do and offers advice and an independent perspective. This is the "I'll give advice and ideas" category. Moving back a little, there's "I'll provide guidance," "I'll train you," and "I'll help you do it" (which falls right before the aforementioned "I'll do it for you").

Because the time slots I've normally had available have been typically short (1–2 weeks), my type of consulting has usually been in the advice-guidance-training arena. However, since I've moved more into Python (with UIs in Flex), the productivity is high enough that I've been able to build or help build solutions even within short consulting visits.

How Did I Become a Consultant?

I made a conscious decision to become a consultant, but getting there seemed to be a series of fortuitous accidents: I began college as a journalism major, changed to physics, then added engineering. After that I discovered I wasn't ready to join the real world and so got a master's degree. For a while, I even thought having a Ph.D. would make me more desirable as a consultant; fortunately that failed. Later the journalism background and my struggles to learn physics—I was a pretty bad physicist, but it taught me to throw myself up against intractable problems—converged when I started writing about computing. I decided writing would market me as a consultant, but in hindsight I'm certain there must be a more direct way.

Over time, I've settled on a number of factors that I think are essential in order to become an independent consultant.

"Consultant" Is Part of Your Core Identity

I was 15 when I decided I wanted to be a consultant. The primary appeal was being independent, and that continues to be a positive part of it. But at the time I had no idea what I was going to actually do or how to go about it. For me it was a lifestyle decision.

Starting your own business that only has one employee (you) is easier in many ways than starting a business with employees, but there are still plenty of challenges. Initially, you'll have to work through the process of rewiring your brain so it doesn't think that, without cubicles and bosses, it's constantly the weekend. Or lunchtime. This doesn't happen overnight; indeed, discovering your best work patterns seems to be a lifelong challenge. You must find or invent your own structure.

You'll make lots of mistakes (more on that later). Friends and admirers won't understand the obstacles you face—in fact, they don't want to, instead preferring to fantasize that your life is all weekends and lunch and overnight success. You'll learn to redefine success and failure. And you must regularly revisit the question of "how am I doing?" to discover whether you're just following what's easy and profitable or if you're actually moving along the path that makes you happy.

If "consultant" isn't firmly ensconced in how you describe yourself to yourself, you might not be able to overcome all these challenges. That's also a good thing to discover. If you force yourself to become a consultant when that's not who you really are, it's not good for you or your clients.

Me, I'm in this for the long haul. I always want to continue learning, experimenting, and growing. I don't plan to retire, so if I take some breaks or there are quiet periods and times of change, that's all part of the picture.

Economic Nerves of Steel

While I was growing up, my father built custom homes as a contractor. As a master craftsman, he didn't bid on jobs because those weren't the kind of customers he wanted. His customers were those who had already decided they wanted a home built by Wayne Eckel. To do that, he had to wait. So I grew up thinking that waiting was just part of the job. And fortunately, in our business there are lots of other things to do in the meantime, so you're never sitting around. You can do research and create products, both of which benefit you as a consultant (note that consulting to support a product-creation company and product creation to support a consulting company are two very different things).

So if you don't know what to do with yourself without regular paying work, you should get a regular paying job. But keep in mind that a regular job is no guarantee of stability—everyone has a two-week contract. Sometimes being a consultant is *more* stable than having a regular job.

One of the important places you need economic nerves of steel is in marketing. No one knows how to market. "Marketing Experts" are only expert in selling their own marketing services—this is nothing to sneeze at, and you may learn something from such people, but don't be fooled into thinking that what works for them will work for you.

You just have to get ideas, try things out, and see what happens—and be ready to fail most of the time. And you can't assume that because it works once, you can stop thinking about it and use the same trick over and over again. A great learning experience for me happened in the early days of both Java and the Internet. I decided that what I really wanted was to get people to come to seminars, so I started giving away "Thinking in Java" on the Web (according to Eric Raymond, he was the first person to give away a book on the Web, and I was the second). Lots of people came, and I thought I had marketing all figured out. Alas, I had made my discovery when there was relatively little on the Internet, and while I was enjoying my success, the Web started filling up around me, reducing my differentiation.

Internet marketing is challenging and requires you to keep thinking differently. Read Seth Godin's blog and his books as a starting point.

Relentless Learning

This is true of our profession in general, but it is especially important as a consultant. The only unique thing you bring to the table is your ideas and insights, and you must be constantly feeding your brain in order to generate those.

There are some topics that take many years to understand. Concurrency, for example, is something I've been periodically flinging myself at since graduate school, and over the years it's begun to seep in. Only because I am constantly trying to learn one thing or another do these concepts eventually solidify (generally in a time and place of their own choosing). In our profession, you must be ready for a long commitment in order to learn some of these concepts.

Your feed reader is a good way to get new information, if used judiciously (only a few entertainment feeds). I'm always reading a book that expands business or programming ideas. I've found that podcasts are an excellent way to get new ideas. It's like going to a lot of different conferences and being able to pick and choose the best presentations, but without the travel time and costs. The right conferences can be very intellectually stimulating, as well (these days, my preference is for open-spaces style conferences).

Relentless Experimentation ... and Willingness to Fail

This can be particularly difficult because we've been trained to find the right answer, apply it, and make no mistakes. Anything else is considered failure.

Especially in the age of the Internet, we've been learning that the key to success is to make mistakes as rapidly as possible and to learn from each one and try again. Indeed, success and innovation on the Internet is based on the ability to cheaply make large quantities of mistakes.

The cost of experimentation in your consulting business is both financial and often emotional. Sometimes failure is just annoying, and sometimes it feels bad and scary. But without it, you don't learn much, you don't grow as a consultant, and you aren't very valuable to clients. The motto of the honest consultant might even be: "We make mistakes so you don't have to."

Diversity

I think the primary reason I can be successful at (my kind of) consulting is that I always have other projects. It's good to be learning and productive while you're waiting for the right job to come along, and that's one reason I keep writing books and creating other kinds of learning materials and conferences—these can supplement your income, but they are also a way for potential clients to get to know you, so it's another kind of marketing.

Having multiple projects also keeps you growing and expanding.

Your Personal Journey

Many people have big problems when they follow the path that seems to have been laid out for them and it comes to an end. An academic, for example, might get a Ph.D., do research, publish papers, distinguish themselves, and then wonder "is that all there is?" In the corporate world, you can climb the career ladder and then begin to wonder why.

To be my kind of consultant, you start by breaking the ladder and muddying the path. You not only have to be ready to do this, you must *want* to. For many this will be difficult or impossible, and even if you can accomplish it there will be numerous periods when you regret the lack of structure and miss the camaraderie of the workplace. Many other times you will wonder how people in regular jobs can live within such bonds.

In your consulting services, you are offering "thinking outside the box," and to do so, you must actually live outside the box. Getting there, and staying there, is a constant battle.

People will be threatened by this and try to stop you. While in my longest traditionally corporate job, early out of grad school, I began telling people that I wanted to be a consultant. They responded by saying it couldn't be done, pointing out people who had tried and failed, and making very compelling arguments why it was impossible. Apparently this is standard group behavior when someone tries to break the social contract and go against the belief system; overweight families, for example, will try to feed a dieting member.

A Mission

In recent years I've discovered that making money isn't enough. I've known this since I was a child, but as Morpheus states in *The Matrix*, "There's a difference between knowing the path and walking the path." If your only goal is to make money, for a while you will be entertained, but eventually you will begin to look elsewhere for meaning.

To continue to progress in your chosen profession, you need a compelling, soul-satisfying mission. I've only just realized that for me it's about *connecting*. I can never write without imagining a room filled with people hearing the words. When I speak in person I want lights to turn on in the eyes of the audience. I happily give up control during Open Spaces conferences because I know people get so much more out of discussions than listening to me lecture. And when I consult, the greatest satisfaction comes from helping people make a shift, no matter how small, that improves their understanding, their designs, and their work experience.

All these things are wonderful and terrifically compelling. However, I still don't think it's enough. Until you find something that is outside yourself and bigger than you, it feels like there's something missing, and projects that don't have this component will eventually lose steam and run down.

I've always wanted to do something to improve the world. People have written me and told me that one or another of my books has had a big effect on their life, but couched in economic terms. While it's good to know someone else is better off because of my work, it never quite feels like enough. And although I have traveled broadly, I'm not so sure that I could do something where I pull up stakes and go to another country and make some kind of big impactful change there (actually, I don't even know what that would be).

So while I might not be able to do something directly, like solving the energy problem or developing new perspectives on disease, I think I can help give tools to other people who can solve these problems (in the same way that Open Spaces conferences get people communicating as well as starting their own conferences once they see how easy it is and that it works).

Programming is just a different kind of writing. Almost everyone in the developed world writes, but only a few are considered good writers. What I'm trying to achieve with my current project, an open-source book called *Python 3 Patterns, Recipes and Idioms*, is to create better writers. I think that a few of those writers—because they can then solve programming problems more easily—might just be able to help solve some of the bigger problems in the world. Because the book is open-source (which means, for example, that it can be translated easily), it just might reach someone, somewhere who has the motivation to make something really important happen.

Go Easy on Yourself

This may be the most important point because you'll have lots of failures. If your two choices are overnight success or abject failure, it's not going to work. This is not to say that when you get up a little speed and then smack into a wall, it isn't going to hurt. Life will be a lot easier if you can accept that you've crashed and burned, then eventually pick yourself up and brush off and try something else. In the end, the key to quickest success is to learn to fail fearlessly, then learn from the failure and try another experiment. And another, and another.

What About Forming a Consulting Group?

On several occasions, discussions have arisen among different consultants I know regarding whether and how to form a consulting group. This is generally motivated by two goals: an attempt to produce a more consistent flow of clients and a desire for camaraderie.

Especially if your consulting is of the less-specific advice-and-guidance sort, marketing is tough. I have always felt that the client must be developed and aware enough before they know how to use a consultant (Gerald Weinberg's "Secrets of Consulting" reinforces this idea), and such clients do not seem that common. My friend Scott Meyers once told me he thought it took five years from when a client first read your book to when they were ready to hire you—he went on to wonder how consultants who are just starting can survive long enough for this "book effect" to kick in.

One suggestion was for a group of consultants to collectively hire a marketing person for one year, and this person would theoretically pay for themselves through commissions after that first year. This assumes, however, that all consultants in the group are more or less equal, and selling the services of one will be equivalent to selling the services of another. This desire to treat all programmers as interchangeable commodities is a general problem in our industry and becomes clear when looking at marketing consulting services.

The interchangeability myth seems to reduce most consulting firms to command-and-control organizations, forcing the consultants to conform to whatever the organization seems to be good at marketing rather than emphasizing and exploiting each consultant's natural talent. I believe this happens out of reflex, just as the reflex of a conference organizer is to set up a bunch of eyes-forward presentations like every other conference they've seen. We have no other training, so we can't think any other way. I believe it's possible to learn to think differently—in fact, I think this is an essential talent for a consultant—so one day we may be able to create a group that helps market consultants for their individual talents. However, I think this will require the same kind of mental shift that Open Spaces conferences require.

In the meantime, I think the only viable consulting group is one that emphasizes camaraderie. Although financially this is far less compelling, it is personally quite attractive because consultants often become isolated working on their own and encounter issues that can only be understood by other consultants. I know of one such group that works this way, the Atlantic Systems Guild that Tim Lister belongs to. I don't think they share much in terms of resources, but they regularly communicate and have retreats a couple of times a year. It's basically a support group for consultants.

I think the ideal consulting group would be both a support group and provide marketing and other benefits. And because I'm lazy about such things, it would have to be self-organizing, just like Open Spaces conferences are. But I have yet to envision such an organization, and that's why I haven't started one.

Resources

Secrets of Consulting, by Gerald Weinberg. Weinberg is the "consultant's consultant," and this is, I believe, his most popular book: short, pithy, and filled with insights for cracking tough consulting problems. It includes the phrase he is probably most famous for, "No matter what they tell you, it's always a people problem."

Peopleware, by DeMarco & Lister. Entertaining ideas and mind-twisting results from serious studies about how we work—and how organizations constantly make it hard to work. Basically, "why Dilbert is true."

Waltzing with Bears, by DeMarco & Lister. Not about consulting per se, but the kind of thing you must be able to do. In this case, introduce somewhat radical (albeit true) ideas about risk management to project development.

Multiple books that have been accumulating hopefully on my shelf about how to market yourself as a consultant, start out as a consultant, be successful as a consultant, etc. I haven't read them yet, and it could turn out to be just an extension of the self-help book publishing industry. The fact that there are so many makes me wonder.

Technical podcasts like *IT Conversations*, *The Java Posse*, *Software Engineering Radio*, and many others. Freely available on the Web.

TED Talks, freely available as both audio podcasts and streaming videos. Short (less than 20 minutes) talks that are not focused on computers or programming, but which expand your ideas and the way that you think about the world and about problem-solving.

⮑

It's Been Fun So Far

By Michael Hugos, Center for Systems Innovation

I collaborate with colleagues and clients through an organization I founded called the Center for Systems Innovation [c4si]. This means I write books and a blog and that get me opportunities to speak at conferences and seminars. Sometimes people like my ideas and invite me to work with them and their companies. I focus on mentoring groups of business and IT people to use a rapid (you could say "agile") application development method for developing information systems. Previously, I spent six years as chief information officer of a national distribution company where I developed a suite of supply chain and e-business systems that transformed the company's business model. Prior to that, I was a practice director at a global IT services and consulting firm.

I won the CIO 100 Award in 2003 and 2005, won the *Information Week* 500 Award in 2005, and in 2006 was selected for the Computerworld Premier 100 Award for career achievement. I earned my MBA from Northwestern University 's Kellogg School of Management. I've authored several books including *Essentials of Supply Chain Management*, 2nd edition, and co-authored CIO *Best Practices: Enabling Strategic Value with Information Technology*. My newest book is *Business Agility: Sustainable Prosperity in a Relentlessly Competitive World*.

As the saying goes, "Everyone here is on their way to somewhere else," so I'm a work in progress. Some days I like what I do, and other days I like where I think I'm going more than what I'm doing that day.

I Learn More from Failure than from Success

When I succeed, it just provides evidence for what I already suspect—that I'm a genius. When I fail, it forces me to face some unpleasant facts, and sometimes I learn something new in that process. My failures group into three main categories. The first category is learning to manage project scope. The second category is learning to manage my desire to please my clients. And the third category is learning to manage my relationship with people in authority.

Regarding the first category, all useful systems have an infinite number of possible features, which leads to the second category where my desire to please has (more than once) induced me to try building more of these features than was realistic considering time, money, and people available. One of the most educational failures I ever had was a project where I committed to develop a newspaper distribution and billing system for a newspaper and magazine distributor. I let the client talk me into adding more and more features while my company was in the middle of programming the originally agreed upon features. I wound up losing money, the project took too long to finish, and the client was not happy. It taught me to zero in on the most important features and rigorously limit scope so as to get the first version of the system delivered quickly. That made clients happy because they had something they could start working with right away. Then I could always add more features if clients wanted them. I learned it was also a good way to build trust with the clients and get follow-on work.

Regarding the third category, my relationship with people in authority, I have driven a succession of bosses nuts with my headstrong behavior and my need to point out flaws in their plans and suggest better ways to do things. I find most people in positions of authority do not take kindly to that type of behavior from an employee, but they do respect it when it comes from a highly paid consultant. So I figured it makes more sense for me to be a highly paid consultant than to try to be an employee.

The Intermittent Rewards of Success Are Addictive

Ask any gambler or stock trader or any casino operator or behavioral psychologist; the most powerful behavioral inducements are rewards that happen sometimes but not all the time. If rewards happen every time you do something, then you take it for granted and become indifferent; you stop learning. When rewards are uncertain, you appreciate every reward and keep trying and learning new things to get those rewards. Consulting is a great place to find intermittent rewards.

The rewards of success depend on skill and also on a host of things you cannot control (known as luck). So I practice learning the lessons from my failures, and I focus on doing things I like so much that I would even do them for free because sometimes I do wind up doing them for free (when the rewards don't come).

I also cultivate an active interest in non-IT-related subjects because that is where I often get insights and random ideas that I sometimes apply with brilliant effect in my consulting practice. My areas of non-IT interest lie in the performing arts like theater and dance and in the study of history. I learn about audience interaction and communication from the performing arts, and I learn from mistakes others have made through my study of history.

The IT profession as we have come to know it these last 30 years is changing rapidly. Fixed ideas about what it means to be a developer or an IT consultant are a sure way to miss new trends shaping the profession. Don't fall in love with your opinions; be the first to admit your mistakes and adopt better ideas when you see them. Try to stay humble in the face of your occasional successes. If you can do these things, you might have an IT consulting career that will be fun and last for a while.

🖚

15 Bytes of Consulting Wisdom

By Deborah Kurata, President, InStep Technologies, Inc.

Much of this book describes how to be a consultant for a consulting firm. There is another option: You can be independent.

Being an independent consultant allows you to select which clients to work for, set your own hours, and get 100 percent of your bill rate. But with these rewards, you also take on 100 percent of the risks. You have to find your own clients, pay for your own office equipment and supplies, find ways to train yourself, get the client to pay you, and you don't get paid when you are on the bench.

Some people carefully plan their career to become an independent consultant; others just fall into it. I fit into the latter category. I am an independent consultant and code junkie. This is my story.

I started out with a Math and Physics degree, but I had worked at the college's computer lab writing computer-based training software on a PDP 11-45 and loved it. So my first job out of college was developing software. I worked my way up, learning everything I could about writing good code.

Lesson Learned #1: Learn everything you can from your current employer before you start out on your own. Be sure to pay attention to all areas of software development including architecture, design, and good coding practices.

I later found myself in project management positions and then the Software Development Manager and soon realized that I needed to know more than just good coding techniques. Since I was lucky to be living in Williamsburg, Virginia, at the time, I was able to earn an MBA from The College of William and Mary while working full-time.

Lesson Learned #2: Being an independent consultant means that you will not only be coding, but will be managing clients and running your own company. Picking up some management or basic accounting classes could be helpful.

Getting my MBA helped me make a move to a Silicon Valley company in California, where I was able to expand my software management experience and learn how to code for PCs using C++. After I spent several great years there, the company was bought out by a firm in the Los Angeles area. With a house, a family, and another child on the way, I was not interested in making the move to LA. So the company helped me to set up a home office. My independent consulting career had begun.

Lesson Learned #3: Consulting back to your prior employers is one of the easiest ways to start your independent consulting career. They know your skills and your expertise, and you know their projects.

As the work for my prior company transitioned to a new team in LA, I started to look for other projects. Luckily, I had met Alan Cooper (the "father of Visual Basic") through some colleagues, and he hired me to work with him on a project. I learned vast amounts from him including how to design for the user and how to be a good independent consultant. He also got me hooked on Visual Basic because I could do so much so much faster in VB than I could in C++.

Lesson Learned #4: One of the hardest things about independent consulting is to find that next project while you are still in the heat of the battle on your current project. But it is something you must do if you want your consulting work to provide a steady income.

Lesson Learned #5: Take every opportunity to get to know the other people at your current employer and their colleagues. The chance of getting a lead to that next great project increases the more connections that you have.

Working in my home office all alone and using a new programming language led to a sense of loneliness and frustration. How do I figure out the best way to code? What can I do if I get stuck on a problem? I sought out answers and found solutions through two means: the local developers group and the news groups (which at that time was CompuServe.)

Lesson Learned #6: Find ways to connect to other developers. Check your local area for developer organizations or code camps. Locate developer news groups, forums, or chats on the Internet.

The developers group and news group helped me in amazing ways. I finally had other developers to talk to. We could discuss the pros and cons of one programming technique versus another or the best development tools. I also met other talented independent consultants, some of which I later hired as my company grew.

Lesson Learned #7: Get involved. Ask questions. Meet people.

One of the other members of our local developers group was Robert Scoble, who at the time worked for Fawcette Technical Publications (a technical magazine publisher and conference producer). He talked me into writing articles, which then led to speaking at technical conferences. Writing good articles and speaking intelligently on topics at conferences required me to complete a significant amount of research on the topic. This extensive research clarified the topic for me as well, making me much more knowledgeable.

Lesson Learned #8: Become an expert. Most companies looking for consulting assistance want an "expert." The best way to become an expert on something is to explain it to others. Write magazine or Web articles, make presentations at your local user group, and teach others on your project team.

The magazine articles and speaking engagements led to a book deal. My first book was *Doing Objects in Microsoft Visual Basic 4.0*. This provided an opportunity for me to share everything I had learned about designing and developing object-oriented software and how to apply that knowledge to a language that was not entirely object-oriented.

Lesson Learned #9: With the huge time investment required to write a book, you won't make any money from the book deal. But a book gets your

name out there. Being well-known in your field is your best marketing strategy.

I started to get phone calls and emails from other developers asking for training or assistance with projects. My company was growing. I looked to my developers group to find good talent and surrounded myself with people I could learn from. I got real office space. My spouse joined the company, as did one of his work colleagues. The consulting life was good.

Lesson Learned #10: If you find yourself with more project work than you can do, consider first contracting with other independent consultants. They know more about managing the client and engagement, and you don't necessarily have to find them their next project.

Lesson Learned #11: As soon as you hire an employee or employees, you have a significantly larger responsibility. First, there are many government regulations that come in to play as soon as there is someone else (just keeping up with the government-required posters can be a big job). Second, you are responsible for their livelihood. You have to pay them regularly, regardless of whether you are getting paid by the client. You have to find them their next project and so on. So be sure you are ready before taking this step.

Lesson Learned #12: When your company becomes more than just you, find yourself a good part-time administrative assistant. Let that person handle the invoicing, bill paying, poster posting, filing, and other administrative tasks.

Then came the Internet craze. Many of our most talented developers left us to make their hoped-for millions at startup companies. As our workload increased, we struggled to bring on enough talented developers. We assigned new, technically skilled developers to projects without providing them enough training in client etiquette. (The majority of our prior hires had been independent consultants, and this had not been necessary.) For the first time, we started to get client complaints. ("Why is Joe playing Solitaire during our design meetings? We don't want to pay for his time if he is not even paying attention.")

Lesson Learned #13: Rapid growth can hurt you just as much as no growth. It is much better to turn down work than to take on work that you don't have the people to complete successfully.

But soon, the Internet bubble burst. And to add to our difficulties, most of our large clients received the directive from their management to send all consulting work offshore. We found ourselves without work for the first time in many years. It took a long time to mentally recover from the sadness of laying off employees and downsizing the company.

Lesson Learned #14: In today's economy, be sure you can sustain your growth before making the big step of hiring permanent employees.

So now we are lean and again finding happiness in the pleasure of designing and developing software. We find enough consulting projects to keep ourselves pleasantly busy and yet have time to keep up with the latest technology. Consulting is fun again.

Lesson Learned #15: It was great to work with a large team of talented developers and manage lots of interesting projects, but it was also very stressful. And it was difficult to find time to actually code or keep up with technology. Decide where your pleasures lie. Life is too short; consulting should be fun.

〜

Learning from Your Mistakes

By Ted Neward, Principal Consultant, ThoughtWorks

I'm a Principal Consultant for ThoughtWorks, and prior to that, I was the Principal of Neward & Associates, my own consulting firm. I write, speak, mentor, and consult on a variety of technical topics, including Java, .NET, XML services, enterprise systems, programming languages, and virtual machines. Yes, I have no life.

How Did I Become a Consultant?

Originally, I never expected to be a software development guy; I'd always assumed I'd either be a fiction author or work for the CIA or DIA in foreign intelligence work. My degree is in International Relations; I spent most of my college years studying economics, political science, psychology, sociology, history, and foreign languages; and I'd tagged as my "hero" (the guy with the job that I wanted) Jack Ryan, of Tom Clancy book fame. But I spent a lot of my spare time in college playing around with C++ and Windows programming, and a roommate double-dog dared me to interview for a programming position in town, which I almost got, much to my surprise. That was the wake-up call that maybe, just maybe, I was really more interested in programming for a living because if it was what I was doing with my free time, and people thought I was good enough at it to get paid for it...

I finished my degree, took a couple of C.S. courses just to see what was there, and when I graduated, I found an employer willing to take a chance on somebody who seemed to know what he was doing despite the lack of a degree in Computer Science. That led to a contracting job with Intuit on Quicken, and from there, I now had the "experience" to back the assertion that, yes, I really did know how to code my way out of a paper bag.

Quite bluntly, I've gotten very lucky with the opportunities that were thrown my way. In 1995 or so, I was offered a chance to write a book on Borland's C++ Windows framework (OWL), and that led to an association with the publisher (Manning), who then asked me to write a book on Java, which then led me to teach at DevelopMentor, which then led me to .NET, which then led me to write DevelopMentor's course on C#, which then led me to co-author a book on C# (*C# In A Nutshell*) with another publisher (O'Reilly), who then asked me to co-author another book (*SSCLI Essentials*), which then led me to know a number of the folks at Microsoft, all while another DevelopMentor buddy asked me to speak at a conference he was track-chairing, which led to more conference speaking, and so on. I'm living proof that sometimes it's about both what you know and who you know.

How I Have Failed

I've failed on projects before, and I've failed with clients before, but I don't think that I've failed me or my career.

One failure was a classic YAGNI (You Ain't Gonna Need It) failure. While at a client site working on some C++ code for them, I found their diagnostic logging system to be really entirely too simple to be credible. It was a standard function call to write out to a file, and I found it horribly limiting and completely lacking in flexibility. (Veterans can already see it coming, I'm sure.) I sat down and rewrote the whole thing, using C++ streams and macros and flexible logging levels, not too far removed from what we see today in systems like log4j or System.Diagnostics.Trace, and even wrote a few C++ macros to help make it easier to use. Only problem was, you couldn't view the log file while the applications were running—pretty much a necessity for the diagnostic engineers—and I couldn't figure out how to open the C++ file stream with the right Windows-specific flags to allow others to view the file. After I left, I heard that the client ripped out everything I did on that logging system and went back to the old stuff. Lesson learned? Make sure you know what's important to the client before you go refactoring the code.

Another failure was a classic consultant mistake, in that I allowed dislike for the new CTO to overshadow how I could best help the client (and myself). When asked by the new CTO to evaluate some code—in essence, to do a code review on it—I discovered that the codebase wasn't in source control, and in fact, the most recent code was on a floppy disk in the (lone) developer's shirt pocket, and nobody else had access to it. The code was sloppy and messy classic VB code, and during the review itself, I took great pains to point out that this was classic "cowboy code written by a cowboy developer, and were it my company, I'd fire the guy until he could learn to write code professionally." All of what I said was true, but the developer was the CTO's pet coder, and he let me go that afternoon.

Some developers may be asking themselves, "Where's the failure here? You were right, you said as much, they were stupid. How were you wrong?" I'd also been discovering this new technology, called Java, that I thought could be of huge benefit to the company, and I was getting interested in it myself. I found out later, about six months after I was gone, that the company ditched its current projects in favor of building an all-Java backplane, and had I taken a more politically-savvy tone during that code review, I might have found myself as the chief architect of an all-Java backplane project as early as 1996. Instead, I was back to working on a C++ project and wouldn't touch Java in a professional manner until 1998. Oops.

Secrets to Success

Quite bluntly, the key to success, in my opinion, is two-fold.

One arm of your career clearly has to be technically oriented. The savvy consultant is always looking at every technology that she can get her hands on, whether it's directly relevant to her job at the moment or not. Currently working on a .NET project? Look at Java and J2EE, so you can see what a platform that predates .NET by five years looks like. Look at Objective-C and MacOS/Cocoa/iPhone development so that you can get familiar with what programming that platform is like and can do. Look at Ruby and Rails and other dynamic languages, so you can see how programming with a different mindset opens up new avenues of design approaches and implementation ideas. You cannot allow yourself to get caught up in religious debates or crusades; every time somebody starts to engage you in a debate about how much better the Mac is over Windows, take the opposite position and argue with them, not because you believe it, but because you want to see how well you know the issues at stake. It will also ensure that you never fall into a rut of thinking that "X is always better than Y" because quite frankly, it's never been true, and it never will be, for any two tools, languages, platforms, or libraries.

The other arm of your career has to be political, however. You have to have decent social skills because half of the consultant's job is negotiating the much murkier and trickier world of human relations. It's not always sufficient to rest on the strength of your technical arguments—there will always be that one scenario where the right thing to do is to actually keep the old codebase and make it limp along for another five years, despite the clear advantages of rewriting the thing from scratch. Not all the arguments that matter are technical ones—human reasons ("I can't really describe what I do" means "I don't want you to write software that makes my job superfluous") and business reasons ("We like the old system" means "We don't want to go through the hassle of having to relearn a new system, not when learning the old one took us five years of blood, sweat, and tears") will always come up to stand in the way of technical reasons, and you have to be able to see your way through them if you're to be of any use to the client … and thus too valuable to fire at the next round of budget cuts.

A large part of that political arm is also who you spend your time with. As Chad Fowler puts it in his excellent book *My Job Went to India*, you should be surrounding yourself with people smarter than you so you can learn from them. It's amazing how quickly you can learn a subject when you're surrounded by experts, and it's easier than ever to be surrounded by experts, thanks to social tools like mailing lists, IM, Twitter, IRC, and conferences. It's hard on the ego, but it's like nitrous oxide for your career and technical abilities when you do—not only will you get smarter, but those connections might just lead to the Next Big Thing for your career.

Remember, it's not always about what you know; who you know (and what they think of you) plays a big part in getting those opportunities that will advance your career to that next level.

〜

The Many Ways to Fail

By Derik Whittaker, Software Developer, AllscriptsMisys Healthcare

I guess you could say that I don't fit the stereotypical mold of a software developer. I did not start writing code as a kid (although I did have an old Texas Instrument in the late '80s), nor am I gamer. In fact, I was a senior in high school when I received my first real computer (a Pentium-90 with 8MB of RAM; those were the days), and it was about that time I created my first program, which was a screen-saver type of application in QBasic.

When I decided on a major in college, I had no intention of working with computers; I wanted to be a kinesiologist. However, I could never stop playing (read that as breaking, then fixing) with the computer my parents had gotten me. After about a year of everyone telling me to switch majors, I finally listened. From that point on, I have never looked back and to this day love writing code more than anything else.

When it was time to get a real job (one that actually could pay the bills), I knew I wanted to start off my career as a consultant. My plan was to bounce around from project to project and language to language in an attempt to figure out what aspect of software development I enjoyed most. The initial goal was to only consult for a few years in order to gain experience and broaden my horizons. But things changed when the Tech bubble of the late '90s, early 2000s burst and jobs were scarce. I was on a long-term project, and since jobs were hard to come by, I stayed put.

The one thing that I learned from the tech bubble bursting is that you can never stop learning. Your goal as a software professional (regardless if you are a consultant or work for a big corporation) must be to learn something new. Learn a new language, a new design pattern, etc. The day you stop learning is the day you are no longer marketable. And when that happens, kiss your career goodbye.

How I Have Failed

Sadly, failing in IT is very, very easy and all too common. Any developer who tells you he or she has never failed is either a flat-out liar or has never worked on any project larger than a "hello world." In fact it is so easy to fail in our industry, it is possible to fail when you meet all your "defined" goals. You must learn early to accept the fact that the definition of success is defined by others, and we have very, very little ability to control it. Learning to accept failure and to learn from it is a critical part of our job. If you are not up for the task, you may be in the wrong career field.

Of all the projects I have worked on during my career, both successful and the not-so-successful, one project stands out above them all as the failure to end all failures. Unlike some projects, which can fail because of a single item not going as planned, such as going over budget, missing deadlines, or simply not getting the application correct, this project failed at all of these and so many more. This is a brief story of this project and how we failed.

The project started off like most typical new projects. We had a clean slate to work with (this was a Greenfield application), we had a pretty good understanding of the desired functionality (we were replacing a "legacy" system), and we had an eager team ready to rock out some goodness and a management team that had our backs.

Soon after we started the planning for the project, it became very clear to the team that given conditions outside of our control (hard deadline), we needed to make a few changes to the team in order to have any chance at success. The two changes we decided to make were to move from Waterfall-based development to SCRUM and to bring on a few new developers to help out with the project.

As I said above, this project was a massive failure, and we are about to find out why.

Moving to SCRUM

When we made the switch over to SCRUM, we did so with no one on the team having any prior experience with any type of Agile development. That was not a real problem. The problem was that not all the team members bought into the various Agile concepts, such as time-boxed iterations, estimating by providing story points, and not planning every aspect of the project to the last degree up front.

Adding Developers

When I say we added developers, I am not talking 1–2 developers. Our organization bought into the concept that "nine women can make a baby in one month." Basically we took our team from 6 full-time developers who all averaged one year experience with the company to 12 developers. Not only did we bring on 6 new developers, which meant interviewing hundreds of candidates, we did this while the project was in midcycle. As the new developers came onboard (about 1–2 a week for a month), we had to not only complete our assigned tasks, but we had to ramp them up on the project. I would estimate that we lost a solid two to three months of productivity bringing on these new developers.

Scope Creep of Massive Proportions

Face it, every project has scope creep; it is the nature of the beast. It is up to the team to manage the extent of scope creep you allow into your project. A good team with solid leadership knows how to persuade management to keep the changes to a minimum. Sadly, this was not the case for our team. When we started the project, we got assurances from the management team; we were going to do a "complete replication, plus one feature." As we all know, this turned out to be a little white lie. As the numerous feature requests rolled in, our development manager simply let them get added on to the list. We never forced our business leaders to make the tough choice of what goes and what stays. About six months into the development, we had increased our scope by about 40–50%, yet the date did not change.

Team In-fighting

As the months rolled on, the frustration began to mount within the team. This led to a pretty bad case of team in-fighting. When the project started, we were a "band of brothers," we went to lunch as a team, we had beers after work as a team, and we even hung out on the weekends from time to time. Somewhere along the way, this all changed. The reason for the change was simple. As the team was failing, we all tried to do what we could to help save the team. This meant we stepped on each other's toes, meant we went around each other's backs, and worst of all, it meant we started to blame each other for things that were out of our control. At the end of the day, we all had the best intentions at heart, but that was not enough. This did NOT help the team in any way....

Most teams could probably weather any one of the above and still have a shot at being successful. However, for each additional issue your team faces, the chances of success decrease. As I look back on this project, it is pretty clear we never had a fighting chance to succeed. Learn from my mistakes and don't let this happen to you and your project.

How to Be Successful

Being successful in the IT industry is actually easier than you may think. I believe it takes more effort to fail than it does to succeed, not to say that being successful is easy. Being successful is all about the "little things" and how you pay attention to the details. Over my career I have had to learn what creates a successful developer and a successful project.

Become a Teacher/Mentor

Everyone has heard the saying, "Give a man a fish and he eats for a day; teach a man to fish and he eats for a lifetime." This saying holds especially true in software development. If you find yourself in a position where you have more experience or knowledge than someone else on your team, it is your responsibility to mentor that person until he or she has a solid understanding in that particular area. If you do this, you will actually realize two things. First, you just helped to make someone on your team more knowledgeable, which in turn makes your team better. Second, you will have taught yourself a few things, in particular in how to better convey your thoughts.

Become a Continuous Learner

If you feel like what you know today will allow you to be successful for the rest of your career, you are in for a rude awakening. Take a look around; the technology we use today is vastly different than the technology used even two years ago. Because of this fact, if you do not set out every day to learn something new, you will fall behind. Learning something new can be as little as learning a new design pattern or as big as learning an entire new language.

Network, Network, Network

Expanding your network is almost as important as being a continuous learner. The benefits of building a large network are two-fold. First, having people you can contact when you have a question or issue is invaluable. Almost every technical issue you will encounter in your career has already been solved by someone else. If you have a large group of peers you can reach out to for help, you can save yourself both time and heartache. The other reason is that throughout your career you are going to move from job to job. When this happens, having a large network can pay huge rewards. The simplest example of this is having the ability to tap this network to find your job.

Have Fun, Love What You Do

The number one tip I can give about being successful is to have fun. Find something you enjoy and are passionate about and do it. If you ever find yourself in a position where you dread doing your job or going to work, then move on to something else and become passionate about it.

As a parting shot, if I could provide one piece of advice to anyone who is looking to get into the software industry, it is this: Find something you love, pour your heart and soul into your work, and don't look back.

⮞

Lessons from the Trenches

By Chris G. Williams, Senior Consultant and Technology Evangelist, Magenic

I'm supposed to start this off by telling you, dear reader, a little bit about who I am, where I work, etc. So, my name is Chris G. Williams, and I can honestly say I have the privilege of working with some of the best folks in the industry. I'm also proud to say that I share an employer with a fair number of those same people.

I am a Microsoft MVP working for Magenic Technologies as a Senior Consultant and Technology Evangelist, but I also work with the greater technical community on a regular basis via INETA (the International .NET

Association) and the numerous .NET User Groups, Code Camps, online communities, and technical conferences both small and large around the country. I also tech-edit books for O'Reilly Media; write the occasional article for CoDe Magazine; and pretty much live my life via social media, stretched between Twitter, Facebook, and my blog.

You may be wondering, as I often find myself doing, how exactly I got to this point. How did I become someone who gets invited to travel across the country to speak at community events and write essays in consulting books?

Ultimately, it was a combination of good and bad career decisions, along with a willingness to go and speak pretty much anywhere and at any event (no matter how large or small). I've also spent a lot of time cultivating a strong network of friends and colleagues who sometimes had more faith in me than I did.

I started writing code when I was nine years old, and I'm doing exactly what I have wanted to do my entire life. I never really had any other career aspirations. (It always amazes me when I meet people in this industry who never touched a computer before college.) Of course, I had no idea what a consultant or a technology evangelist was back then; I just knew I wanted to write software.

My career path looks a little like one of those "Family Circus" dotted-line cartoons that wanders all over the neighborhood. So far, I've developed software for the U.S. Navy (as an enlisted man and a civilian), publicly and privately held software companies, big tobacco, big oil, retail auto parts, and a dot-com failure. I've worked at more than one place that could rightly be termed a sweatshop and eventually ended up at Magenic, where I've been ever since. In abbreviated form, my career path looks something like this: I developed fleet software again as a DoD civilian employee. After that, I pulled my first stint as a consultant (working at a well-known tobacco company and then a not-so-well-known dot-com failure). In the post-9/11 tech industry drought, I left consulting for a "safe" job leading a development team at a well-known automotive parts retailer. I followed that with some time on a product team at a large software company, shipping a couple versions of a specialized Web application. Eventually, I returned to consulting only to wind up at the worst (and shortest) job of my entire career. After leaving it, I joined Magenic, where I've been ever since.

So, you can probably tell I love what I do, but it wasn't always good. I've definitely made a few mistakes along the way. Some of those mistakes were just bad career choices, while others were due to my own inexperience. I'd like to share a couple of the lessons I learned the hard way, so you won't have to.

I Call This Lesson "Listen to Your Friends…"

I had been away from consulting for a few years, and while I enjoyed the relative stability of being an employee, I missed the pace and challenge of consulting. I also really missed the money. It's a trade-off. With risk comes reward. Consultants, as a general rule, make more money than traditional in-house developer employees do.

In my case, I had a good job with a great team and challenging work, but I was making significantly less per year than I had been a few years prior as a consultant. The conventional wisdom at the time was something along the lines of, "Yes, but that was during the dot-com boom, and nobody makes that kind of money anymore." So imagine my surprise when after a chance meeting at a .NET User Group, I found myself across the table from the development manager at a small consulting company staring at a number that was roughly $30,000 more than I was making at that time.

I knew a couple of guys who had previously worked there. Turns out, they had both left. Each of them tried to convince me that, just maybe, this place might not be a good fit for me (or anyone, for that matter.) They shared stories of their frustrations with the management and the draconian policies in place. Naturally, I didn't listen to a word of it. Maybe it was arrogance on my part, or maybe it was just the lure of a significant pay raise; either way I was convinced that what happened to them wouldn't possibly happen to me. I could handle it.

To their credit, they actually lasted a lot longer there than I did.

To put it nicely, it was a nightmarish vision of software developer hell. The project managers were a vicious bunch that would deliberately hold onto bad news until status meetings so they could publicly eviscerate whatever developer was responsible. I saw this happen on more than one occasion. Documentation wasn't just a big deal, it was everything. Time tracking was literally more important than the tasks you were tracking. Functional design docs, technical design docs, and requirements docs each numbered in the hundreds of pages. I spent most of my first month generating documentation by writing code (class and method definitions) in a Word document.

I think I lasted three months, maybe. One day, I went in and quietly cleaned out my desk, emailed the manager on an eight-minute delay (giving myself just enough time to get out of the building), and walked out, never looking back. I also apologized to both of my friends for not listening to them. I found out later there was a pool on how long I would last there, though I'm not sure either of them actually collected.

There's another lesson I would like to share, which may seem counterintuitive to the first one, but life is full of experiences that make you re-evaluate everything you know on a regular basis.

I Call This Lesson "Listen to Your Friends, but Verify Everything..."

I was on a new project with another consultant who had been with the company for a while. Due to a schedule conflict, I started the project a couple of days after the other consultant. Upon my arrival, he informed me that since he was the lead on the project, he had gone ahead and gotten all the necessary requirements and UI mockups and had allocated the work between us. He would be doing the "plumbing," and I would be focusing on the user interface.

It all sounded okay to me, so I dived right in and started working on the application, slavishly adhering to the mockups and handling all the data-binding code in the UI. After a couple of weeks, I proudly announced to the client that I had a prototype I was ready to show them.

We set up a meeting, gathered the team, and I proceeded to step through all the work I had done. The room was so quiet you could literally hear a pin drop. I looked around the room, expecting to see a room full of people admiring my work but instead saw a room full of people who were all staring at their boss, who looked like he wanted to kill someone.

In between very deliberate breaths, he explained that my work looked EXACTLY like the application the company already had that we were supposed to be redesigning. After a few more deep breaths, he asked why I didn't follow the story cards.

"Story cards?" I said, looking first at him and then my fellow consultant, who had developed a strong urge to stare silently at his fingernails at that moment. "I just followed the mockups." His reply, minus a few expletives, was that the "mockups" I used were in fact screenshots from the old application and that everything I needed was in the story cards application.

As it turns out, not only had he not done a very good job of gathering requirements, but he wasn't even the lead on the project. I found out later that I was supposed to be and didn't know it. We eventually made good on the design and made the client happy, but that initial disaster set the tone for most of my relationship with the client.

A little due diligence on my part would have gone a long way. Lesson learned.

Consultopia: The Ideal Consulting Firm

Is perfection possible? No. But it doesn't mean we shouldn't try.

In life, it is natural to imagine, at least at times, what a more idealized state of your life might look like. You are driving in traffic, and you imagine how much better the roads would be if only you could just add a lane here and there to make your and everyone else's commute shorter and therefore life better! If only the highway were arranged in a manner that made it possible for you to get done what you needed, with a minimum of obstructions that, at least in theory, don't really need to exist.

This principle, applied to how consulting firms work, is something I like to call *Consultopia*—a term that describes an idealized technology consulting firm where consultants and clients engage in the ultimate "win-win" exchange. A place where consultants do meaningful work, and clients receive consultants who are engaged, own the work like it's their own, and because of mutually beneficial exchange, both are excited about the possibilities that the results of the work can bring.

⁓

Foundations

A principle of Consultopia is that people do best when they are in a position to thrive. To get there, more basic needs, like food, shelter, safety, and a sense of community, need to be well in place. Although this can be tough in an environment where the whims of business are tough to control, it is, nevertheless, one of the functions that differentiates a *contracting* firm, where employment is based on "is a client willing to pay this consultant right now," from a *consulting* firm, where concerns are separated, allowing demand generation to do its job (generate and produce demand) to a degree that allows the consultants to do their jobs (provide good advice) without constantly worrying about whether there will be work after the next engagement ends.

In Consultopia, demand is always running ahead of supply, even during bad times when demand is hard to generate. Although this concept may sound hard to turn into reality—remember, information technology is an area that helps cut costs (helps in recessions) and expands markets (helps in expansions)—in theory, demand for information technology should be robust despite the economic cycle. Consultopia focuses on how to reach out to executives who need to save money, helps them find ways to do so using technology, and relentlessly delivers on that objective.

Of course, no version of Consultopia could ever work if people don't deliver. Simply liking jobs or having interesting work isn't enough. Engagement is a combination of interesting work and willingness to go the extra mile to execute and make results happen. In Consultopia, all consultants treat engagements as though they are their own personal startups because the work is meaningful, because they feel safe from harm, and because they know that to keep the "cool work" coming, a high standard of excellence in delivery is required. A degree of excellence so high that even if a coworker makes a mistake, the team picks up the slack so that the firm as a whole does not suffer.

To put it another way, Consultopia is not a place for slackers. In fact, to the slacker who just wants to hang out and collect a check, it will feel much more like *dystopia* than Consultopia. Consultopia will assure you are not being physically threatened at work, not sexually harassed, not embarrassed or ridiculed in front of your peers, and so forth, but it won't shelter you from the effects of not treating your work seriously. Although you can expect to be treated with respect, as an adult, and not talked down to, you won't be treated with "kid gloves" either.

In other words, Consultopia exists on the founding principle that coworkers will treat each other with a minimum level of respect and an expectation of being responsible adults. Presuming you are able to meet this standard—one, thankfully, most good software engineers can meet—certain other principles help make the place work.

Upon this foundation, my view of Consultopia depends on three main principles that are deeply ingrained in the culture of the company (see Figure A-1). The first principle, Financial Transparency, rests on the premise that resource allocation is so important that the light of day ought to permeate how each dollar, euro, or yen flows through the company. The second principle, Community of Professionals, rests on the idea that the best work gets done with well-adjusted individuals who work well with others and can check most of the more "dinosaur brain"-based impulses at the door. The last principle, A Mission with Purpose, rests on the fact that people do better work when they are engaged not only by self-interest, but by broader goals that the company deems of interest to a broader community bigger than itself.

Figure A-1 Three principles of a perfect consulting firm.

Financial Transparency

No firm that respects its consultants expects them to accept, as a matter of faith, that the company is solvent, especially in bad times. Good consultants operate on the following principle: Either I know how well the company is doing and therefore how secure my job is, or I assume that the moment I hit the bench, my job is probably at risk. Good consulting firms, because they want to keep and retain good consultants, (1) communicate the financial status of the firm to keep people apprised and in touch with reality and (2) incent consultants in a manner that makes them have a stake in improving the firm's financial position—beyond job security (something that good consultants can easily find elsewhere in the market). Such firms are clear on everything from profitability to bank balances to sales pipelines. This information, in turn, allows a consultant to make an informed decision about whether to stay or go after a given assignment is over.

Bench Policy Transparency

Of course, no consultant should expect to be able to sit on the bench for an extended period of time and not add value, but on the other hand, if the firm is going to fire you the moment you hit the bench, the consultant has been *conned out of risk premium.* Let's put it this way, if you were to accept an hourly position of a fixed contract length, you would demand an amount of money to allow you to even out the periods when you are not working. This is the basis on which most independent consultants who are not affiliated with a firm set their rates. When a firm says "no bench" after someone accepts a salary, what is really happening is that terms are being changed, usually unilaterally, taking away the risk premium. Although the courts will not generally accept such a situation as highway robbery, such snookering of risk premium from consultant to consulting firm does represent a transfer of risk and therefore value.

No good relationship is founded on such a lie. By hiring employees, the consulting firm gains a loyalty and predictability that it would not receive if it operated as a body shop. Such firms are generally able to charge higher rates and sell better work than body shops. In Consultopia, such firms make the risk/reward clear and compensate on a level consummate with the risk, clearly communicating along the way what the financials are.

The best firms communicate clearly what the bench policy is so that the consultants who work for them can evaluate, in the sunshine of reality, what their best deal is. Firms with something to hide usually try to obscure this as much as possible. If you ask a few questions about the policy on this kind of matter, it should not be too difficult to determine whether you work for a good firm or a firm that profits from transferring your risk premium into its profit.

Paycheck Transparency

This next principle is much more controversial. In fact, it scares the heck out of most human resources people, who suddenly worry what might happen in a world that is transparent about what people make. Worries about lawsuits, worries about privacy concerns, and all sorts of issues related to doing something this different from normal practice abound whenever this topic is brought up.

There are all sorts of reasons people come up with not to publish such things. However, there are serious benefits as well. First of all, without the mystery or secrecy, a lot of controversy could be handled up front. Any decision to pay someone very much more than anyone else would have to be strongly justified because there would be no refuge for hiding the decision. In essence, the market would come much closer to clearing; that is, the correct price for an individual's "unit of labor" is much more likely to be correct when it is made in broad consideration of other marketplace information.

As far as privacy is concerned, I'm not sure this issue really holds water. Most people can guess a range by title. And frankly, such information usually gets published anyway, albeit from rumor mills, Web sites like glassdoor.com, and other backroom ways. When this information is released, the biggest thing that will occur in a well-run company is a shrug, a little like suddenly learning everyone's shoe size.

When you really think about it, obscuring salary information preserves a couple of things: a little privacy and the ability of management to make decisions that, when shown in the sunshine, would not be otherwise justified by logic and reason. Usually, these are things like keeping private the salaries of people hired some years ago when the market was low while paying newer people more money as the market improves. Given that the information tends to get out anyway, such tactics rarely work. Make the information public, justify the differences, and if not justified, make the adjustments required to make them justified.

Bill Rate Transparency

On a related note, consultants should be *very* aware as to what bill rates their services are being charged out at. Many firms make this information available in internal reports, but many do not. This kind of obfuscation almost never works out well.

Again, information tends to leak. Bill rate information tends to be prominently displayed on consulting contracts, and these contracts, at some point, end up on a fax machine someone was using to send an expense report or something like that. And if the information does not get out that way, clients themselves, who are harder to control sometimes (much to our dismay), will occasionally leave such things lying around on desks during meetings. Sooner than later, rate information always tends to leak.

The usual reason a company might keep this information secret is fear that if a consultant sees how much money he or she is generating, that person may ask for more money. This is an understandable fear—to some degree. One of the reasons I wrote this book was to help consultants understand the economics of the industry so that when they find out that the bill rate they charge for, when multiplied by the billable hours in a year, is a lot more than their salary, they understand why the difference exists. It is incumbent on company management to help consultants understand why this difference exists because there are indeed good reasons for justifying the taxes, training money, and overhead that have to exist to run a firm.

Of course, some firms charge a hefty premium but fail to deliver on the things that hefty premium should bring them, such as some level of bench, better quality work, training, equipment, and so forth. Although I understand why they would want to keep the information secret, doing so is really a good indicator of a firm with something to hide, which means you should be *very* wary.

How Transparency Is a Win-Win Deal

Financial transparency is a win-win deal for consultant and company. You get to know your clearing price, which gives you a piece of the picture in understanding your market value. The consulting firm benefits to the degree that after the information is public, it is a lot easier to explain any salary differentials that come up (that is, people who bill higher rates probably justify higher salaries). Although such transparency does not guarantee conflict avoidance because there will always be people who are unhappy with where they are, the important part is that it brings such problems out in the open, versus in the background, where they simmer. Efficient markets assume both sides can do reasonable price discovery; limiting price discovery causes market distortion, which is really the source of most issues as they relate to dissatisfaction with pay and benefits.

⮑

Community of True Professionals

Many firms that have serious dysfunctions tend to have ingrained a sense of "us versus them" that makes any kind of collaboration very difficult. Sometimes it is management versus technologists; sometimes it is developers versus quality assurance, as well as many other common forms. The reality of the situation is that once respect for your colleagues breaks down and you start assuming the worst about their intentions, it is awfully hard to focus on the client politics that you normally need to focus on navigating. It is bad enough having client politics that present one set of issues that are a known job hazard; negotiating two is crippling.

How does this happen? The first place to look is in the mirror—admitting that you, I, and every other professional makes mistakes from time to time. This step is key because when you start to become aware of your own imperfections, if you are truly honest with yourself, the imperfections of others maybe won't look so bad!

Another key part of this process—and this takes a lot of discipline for technology people (including myself!)—is to realize that just because you are good at what you do, needing reasonably high intelligence to do it well, it does not make you the master of every problem in the known universe. Knowing and being aware of your own limitations and allowing for the skills and experience of others to complement your own are key to working well with others. A great way to annoy your account executives, project managers, and QA people is to tell them how to do their jobs. I can only imagine they like that as much as you like them telling you how to code!

The Corporate Immune System

Of course, presuming you are not doing your own level best to up the jerk factor at the office, the ideal consulting firm has an "immune system" of sorts that rejects, at least eventually, the people who Bob Sutton was talking about when he published *The No Asshole Rule*. Although ideally you would find out whether someone is, for lack of a better word, an asshole in the hiring process, the nature of assholes is that just like vampires, they tend to be good at camouflaging themselves, revealing their true nature only after firmly ensconced into position.

In good firms that lack a critical quantity of these types of individuals, such people tend to stick out like a sore thumb when they start to act out. Such people survive in good firms for only so long, after which the system will reject their behavior. Ultimately, the person either gets fired or, more likely, finds out that such tactics don't work, quickly leaving to find a new place/victim where his or her tactics are more likely to work (see Chapter 2, "The Seven Deadly Firms").

We Are All Adults Here

When we can get to a place that, while not "asshole-proof," actively has defenses against them, we then move to a place where each and every person is respected as a fellow professional. This means, of course, that we expect coworkers to be able to deal with reality as it is, not as they want it to be—part of why financial transparency is important. It means no "kid glove" treatment, which can be harsh but helps keep people rooted in reality.

But this concept is more than that. It is really part of how people walk, talk, and act in management. It means that although people may be above or below you in a well-run company, it rarely *feels* that way. While there will be differences in responsibility levels, reflective of skills and attributes of those individuals, simply put, the better the organization, the less rank matters—and the more reality matters—in how decisions are made. Not only will people be able to operate with more dignity (that is, not kissing the ring of the boss to keep him or her happy), but decisions will be *better*.

Evidence-Based Decision Making

When you get used to making decisions based on data and evidence, rather than persuasion capabilities and politics, you start to wonder how and why anyone would do things any differently. Admittedly, making decisions via data was not always possible. Without systems capable of measuring performance, that is, good *evidence*, rank and relationship become the only real mechanisms, better than raw chance perhaps, for making decisions. Inertia is powerful!

In consulting, however, we have ample ways to measure performance. We can measure the effectiveness of sales by looking at revenue and profit margin, for example. Engagement management can be measured by client retention. Consultants can be measured by client satisfaction surveys and utilization reports. Recruiters can be measured by close ratios, successful hires, and so forth. Estimators can be measured by how accurate estimates are. Tools exist to capture each and every one of these measurements. Any firm that isn't using these tools is really making a choice to be less evidence-based than it could be and, thus, less effective.

A Mission with Purpose

It is a sad, sad commentary that the chief goal of many organizations is simply to increase the shareholder value of the organization—that is, increase profits and therefore returns. Although such sentiment rarely exists directly on the mission statement, per se, for most organizations, it is the understood goal. While most companies tend to have mission statements that sound noble, the reality—and in fact, for publically traded companies, the *charter*, the reason for existence—is to, as "Chainsaw Al" Dunlap so eloquently put it (ironically enough, as he was looting is own company), "To Create Shareholder Value, Period."

What's Wrong with Money?

Frankly, as much as I reject almost everything Al Dunlap purported to stand for in the 1990s, when he was popularizing the idea of creating profits by firing everyone, I did like the simplicity of mission in his statement about shareholder value. I liked it because it was in such contrast to the mission statements of that era—and for that matter, present day 2009. No dishonesty about whether the company exists to make better light bulbs or to "advance the state of the art" or any such nonsense. Companies exist to make the generation of filthy lucre more efficient.

The good or ill of such a goal can be debated—and often is. But what I find striking is the fact that so few companies actually have "create sustained and ever-growing profits" as their mission statement, when in fact, that is what it is. To me, it begs the question of why exactly do we have mission statements in the first place?

The Purpose of Mission Statements

Of course, when you look carefully, mission statements are not there to state the mission of the organization. In most cases, Al Dunlap's quote about shareholder value, not the text of the mission statement, actually captures the real mission. The real purpose of a mission statement is to obscure the reality and provide the illusion that there is some purpose *other* than economic for a corporation to exist. Such statements are, in effect, a tool of propaganda, designed to help create a sense of engagement among a salaried workforce.

The goal of most mission statements is to make the mission of the organization less transparent. Why would an organization that purportedly respects its people lie about the purpose of the company in the first place? Well, would you really be motivated as a nonshareholder to work really hard to make other people, people who probably don't care that much about you, rich? Of course not. Not nearly as motivated as you would be toward something with a higher purpose, such as "advancing the state of the art in technology," or something like that.

"But I Can Do Charity in My Spare Time"

The argument someone would typically make in defending the idea of a good mission being simply "create shareholder value" is that money itself is just an instrument that represents value. This is an argument I can respect. It is not evil or good; it is just a convenient and liquid form of value that individuals can use to further the ends that they, as individuals, deem important. Why not leave "mission" to charities, nonprofits, and others who receive donations from individuals who are successful in the for-profit side of the economy, where people work for companies, all of which have a mission statement that goes something like "we exist to generate larger and larger piles of cash."

From a human potential standpoint, there are some huge problems with this approach. As it stands, very few people, mostly in Western countries, can afford to really give much to charity or invest much more than money into their work. Moreover, there are many, many people who are passionate about causes who would like to participate but simply by the nature of their day-to-day work have little left to really make much of an impact.

The Paradox of Nonprofits

Most nonprofits, because they are so starved of resources, do not benefit from the talent that is available in the general marketplace because they are generally outbid by for-profit companies. What ends up happening is that the strongly motivated take the lower pay to work for the nonprofit. Anyone who is less than strongly motivated—perhaps willing to get involved in something with real purpose but may still need convincing—generally ends up working in a normal for-profit company by default.

Worse yet, because of the focus on the mission (remember, a nonprofit selects for more "true believers"), the staff at a nonprofit tend to be people who are not all that focused on financials at all, beyond perhaps working to get additional grant money. Over time, this relationship to money—as it is something given to them, not something earned—becomes part of the organizational culture, and most of the talent of the nonprofit ends up spending most of its time getting more funding, not making the organization more efficient (there are exceptions, of course, but the trend is very common).

Toward a Better Mission

So if the nonprofit model is less than optimal, what might be better? Muhammad Yunus, the Nobel Prize–winning economist, wrote a book, *Creating a World Without Poverty*, that, among other things, describes his Grameen Bank organization. This for-profit enterprise makes a compromise: His investors get a moderated rate of return, but the bulk of the profits go into supporting the mission, which in the case of Grameen Bank is "to enable the poor, especially the poorest, to create a world without poverty."

This concept, which he calls a *social business*, actually has some great potential. There are noted downsides, of course, in that such businesses do not have access to capital seeking a high rate of return. However, to compensate for that, such businesses have the *advantage* of having a real principled mission that can attract talent that, while wanting to earn a market wage in a real business, has a desire to do something other than enrich investors. In industries that are less financial capital-intensive, and more intellectual capital-intensive, like software, this is a killer advantage.

We see this even today in how companies such as Microsoft (through the Bill and Melinda Gates Foundation) and Google both invest a lot of their profit into humanitarian causes, allowing their employees to at least have a sense that their efforts are likely to help a mission beyond making some rich guy even richer. Over time, it is more and more likely that even consulting organizations will start to have the same kind of orientation after more of them see the advantage of not just having, but living, a higher order mission.

⤳

Does "Consultopia" Exist?

In a word, no, Consultopia does not exist. The purpose of this appendix is to set a goal—a goal that I think we, as consultants working in this field, as well as owners of consulting companies, should try to push our companies to strive for. True, there will be some companies that are closer than others, but a human reality is that no company is perfect, and if you are in a company that meets at least a reasonable number of the principles set forth in this appendix, you are probably better off than you would be working for the companies described in Chapter 2.

In fact, I would go so far as to take anyone who claims to have built a Consultopia with a huge grain of salt. Before you go work there, perhaps quitting a reasonably good position in a company that at least tries to meet some of these standards, you should look long and hard to make sure you are not being sold a bill of goods. Like a nomad being fooled by the mirage of an oasis in the desert, being fooled by those claiming to have the Promised Land can cause you more harm than good.

⤳

Works Cited

Yunus, M. (2009). *Creating a World Without Poverty*, Jackson, TN: PublicAffairs.

A CONSULTING LEXICON

Every industry has its own indecipherable jargon; tech consulting is no exception.

To make sure that other people have a hard time understanding what we do, we often invent language so we can tell the insiders from the outsiders. Okay, perhaps that is not *the* reason we invent language, but regardless, it is a good idea to acquaint yourself with some terms so you can understand exactly what it means when someone says, "Let's make sure the presales on this small-ball gig isn't overexposed, creating a resource romance too early in the cycle."

A

Agile A family of software methodologies that focus on transparency, results, continuous improvement, honesty, and embracing change—that is, the world as it is, not as we wish it to be. Because it admits that the "process" of software solution development is people-based and usually nondeterministic and therefore hard to negotiate in a fixed-bid manner, it scares the heck out of people who see the world in terms of fixed contracts and certainty of outcome. Generally defined as methodologies, including XP, Scrum, Spiral, and others, which are highly capable of integration of what you learn during a project into an evolving project plan.

Although the Agile community is often accused of engaging in faith-driven development (FDD) as it relates to their methodology, the alternative, Waterfall, with its GANTT charts that specify during which hour a developer will go to the bathroom in three years, turns out to be the pinnacle of faith-driven development. Waterfall pretends, with all the hubris in the world, to predict every detail of an application before a single line of code is written or idea is tested.

Sadly, Waterfall projects eventually have to embrace the same kinds of change that Agile ones do. Unfortunately, in most circumstances, the additional work required to handle the change is paid by the developer in the form of free overtime and weekend work.

Architect   Latin term that means "person who no longer writes code." More seriously, an architect is most commonly the person who designs systems (in the application architect case) or designs an ecosystem for multiple systems to work together (in the enterprise architect case).

Although the former description may be an unfair characterization in some cases, some architects really are in touch with the realities of development and do a great job. However, sadly, there do exist (many) companies that employ architects who have not touched a line of code since the first Clinton administration, and these people actually make decisions about how code gets written. Employing this person is, of course, very much like hiring someone who once did surgery 15 years ago to do brain surgery on your mother, using the same rusty techniques and tools from that era, mixed with a few things he read about in a journal article here and there.

B

Backlog   The amount of work currently under contract but not yet billed. Companies get very nervous when backlog gets low because a dropping backlog usually is a precursor to a spate of low utilization that generally leads to layoffs.

Bench   The state of a consultant when he or she is not billing at a client. Although bench time on occasion is a good way to get a chance to pick up some new skills or get to work on some cool internal projects, even in a well-run firm that can afford a bench, it is not a place where you really want to be for long.

In nearly every consulting firm, at review time, utilization—that is, the ratio of billing hours to overall hours—is a key performance measure on which your raise will be determined. Having a ton of bench time does not help you in such a case.

Being on the bench in a firm with declining sales is especially risky because the amount of time from "hit the bench" to "layoff" is usually contracted drastically.

Also known as "the Beach," "Between Projects," "Consultants in Transition," or "The Clock Is Ticking."

Billable Hour   A unit of work from a consultant. Unfortunately, the term gets married to the term *resource*, which leads to a mode of thinking that one billable hour from one resource is equivalent to a billable hour from any other resource, which any experienced technology person knows to be laughably incorrect.

The amount of productivity from one billable hour, when dealing with programmers, often varies by over 1000 percent. This variability, because it is difficult to determine by traditional methods like resumes or interviews, often gets randomly distributed across projects, and this is one of the reasons why results from actual software projects have so much variation.

Body Shop   A firm that provides people for money, without much discretion beyond what is claimed on a resume. Most body shops don't really know what the skills of their people are, beyond what is on the resume and is matched through keyword search. Rates are lower because a body shop is really just a recruiting operation and a temp agency that provides labor. Because technical capability is hard to assess, especially for recruiters who lack technical background most of the time, the quality of people from body shops ranges from highly variable to routinely very low. Also see *Contracting*.

❧
C

Career Path   The trajectory or arc of your career that leads to your being able to leverage your experiences to do more and more meaningful work as you progress through your career. It is important to note that even the most successful people have career paths that are not always straight up; setbacks will occur. Keys to success: leverage the setbacks, learn from them, but continue to pursue your career with enthusiasm and engagement.

Client   The lifeblood of each and every consulting firm and the main economic reason why consulting firms exist. Most good consulting firms do everything possible to act in the clients' best interests, finding a good "win-win" scenario where, when an engagement completes, clients get a solution that saves them money or makes them money far in excess of the fees charged by the consulting firm.

The best client relationships are truly partnerships, allowing both sides to experience profit from the deal, doing what they individually do best. This situation tends to break down when one side or another uses leverage to take advantage of the other, be it a consulting firm using the client as a dumpster engagement or the client demanding fee reductions when it gains knowledge that the consultancy just ended an engagement elsewhere and therefore is sensitive to further additions to its bench.

"Come to Jesus" Meeting   A meeting where some hidden problem is finally revealed to a stakeholder, usually with an expectation and bracing for something very bad to happen as a result. Such meetings tend to have a premeeting, a meeting to plan the premeeting, post meetings, and all sorts of ceremony, due to the stakes involved. They are usually the result of some combination of "yes man," "vampire," and "faith-driven development" converging with the inability to hide poor results any longer.

Consulting   The act of providing expert advice, assistance, and accountability for results from one person or organization (a consultancy) that has expertise or solution delivery capability to another organization (a client) that does not possess that expertise or solution delivery capability internally. The consultancy can then be in the expertise and solution delivery business, while clients can concentrate on what *they* are good at, which is typically something other than solution delivery or expertise in a given specialty (such as technology).

By contrast, contracting is about delivery of a particular person to a client that makes a specific order for a person who meets a certain specification. This practice, also known as *staff augmentation*, is not an exchange of high-order expertise or delivery capability, but an exchange of people, and is really a different business model. Both are valid business models, but because consulting has a higher premium attached to it, there often exists a motivation for contracting firms to call what they do *consulting* when it is, in fact, nothing more than *contracting* because it allows for the contracting firm to attempt to charge higher rates and attract a higher caliber of talent. This model usually works only in the short run, however, because contracting firms tend to see people as *resources* and generally do not have broader institutionalized expertise, methods, and group values that are required for effective solutions delivery.

Consultopia   The world's best consulting company. Noted for the fact that, just like Santa Claus, the Easter Bunny, and the Loch Ness Monster, it probably doesn't really exist.

Contracting   A business model, often confused with *consulting*, that relies on clients putting out "orders" for people (often called *resources*) that the contracting firm fills by finding contractors in the open market. Contracting firms provide people who work for hourly wages. Consultants provide solutions and expertise. See *Body Shop*.

Cycle   Usually referred to either as a "sales cycle" but can also mean "unit of work," as in "don't spend too many cycles chasing that bad deal." The former meaning refers to the process of finding work. Shorter sales cycles are good because that means business gets built faster. The longer the sales cycle is, all other things being equal, the more chances are that things can go wrong and that the project isn't really very important (that is, if it were important, there would be more urgency and, thus, not such a long cycle).

D

Delivery   The general term used to refer to the people who make good the promises made by the account management, sales, or demand generation side of the organization. Ideally, the latter are somehow incented to make sure the promises are realistic, such that the fees charged for delivery might actually be paid.

Documentation   Rarely read stacks of paper that are produced so that people can feel good about the actual product (software). Although not all documentation is bad, there is probably a right level of documentation that exists between the developer nirvana of *no* documentation at all (that is, if it was hard to write, it should be hard to understand) and the stereotypical PHB nirvana of three pages of documentation per line of code.

Dumpster Engagement   In some consulting companies, there exists one or more projects where low performers can be dumped and allowed to bill for an indeterminate amount of time, mostly because the person whose organization is paying for the work has "checked out" and could not care less whether anything really gets done. A good sign you are on a dumpster engagement is if, when you start the project, you seem to have lots of time to do very little and there seem to be no visible repercussions.

If you are a high performer, you might find such an engagement enjoyable for around a month, as you surf your way to the end of the Internet, write six open source projects, and blog like a maniac. However, doing nothing gets boring after a while, and after gaining a lot of weight from boredom, you usually seek to move off the engagement before you have to explain to your doctor why you gained 50 pounds in six months.

E–F

Engaged Employee   A person who works with focus, enthusiasm, proactivity, and persistence (Macey et al., 2008), usually from intrinsic incentives, that is, without obvious incentives related to cold hard cash. Engaged employees usually act on something they believe in, usually are not motivated by fear, usually have good relations with their coworkers, and usually have good reason to believe that they will be treated as dignified professionals and not peons in somebody's chess game.

Faith-Driven Development   A development practice also known as *code 'n pray* or *Waterfall*. It relies on an ever-knowing business analyst to write an Old Testament–like book called *The Requirements* or a noncoding architect to write a New Testament–like book called *The Design*. When they are done and cast in stone tablets, a developer (you) is called upon to code the system. The result is a situation that resembles the last chapter in the New Testament, called "Revelations," in which the forces of good and evil fight on a giant battlefield, with massive bloodshed (a process known as *Testing* or *Quality Assurance*). Afterward, there is a promise of a thousand years of utopia. Sadly, it seldom ends this well.

Fee Fight   In a case where a project is being fulfilled with multiple business units from a consulting firm, especially if those business units have different P&Ls, an internal fight often ensues for who gets the billable hours and credit for the fees generated from the engagement. Between offices or departments that lack trust, almost every issue where work together becomes required results in a fee fight. Also happens frequently when firms partner up.

Fixed-Bid Contract   A triumph of hope over experience for those who have done projects involving them and yet insist on continuing in this manner; it is the idea that you can fix costs for something where the product, in all but the most trivial cases, is not only barely defined, but probably subject to change.

Most clients who insist on fixed-bid contracts either (1) have little experience with software development, (2) just got burned by a different consulting company that was using them as cash cows/dumpster engagements and therefore actively distrust the entire industry, (3) have little interest in actually delivering useful software but just want to get it done, regardless of quality, or (4) simply refuse to acknowledge reality and choose to engage in magical thinking.

Although such contracts are understandable, it is incumbent on our industry to educate clients on why fixed-bid contracts do not work for all but the smallest projects. Sadly, because there will always be opportunist consulting firms that bank on a business model built on telling clients what they want to hear and then, through tools like forced overtime, delivering on shaky promises, it is a practice that is unlikely to end soon.

G

Go Native   The process some consultants go through when (1) they spend a ton of time at a client such that they start to identify as employees of the client or (2) regardless of time spent at a client, when the client's and consulting firm's interests cross (that is, hiring competitors), they stop representing the interests of the firm. Common in contracting firms acting as consulting firms, where the contractors who know the gig are simply trying to get hired and are mixed with people from the same firm who are under the impression that this is a consulting engagement, not multiple contractors on a project.

Guru   A developer with an industry-level reputation on one or more technical topics. Usually someone who has made a major contribution to a well-known product or open source project or has some other high-profile accomplishment appreciated by other developers.

H

Happy Consultant   A consultant who is paid well, doing work that matters, is mentally healthy, with supportive coworkers, and has a realistic schedule. A consultant who tends to be engaged in his or her occupation, which leads to amazing results. A happy consultant tends to be the kind of person who not only goes overboard for clients, but also goes out and evangelizes the merits of the firm he or she works for. See *Engaged Employee*.

Hired Scapegoat A consultant brought in for the specific purpose of becoming the official person to blame for things gone wrong on a project. A typical scenario is the two-and-one-half-year project that is going badly. All this time has gone by, and the CIO, in an attempt to keep his job and have someone to fall on the sword, hires a consulting firm to bill for six months, screw up, and take the blame when everything goes wrong.

Although such projects result in short-term billing, they are risky because lawsuits frequently result. This means that if the firm in question has any sort of assets after the big fail, they are gone, and the resulting consultants will be gone too. The best way to avoid a hired scapegoat gig is to watch for small firms that suddenly have impressive contracts with big companies, needing to expand from 2 to 30 people in a weekend. Although not all such engagements turn out to be of the hired scapegoat variety, it is not a bad idea to make sure and ask a few questions.

I–J–K

Independent A consultant who is not affiliated with a major firm and works through body shops, contracting organizations, or sometimes directly with clients to engage in development work. A great way to go if you are great at sales, marketing, self-discipline, accounting, and, oh yeah, technology work.

"Jesus" The alternative name of the salesperson hired in a recession to whom all the hopes of the organization are pinned. Rarely does this strategy work. No really good account executive in his or her right mind would walk away from a successful book of business and currently in-progress sales cycles (and as a result, expected income in the near term) for the prospect of building a new pipeline, which will take longer in a recession and therefore become lower or sporadic income in the near term.

L–M

Magical Thinking   In business, eschewing the information being provided by evidence and observation—probably because of some level of unpleasantness/bad news involved—and replacing that with things like hope and faith. Although hope and faith are nice from a disposition standpoint, failing to temper hope and faith with reality usually has devastating results when such hope and faith are used as an excuse not to communicate bad news.

> **Example:**
>
> *Project Manager:* Hey, the tasks on the project are being completed at three times what the estimates were. Maybe we should let the client know and re-estimate the system.
>
> *Engagement Manager:* That's okay, we just have to have *faith* that the team can catch up. If the client finds out about the problem, the whole project will be canceled.
>
> *Project Manager:* Eh, okay… let's *hope* it works out.
>
> …cut away, 6 months and one lawsuit later…
>
> *Engagement Manager:* Boy, it sucks to have to go to court and do all these depositions because we got sued.

Management   The people who arrange the delivery work or the people who arrange the people who arrange the delivery work. The contradiction in many firms is that consultants tend to have the lowest overhead, which means as little management as possible, yet that same pattern results in fewer management opportunities, especially for those cases in which the advancement path is perceived to be management.

The best firms find a way to combine management with billing, usually a model around engagement management that allows the "manager" to have a role that spans multiple projects, billing a little in each one and forming client relationships that make that person an essential leader in the firm.

N

Network   The group of people who are familiar with your work, your skills, and your capabilities who, based on evidence of work you have done, act as your advocate if and when you might need work in the future. Generally, it is best to build a network not when you need it, but when you don't. The best reason to be in consulting is that, despite some of the issues in this occupation (as there are with all others), you tend to grow a large and diverse network based on the nature of the work.

Nonsolicitation Agreement   A document, generally signed in blood when you join a consulting company (okay, I kid…a little), that says thou shalt not steal our clients or consultants if you ever leave—for at least a year. Unlike a noncompete, which is frequently unenforceable, nonsolicitation agreements are generally, in the United States, quite enforceable and often *are* enforced.

O–P

Overhead   People who work at a consulting company that neither sell work, bill work, or own the company. Probably the worst place to be during a recession because most consulting firms tend to remove nearly all overhead positions and operate with as few people as possible when numbers are declining.

Person   The proper term for the individual who works on a project. Contrast *resource*. People are the brilliant machines that, without programming, invent things on their own and find solutions to problems without always having to have a proscribed process to make it work. On the downside, they require food, breaks, motivation, and work best when given things to work on that, they feel, will help other people too.

PHB   Acronym for *Pointy Haired Boss*, from the "Dilbert" comic strip. This person typically refers to people as *resources* and, when firing people, might use a term like *rightsizing*.

Process   A series of steps designed to be repeated by others so results can occur regularly. Process is okay by itself, but when applied to the wrong disciplines, it can be a problem. This is especially important to those who would prefer to wish away the human element from the act of software development. To such people, process becomes the altar at which managers pray so that perhaps they can play a lot of golf rather than do the hard work of being leaders to a team and actually being responsible for inspiring the team to generate results.

Proprietary Development Methodology   A true mark of an ambitious consulting firm in the 1990s was the creation of its own proprietary software development methodology. Usually exists solely for marketing purposes in an attempt to distinguish its processes from the competition; such methodologies are rarely actually used.

Thankfully, there are plenty of methodologies that have actual usage, peer review, and lack of proprietary lock-in. RUP, Scrum, Agile, XP, and Lean, among others are all well-known, practiced methods that have delivered results for clients. Most modern technology consulting firms have moved beyond prop methodologies, realizing that *any* firm can rebrand such a thing, and therefore it is almost never a competitive advantage because execution, discipline, and talent matter much more than process.

To that end, most clients, after having been sold the false promise of prop methods for years, realize that there is virtually no upside in using an unproven proprietary methodology over the common peer-reviewed ones that have actual surveys of results behind them.

Purple Squirrel   The term for the mythical individual who meets the following requirement in a job ad: "Looking for a Java/C#/Erlang/SAP/FoxPro programmer (15 years of experience in each required) with 12 years of experience with the System.Linq.Expression namespace writing overloads of the Add method. Top-secret security clearance is required. Must have experience in the nonprofit environmental industry as well as 20 years of work in the oil services business working for companies like Halliburton. All these requirements must be met for your resume to be considered." This person is called a *purple squirrel* because, like the mythical creature, he or she does not really exist.

Most notably, a good way to judge whether a consulting company is really a consulting company or a body shop masquerading as a consulting company is to look at its job ads and determine how many look like purple squirrels. Consultancies have latitude to determine the requirements, whereas body shops take specs from procurement groups that might put in an "order" that sounds like something you might hear when the person in line in front of you is putting forth a particularly obnoxious coffee order ("Double skim gingerbread half-caf soy with a bit of room latte").

Q–R

Resource   A horrible term for people invented by a horrible, pointy-haired boss at some point in the 1980s when the thought of thinking of employees as *people* became too much for his soul to bear when he started to downsize (or *rightsize* or *jollysize* or *happysize*—whatever term for *firing* is currently in vogue).

A sure sign of a total jerk is the frequency with which he or she uses the term *resource* to refer to *people*. The term tries to productize people into something that lazier consulting firms can then attempt to slap a SKU code on (imagine a SKU and a bar code on the forehead of something like a "C# Resource"). This term helps perpetuate the project management fiction that people are interchangeable units that a project manager can rearrange when trying to get projects done. In essence, this term is a tool for helping delay the reality that people are not units, but unique individuals, and that you can't manage projects by GANTT chart alone.

Resource Romance   The condition in which a client "falls in love" with a person too early in the sales process. Some sales pursuits are sufficiently long that the person who is introduced to the client early probably won't be available by the time the client makes a decision. Resource romances are tough because the deal becomes dependent on a particular person, which makes for a difficult problem when the process of closing the deal tends to be longer than the shelf life of the consultant.

If you ever wonder why some sales groups don't want to push you into a sales process in the first or second meeting, having lost a deal because of a resource romance once or twice might help you understand such hesitancy.

Rightsize   About one of seven dozen terms (like *happysize, jollysize,* and *orgasmosize*) that really means "you're fired!"

ROI (Return on Investment)   The goal of every project you will ever do in consulting. Nobody spends money on a project for charity purposes.

S

Sales   Generally speaking, the part of the organization chartered with generating demand. Typically via networking with prospects, cold calling, eating a lot of lunches, and playing a lot of golf, an account executive who does his or her job will work with clients to help them find ways to leverage technology to either save money or increase revenue.

Of course, for every good sales professional in consulting, there is probably someone who works the politics of the organization to find clients from whom he or she can simply milk commissions without adding any value whatsoever; see *Vampire*.

Smallball   The process of spending three months and several weeks of dedicated time writing proposals to chase a deal for three days' worth of work worth a total of $1,500, with a vague promise of work "in the future." Any project pursuit in which there is a reasonable chance that you could have actually completed the work being sold during the pursuit process (for example, six months of pursuit chasing a one-month project) is probably *smallball*.

Having lots of smallball is the sign of an unfocused sales group that is not doing a particularly good job of qualifying potential clients before investing lots of time into rabbit holes. Although everyone has to start somewhere, and doing some smallball to break into clients is a hazard of building a technology consulting business, a good way to know whether a firm is in trouble is if *most* deals are four- and five-figure deals for less than four weeks.

T

T&E (Time and Expenses)   Because a consultant sells hours, generally, you report your time on a regular basis so clients can be billed. If you are traveling, you also have expenses (hotel and so on) that need to be billed. Failure to report time and expenses causes serious billing problems; most consultants need to be reminded only once to make sure to report such information on time because consequences of report failure are usually pretty severe.

Technology, The Business Of   What some technology consulting firms forget they are in the business of. When clients are looking to select a technology consulting firm, they are not looking for the firm that is the best at selling technology. Rather, they are looking for the most competent, creative, and disciplined technologists.

Because the struggle in many firms is selling work, there is often an unhealthy focus on that to the exclusion of focusing on being very excellent at delivery of work. Sadly, many firms become so sales-focused that they churn through clients, failing to build relationships because they treat delivery as an afterthought. If a firm fails to invest in delivery—spending to hire good, creative people who can make good on the promises of sales—the best sales group in the world will always be running uphill against a merely competent sales group who can bring in clients that a delivery organization will *retain for a long period of time.*

Time and Materials Contract   A contract that specifies that clients will pay you for your time and materials required to build a solution. Most such contracts are cancellable with a certain amount of notice but require payment for services rendered based on hours worked. Preferred to fixed-price contracts for solutions that have fixed scope because scope is rarely, if ever, fixed, even if it says so in the contract.

Transparency   The act of being honest and forthright with your clients, employees, and partners about the progress of a project, the financial health of the company, or other matters of consequence. Transparency thrives in scenario where participants in a market are engaging in win-win relationships. When information is hidden, the tendency is to use the secrecy as leverage to win rewards that are not due to the person or organization hiding the information. For example, hiding project status information results in being paid for work that isn't really being completed. Hiding financial health information during the interview process deprives incoming employees of risk premium (higher salaries or equity) they would ask for in exchange for moving to a less creditworthy company.

Lack of transparency is generally thought to be the root cause of the Mortgage Crisis of 2007–08, which is the major cause of the global recession being experienced as of the time this book went to publication in 2009.

U

Utilization   The ratio, expressed as a percent, of actual billable hours over total full-time hours (in a year, usually 2,080 or perhaps 2,080 minus holidays). Typically measured at an individual level, office level, and company level.

Utilization Target   In some organizations, you are given a target for your ideal rate of utilization. This number can be as high as 100 percent in sweatshops, to a more typical number around 80–90 percent, to a lower number if you have marketing or other responsibilities mixed into your job description. Generally speaking, nobody complains if you are over, and if you go under for long, it can be bad for your career at a given company.

V

Vampire   A person who, despite having the appearances of a sales professional, really sucks the blood (profit) from an organization, leaving about a year later with the organization in a severely weakened state. Such a person usually pretends to sell, but rather than doing the hard work of meeting clients, finding solution delivery opportunities, and then helping to form teams to capitalize on the opportunity, comes into a company and tries to make quota by inheriting accounts from other account executives who, after working for two months with such a person, get disgusted and leave.

The tragedy of this situation is that the person is generally great at managing up the organization (that is, can sell well enough to get in and convince management to let him or her manage some big accounts) but lacks the desire to apply these sales skills to any external audience.

Most good firms can discover a vampire in their presence somewhere between 3 and 12 months. However, the damage done is usually immense.

Vendor Management   The procurement department that works for larger organizations and sometimes is charged with hiring consultants. Although there are some good exceptions, frequently, such organizations have incentives to lower hourly rates, a practice that works against the interests of the firm given that there is no real equivalence between one billable hour and another (see *Billable Hour*).

Although most consultancies would be happy to work with vendor management programs that know how to properly judge consulting talent, or at least work with those who do, sadly, many such departments are run similarly to the way one would run a department for procuring steel to build a plant, which, in a business where the best results come from collaborative work over contract-driven work, tends not to work out well.

W

Walking Wounded, The   After a major layoff in a consulting firm, the people who remain (1) are usually very nervous about their jobs and (2) as a result, lose a good deal of productivity because of sinking engagement levels linked to dropping feelings of safety. This behavior usually occurs as a side effect of dropping sales during recessions, when the overall universe of opportunities is becoming more limited.

While in bad times layoffs may be a necessity, most good firms are transparent about how such layoffs will occur so people can at least plan for them (for example, "when our utilization is below *X*, we can allow *Y* of bench time" and so on). When there is no transparency, the walking wounded effect tends to be very high because the rumor mill replaces the actual information that might come out.

Waterfall   See *Faith-Driven Development*.

X–Y–Z

Yes Man (Woman)   Generally speaking, a project manager who reports great progress until about five days before the project ends, at which time he or she goes into the Witness Protection Program, vanishing from the earth. Some of the biggest settlement checks a consulting firm ever writes are caused by a yes man working on a project using one of the methodologies that depend on faith-driven development.

Works Cited

Macey, W. H., & Schneider, B. (2008). The meaning of the employee engagement. *Industrial and Organizational Psychology: Perspectives on Science and Practice.* Malden, MA: Wiley-Blackwell Publishing.

Index

A

account executives, 73-76

account managers. *See* engagement managers

accounting. *See* Smelzer and Melzer Accounting example; support personnel

adaptation to change, 274-276

adjustments in sales pipeline valuation, 138-139

advice from experts

adaptation to change, 274-276

independent consultants

consulting group formation, 288-289

definition of, 281-282

lessons learned, 293-297

resources for information, 289-290

skills needed for, 277-288

intermittent rewards, value of, 292-293

keys to success, 305-306

learning from failure, 291-292, 299-305

learning from others' experiences, 308-309

resistance to client demands, 276-277

skills needed for success, 300-301

verifying requirements, 309-310

Agile development

defined, 325

Waterfall development versus, 146

alcohol, drinking at company functions, 234-235

anger management, 250

annual revenue, asking about, 128-130

appearance (hiring criteria), 98-101

appointment stage (sales process), 61-63

sales pipeline valuation, 138

architects, 326

articles for maintaining skill set, 108-109

B

backlog
  defined, 14, 326
  explained, 16-17
balanced life (hiring criteria), 98, 123-124
belonging (on Maslow's hierarchy of
    needs), 185
bench, defined, 327
bench policy, 314-315
  asking about, 145, 151-152
bill rates, transparency in, 316-317
billable hours, defined, 327
billing consultants, asking about, 128,
    132-133
blogs
  company sponsorship of, 153-154
  for maintaining skill set, 108-110
body language when answering
    questions, 127
Body Shop example, 40-44, 241
  dysfunction in, 29
  interviewing, 43
  prognosis of, 43
  working conditions, 41-43
body shop ratio, 133
body shops, defined, 327
book policy, asking about, 156
books for maintaining skill set, 108-109
BOZO Consulting example, 30-34
  dysfunction in, 29
  interviewing at, 33-34
  prognosis of, 34
  working conditions, 31-32
brand building, 202-206
  external branding, 204-206
  internal branding, 203-204

broad skill set (hiring criteria), 98,
    107-112. *See also* continuously
    learning
  developing as survival strategy, 164-166
  resources for maintaining, 108
burnout, handling, 187-189
business developers. *See* account executives
business focus areas for continuous
    learning, 198-199
business-related questions, asking during
    interview, 127-136
  annual revenue, 128-130
  billing consultants, number of, 128,
    132-133
  exit strategy, 128, 135-136
  net income and EBITDA, 128, 130-131
  operational reports, 128, 134
  target growth rate, 128, 133-134
  target profit margin, 128, 131-132
business results, enthusiasm for, 118-119
"butts in seats" stage (sales process), 62,
    69-70
  sales pipeline valuation, 139

C

cancelled projects, 69
career paths, 207-208. *See also* career-
    limiting moves; survival strategies
  defined, 328
  entrepreneur track, 226-229
    reasons to avoid, 229
    reasons to pursue, 228
  evangelist/guru track, 223-225
    reasons to avoid, 225
    reasons to pursue, 225
  flexibility in, 229-230

for independent consultants, 286

management track, 208-218

    consulting managers, 209, 214

    engagement managers, 209, 213-214

    general managers, 209, 215

    project managers, 209, 211-212

    reasons to avoid, 217-218

    reasons to pursue, 216-217

    senior managers, 209, 215-216

    solution architects, 209, 212-213

    team leads, 209-210

sales track, 218-223

    reasons to avoid, 222-223

    reasons to pursue, 221-222

career-limiting moves, 231-232

envy (comparison with others), 251-254

    consulting companies, moving among, 253-254

    projects, moving among, 251-253

gluttony (overconsumption), 232-235

    drinking at company functions, 234-235

    expense account abuse, 233-234

greed (love of money), 238-243

    fraud, 239-240

    overpricing yourself, 241-243

lust (sexual attraction), 235-238

    dating clients/coworkers, 236-237

    pornography at work, 238

pride (overconfidence), 254-257

    gold-plating code, 255-256

    humility versus, 256-257

sloth (laziness), 243-248

    loafing on the job, 243-246

    low-quality code, 246-248

wrath (office drama), 248-250

career satisfaction. See thriving in technology consulting

cash reserves for entrepreneur track career path, 227

challenges faced by consultants, examples of, 91

    code quality, 92-93

    late projects, 91-92

    misrepresentation of skills, 94-95

    scope creep, 93-94

change

    adapting to, 274-276

    of jobs, 7-9

CHEAP Consulting example, 44-47

    dysfunction in, 29

    interviewing, 46

    prognosis of, 46-47

    working conditions, 45-46

chief evangelists. See industry gurus

chief executive officers. See senior managers

chief financial officers. See senior managers

chief operating officers. See senior managers

chief scientists. See industry gurus

chief technical officers. See industry gurus

client partners. See engagement managers

client turnover, determining, 33

clients

    contract extensions, as survival strategy, 174-175

    dating, 236-237

    defined, 328

    employee-to-consultant ratio, asking about, 145, 149

    providing value to, 160-162

reassignments, avoiding asking for, 172-174

resistance to demands of, 276-277

clothing. *See* appearance (hiring criteria)

CM. *See* consulting managers

code

  gold-plating, 255-256

  quality, 92-93

cold calls, as source of appointments, 62

collaboration, asking about, 145-147

"come to Jesus" meeting, 328

commission struction for sales, asking about, 137, 142-143

communication. *See* writing skills (hiring criteria)

community involvement questions, asking during interview, 153-156

  blogs, 153-154

  conference attendance, 153, 155

  consultant writing/speaking engagements, 153-155

  investment in consultant skills, 153, 155-156

company functions, drinking alcohol at, 234-235

competition at proposal stage (sales process), 66

complementary skills, developing as survival strategy, 164-166

conferences

  company support for attending, 153-155

  for maintaining skill set, 108-110

consultants

  challenges, examples of, 91

    code quality, 92-93

    late projects, 91-92

misrepresentation of skills, 94-95

    scope creep, 93-94

  company investment in skills of, 153, 155-156

  hiring criteria, 98

    appearance, 98-101

    balanced life, 98, 123-124

    broad skill set, 98, 107-112

    enthusiasm, 98, 117-119

    interviewing skills, 98, 101-107

    network development, 98, 121-122

    scarce commodity, 98, 112-114

    team player, 98, 115-117

    technical community activity, 98, 114-115

    writing skills, 98, 119-121

  independent consultants

    consulting group formation, 288-289

    definition of, 281-282

    lessons learned, 293-297

    resources for information, 289-290

    skills needed for, 277-288

  job responsibilities of, 74, 90-91

  reasons for hiring, 9-10

    employees versus consultants, 11-12

    technology as human replacement, 10-11

  skills needed for success, 300-301

  writing/speaking engagements, asking about, 153-155

consulting

  benefits and drawbacks of, 24

  career paths, 207-208

    defined, 328

    entrepreneur track, 226-229

evangelist/guru track, 223-225

flexibility in, 229-230

for independent consultants, 286

management track, 208-218

sales track, 218-223

contracting versus, 329

defined, 328-329

number employed in, xxviii

pipelines in, 59-61

reasons not to choose, 259-260

greed, 269-270

lifestyle/responsibilities, 265-268

personality incompatibilities, 263-265

risk tolerance, lack of, 260-263

single product focus, desire for, 269

recruiting pipeline, 70-72

sales process, steps in, 61-62

appointment stage, 61-63

"butts in seats" stage, 62, 69-70

contract stage, 62, 67-68

first meeting stage, 61, 63

proposal stage, 62, 66-67

signature stage, 62, 68-69

technical meeting stage, 61, 63-66

thriving in. *See* thriving in technology
consulting

understanding of, demonstrating during
interviews, 106-107

consulting agreements. *See* master
consulting agreements

consulting companies

Consultopia example, 311

defined, 329

financial transparency, 314-317

mission statements, 320-323

principles of, 312-313

professionalism in workplace,
317-319

contracting companies versus, 42, 312

economics of, 13-14

backlog, 16-17

hourly rate, 17-20

overhead, 21-24

profit margin, 15-16

revenue, 14-15

utilization, 21

evaluating for employment, 27-28

job responsibilities within, 73-74

account executives, 73-76

consulting managers, 73, 81-82

engagement managers, 73, 76-78

general managers, 74, 86-87

industry gurus, 74, 84-85

marketers, 74

presales specialists, 74, 82-84

recruiters, 73, 78-81

senior managers, 74, 87-89

support personnel, 74, 89-90

technology consultants, 74, 90-91

moving among, 253-254

questions to ask, 126-127

business-related questions, 127-136

community involvement questions,
153-156

delivery-related questions, 144-152

sales-related questions, 136-144

selection criteria, 98

appearance, 98-101

balanced life, 98, 123-124

broad skill set, 98, 107-112

enthusiasm, 98, 117-119

interviewing skills, 98, 101-107

network development, 98, 121-122

scarce commodity, 98, 112-114

team player, 98, 115-117

technical community activity, 98, 114-115

writing skills, 98, 119-121

types to avoid, 28-30

Body Shop example, 40-44, 241

BOZO Consulting example, 30-34

CHEAP Consulting example, 44-47

FEAR Consulting example, 34-40

Personality Cult Consulting example, 47-50

Push the SKU example, 54-57

Smelzer and Melzer Accounting example, 51-54

consulting groups, forming, 288-289

consulting managers, 73, 81-82

on management track career path, 209, 214

Consultopia example, 311

defined, 329

financial transparency, 314-317

bench policy, 314-315

bill rates, 316-317

pay rates, 315-316

mission statements, 320-323

principles of, 312-313

professionalism in workplace, 317-319

continuously learning, 195-199, 280, 284-285, 300, 302, 305. *See also* broad skill set (hiring criteria)

business focus areas, 198-199

process focus areas, 197-198

technology focus areas, 196-197

contract extensions, as survival strategy, 174-175

contract stage (sales process), 62, 67-68

sales pipeline valuation, 139

contracting

consulting versus, 329

defined, 329

contracting companies

Body Shop example, 40-44, 241

consulting companies versus, 42, 312

contracts, types of, 67-68

core identity as consultant, 283

"corporate immune system," 318

corporate IT software developers, job security, 8

corporate network diversity

defined, 4

lack of, 5

coworkers, dating, 236-237

Creating a World Without Poverty (Yunus), 322

critical thinking skills at Personality Cult Consulting example, 48-49

cycles, defined, 329

D

dating clients/coworkers, 236-237

deal qualification, 140

decision making, evidence-based, 319

delivery. *See also* "butts in seat" stage (sales process)

defined, 330

role in estimation process, 136, 141-142

delivery-related questions, asking during interview, 144-152
- bench time activities, 145, 151-152
- client employee-to-consultant ratio, 145, 149
- fixed-bid work, 145, 148-149
- mistakes, learning from, 145, 152
- nonstandard development tools, 145, 150-151
- project management, 145, 150
- software development process, 145-146
- travel requirements, 145, 147-148
- work location, 145-147

demand
- balancing with supply, 72
- Consultopia example, 312

developer-hours, interchangebility, 44

directors. See general managers

disagreements between technology consultants, 90-91

documentation, defined, 330

downloading bits and experimenting for maintaining skill set, 108, 111

drinking at company functions, 234-235

dual pipeline management, 72

due diligence research, 102-103

dumpster engagement, 330

Dunlap, Al, 320

E

early technologies, selecting for specialization, 113

EBITDA, asking about, 128, 130-131

economic downturns, surviving. See survival strategies

economics of consulting companies, 13-14
- backlog, 16-17
- hourly rate, 17-20
- overhead, 21-24
- profit margin, 15-16
- revenue, 14-15
- utilization, 21

EM. See engagement managers

employee hiring in entrepreneur track career path, 227

employee turnover, determining, 33

employees, consultants versus, 11-12

engaged employees, defined, 330

engagement, Consultopia example, 312

engagement managers, 73, 76-78
- on management track career path, 209, 213-214

enjoying your work, 186-191
- burnout, handling, 187-189
- fun, reintroducing, 189-190
- sense of ownership, 190

enthusiasm (hiring criteria), 98, 117-119

entrepreneur track (career paths), 226-229
- reasons to avoid, 229
- reasons to pursue, 228

envy as career-limiting move, 251-254

estimates
- asking about process for, 136, 141-142
- reducing, 83
- responsibility for, 65-66

ethical objections, 191

evaluating consulting companies for employment, 27-28

evangelist/guru track (career paths),
223-225
reasons to avoid, 225
reasons to pursue, 225
evidence-based decision making, 319
executives. *See* senior managers
exercise, self-confidence and, 100
exit strategy, asking about, 128, 135-136
expense account abuse, 233-234
experimenting for maintaining skill set,
108, 111
expert advice
adaptation to change, 274-276
independent consultants
consulting group formation, 288-289
definition of, 281-282
lessons learned, 293-297
resources for information, 289-290
skills needed for, 277-288
intermittent rewards, value of, 292-293
keys to success, 305-306
learning from failure, 291-292, 299-305
learning from others' experiences,
308-309
resistance to client demands, 276-277
skills needed for success, 300-301
verifying requirements, 309-310
extended contracts as survival strategy,
174-175
external branding, 204-206

F

failure, learning from, 273-274, 285,
291-292, 299-305
failure patterns. *See* career-limiting moves

faith-driven development, 331
"farmers," 77
fear, avoiding, 157-160
FEAR Consulting example, 34-40
dysfunction in, 29
interviewing, 39-40
prognosis of, 40
working conditions, 35-38
feature creep. *See* gold-plating code;
scope creep
fee fights, defined, 331
finance. *See* support personnel
financial management. *See* living within
your means
financial transparency, Consultopia
example, 314-317
bench policy, 314-315
bill rates, 316-317
pay rates, 315-316
first meeting stage (sales process), 61, 63
sales pipeline valuation, 139
fixed-bid contracts
asking about, 145, 148-149
defined, 331-332
food (on Maslow's hierarchy of needs), 184
forums for maintaining skill set, 108-110
fraud as career-limiting move, 239-240
fun, reintroducing into your work, 189-190

G

general managers, 74, 86-87
on management track career path,
209, 215
generalists, specialists versus, 113
gluttony as career-limiting move, 232-235

GM. *See* general managers

"go native," 332

gold-plating code, 255-256

greed, 269-270

  as career-limiting move, 238-243

growth rate, asking about, 128, 133-134

guru/evangelist track (career paths), 223-225

  reasons to avoid, 225

  reasons to pursue, 225

gurus, 74, 84-85, 332

H

happy consultants, defined, 332

hired scapegoats, defined, 333

hiring consultants

  reasons for, 9-10

    employees versus consultants, 11-12

    technology as human replacement, 10-11

  selection criteria, 98

    appearance, 98-101

    balanced life, 98, 123-124

    broad skill set, 98, 107-112

    enthusiasm, 98, 117-119

    interviewing skills, 98, 101-107

    network development, 98, 121-122

    scarce commodity, 98, 112-114

    team player, 98, 115-117

    technical community activity, 98, 114-115

    writing skills, 98, 119-121

hiring employees in entrepreneur track career path, 227

hourly rate

  defined, 14

  explained, 17-20

HR. *See* support personnel

human replacement, technology as, 10-11

humility, pride versus, 256-257

"hunters," 77

I

ideal consulting companies. *See* Consultopia example

"immune system," 318

independent consultants

  consulting group formation, 288-289

  definition of, 281-282, 333

  lessons learned, 293-297

  resources for information, 289-290

  skills needed for, 277-288

independent consulting, as possible career-limiting move, 242-243

industrial engineering, 44

INETA, 115

intellectual stagnation, 48

intermittent rewards, value of, 292-293

internal branding, 203-204

Internet surfing on the job, 243-246

interpersonal skills (hiring criteria), 98, 115-117

interviewing

  Body Shop example, 43

  BOZO Consulting example, 33-34

  CHEAP Consulting example, 46

  FEAR Consulting example, 39-40

Personality Cult Consulting example, 49-50

Push the SKU example, 56-57

questions to ask during, 126-127

    business-related questions, 127-136

    community involvement questions, 153-156

    delivery-related questions, 144-152

    sales-related questions, 136-144

Smelzer and Melzer Accounting example, 53-54

technical interviews, 72, 80

interviewing skills (hiring criteria), 98, 101-107

    consulting, understanding of, 106-107

    due diligence research on hiring firm, 102-103

    learning skills and, 105-106

    return on investment (ROI) explanations, 103-104

    technology trivia questions, 104-105

introversion, 265

inventor, meaningful work as, 193-194

IT department jobs, risk in, 260-262

J–K

"Jesus," 333

job responsibilities within consulting companies, 73-74

    account executives, 73-76

    consulting managers, 73, 81-82

    engagement managers, 73, 76-78

    general managers, 74, 86-87

    industry gurus, 74, 84-85

    marketers, 74

    presales specialists, 74, 82-84

    recruiters, 73, 78-81

    senior managers, 74, 87-89

    support personnel, 74, 89-90

    technology consultants, 74, 90-91

job security

    provided by networks, 2-3

    specialization, reasons for avoiding, 7-9

JUGs, 115

L

late projects, 91-92

layoffs

    avoiding. *See* survival strategies

    how to handle, 178-179

laziness as career-limiting move, 243-248

lead generation. *See also* rainmakers

    asking about, 137, 143-144

    as survival strategy, 162-164

leaders, managers/supervisors versus, 6. *See also* management track (career paths)

learning continuously, 195-199, 280, 284-285, 300, 302, 305. *See also* broad skill set (hiring criteria)

    business focus areas, 198-199

    process focus areas, 197-198

    technology focus areas, 196-197

learning from failure, 273-274, 285, 291-292, 299-305

learning from others' experiences, 308-309

learning skills, demonstrating during interviews, 105-106

letters of intent, 68

lifestyle, incompatibility with technology consulting, 265-268

living within your means as survival strategy, 175-178

loafing on the job, 243-246
love (on Maslow's hierarchy of needs), 185
loving your work. *See* enjoying your work
low-quality code-writing, 246-248
lust as career-limiting move, 235-238

M

magazine articles for maintaining skill set, 108-109
magical thinking, defined, 334
"making rain," 70
management, defined, 334
management track (career paths), 208-218
    consulting managers, 209, 214
    engagement managers, 209, 213-214
    general managers, 209, 215
    project managers, 209, 211-212
    reasons to avoid, 217-218
    reasons to pursue, 216-217
    senior managers, 209, 215-216
    solution architects, 209, 212-213
    team leads, 209-210
managers, leaders versus, 6
margin. *See* profit margin
marketers, 74
marketing
    role in independent consulting, 283-284
    as source of appointments, 62
Maslow's hierarchy of needs, 182-186
master consulting agreements, 67
meaningful work, 191-194
    as inventor, 193-194
    turning ordinary work into, 192-194

meetings. *See* first meeting stage (sales process); technical meeting stage (sales process)
mentoring
    in building your brand, 205
    importance of, 305
methodologies
    Agile development
        defined, 325
        Waterfall development versus, 146
    continuously learning, 197-198
    faith-driven development, 331
    proprietary development methodology, 336
    Waterfall development, 326
        Agile development versus, 146
        defined, 331
metrics
    decision making based on, 319
    peformance metrics of consulting companies, 13-14
minors. *See* complementary skills
misrepresentation of skills, 94-95
mission, sense of, 286-288
mission statements
    Consultopia example, 320-323
    purpose of, 320-321
mistakes, learning from, 145, 152
money, love of, 269-270
    as career-limiting move, 238-243
moral objections, 191
motivation for fraud, 239
moving among
    consulting companies, 253-254
    projects, 251-253
multiposition players, 164-166

N

narcissism, 185

needs, meeting (Maslow's hierarchy of needs), 182-186

net income, asking about, 128-131

network development (hiring criteria), 98, 121-122

networking relationships
anger and, 250
building, 3-6
corporate network diversity
defined, 4
lack of, 5
defined, 335
importance of, 306
job security provided by, 2-3
need for diversity within, 4-5
sector diversity, lack of, 5
social networking sites and, 4
at user groups, 114

The No Asshole Rule (Sutton), 318

nonprofits, funding for, 321-322

nondisclosure agreements, 68

nonsolicitation agreements, 164, 335

nonstandard development tools, providing, 145, 150-151

O

office politics
avoiding, 166-168
in career-limiting moves, 248-250
skills needed for, 300-301
on site stage. See "butt in seat" stage (sales process), 62

open source projects as means of having fun with work, 189-190

operational reports, asking about, 128, 134

opportunity for fraud, 239

opportunity size, 138

ordinary work, turning into meaningful work, 192-194

outsourcing, CHEAP Consulting example, 45

overconfidence as career-limiting move, 254-257

overconsumption as career-limiting move, 232-235

overhead. See also support personnel
defined, 14, 335
explained, 21-24

overpayment, avoiding as survival strategy, 168-170

overpricing yourself, as career-limiting move, 241-243

ownership, sense of, 190

P

paid training for maintaining skill set, 108-110

partnering arrangements, 149

partners. See engagement managers

passion for your work. See enjoying your work

paths. See career paths

patterns of failure, 231-232
envy (comparison with others), 251-254
consulting companies, moving among, 253-254
projects, moving among, 251-253

gluttony (overconsumption), 232-235
  drinking at company functions,
    234-235
  expense account abuse, 233-234
greed (love of money), 238-243
  fraud, 239-240
  overpricing yourself, 241-243
lust (sexual attraction), 235-238
  dating clients/coworkers, 236-237
  pornography at work, 238
pride (overconfidence), 254-257
  gold-plating code, 255-256
  humility versus, 256-257
sloth (laziness), 243-248
  loafing on the job, 243-246
  low-quality code, 246-248
wrath (office drama), 248-250
pay rates, transparency in, 315-316
PC Consulting. See Personality Cult
  Consulting example
people, defined, 335. See also human
  replacement
Peopleware (DeMarco & Lister), 290
performance metrics
  of consulting companies, 13-14
  decision making based on, 319
person, defined, 335
personal responsibilities. See
  responsibilities
Personality Cult Consulting example,
  47-50
  dysfunction in, 29
  interviewing, 49-50
  prognosis at, 50
  working conditions, 48-49
personality incompatibilities, 263-265

PHB (Pointy Haired Boss), defined, 335
pipelines
  defined, 60
  dual pipeline management, 72
  recruiting pipeline, 70-72
  sales pipeline. See also sales process
    asking about, 128, 134
    value of, 136-140
  in technology consulting, 59-61
pornography at work, 238
post mortems, 152
practice leads. See consulting managers
presales specialists, 74, 82-84
president. See senior managers
pride as career-limiting move, 254-257
principles of Consultopia example,
  312-313
problems. See challenges faced by
  consultants
process focus areas for continuous
  learning, 197-198
product sales. See Push the SKU example
professionalism in workplace, Consultopia
  example, 317-319
profit margin
  asking about, 128, 131-132
  defined, 13
  in entrepreneur track career path, 228
  explained, 15-16
profitability, maintaining as survival
  strategy, 168-170
project management, asking about,
  145, 150
project managers on management track
  career path, 209, 211-212
project work, defined, 14

projects
    late projects, 91-92
    moving among, 251-253
proposal stage (sales process), 62, 66-67
    sales pipeline valuation, 139
proprietary development methodology, defined, 336
purple squirrels, defined, 336-337
Push the SKU example, 54-57
    dysfunction in, 29
    interviewing, 56-57
    prognosis, 57
    working conditions, 55

Q

quality of code, 92-93
    maintaining, 246-248
questions, asking during interview, 126-127
    business-related questions, 127-136
    community involvement questions, 153-156
    delivery-related questions, 144-152
    sales-related questions, 136-144

R

rainmakers, 70. *See also* lead generation
    value of, 162-164
rationalization for fraud, 239
recession, surviving. *See* survival strategies
recruiters, 73, 78-81
recruiting pipeline, 70-72
reducing estimates, 83
referral programs, 79-80

relationships
    with account executives, 75-76
    building in delivery stage, 69
    with consulting managers, 82
    dating clients/coworkers, 236-237
    with engagement managers, 77-78
    with general managers, 86-87
    with industry gurus, 85
    networking relationships
        anger and, 250
        building, 3-6
        corporate network diversity, 4-5
        defined, 335
        importance of, 306
        job security provided by, 2-3
        need for diversity within, 4-5
        sector diversity, lack of, 5
        social networking sites and, 4
        at user groups, 114
    personality types and, 263-265
    with presales specialists, 83-84
    with recruiters, 79-81
    with senior managers, 88-89
    as source of appointments, 62
    with support personnel, 89
    with technology consultants, 90-91
requirements, verifying, 309-310
resistance to client demands, 276-277
resource romances, defined, 337-338
resources
    CHEAP Consulting example, 45
    defined, 337
    for independent consulting information, 289-290
    for maintaining broad skill set, 108

respect, Consultopia example, 313, 317-319

responsibilities, incompatibility with technology consulting, 265-268. *See also* job responsibilities within consulting companies

return on investment (ROI)

defined, 338

enthusiasm for, 118-119

explaining during interviews, 103-104

providing as survival strategy, 160-162

revenue

annual revenue, asking about, 128-130

defined, 13

explained, 14-15

rewards of success, value of, 292-293

rightsizing, defined, 338

risk premium in bench policy, 314-315

risk tolerance, lack of, 260-263

ROI (return on investment)

defined, 338

enthusiasm for, 118-119

explaining during interviews, 103-104

providing as survival strategy, 160-162

S

S&M Accounting. *See* Smelzer and Melzer Accounting example

safety (on Maslow's hierarchy of needs), 184

salary inflation. *See* overpricing yourself

salary reductions, 169-170

sales

defined, 338

emphasis on. *See* BOZO Consulting example

in entrepreneur track career path, 226

role in independent consulting, 277-281

sales cycles, defined, 329

sales engineers. *See* presales specialists

sales pipeline. *See also* sales process

asking about, 128, 134

value of, 136-140

sales process. *See also* sales pipeline

asking about, 136, 141

steps in, 61-62

appointment stage, 61-63

"butts in seats" stage, 62, 69-70

contract stage, 62, 67-68

first meeting stage, 61, 63

proposal stage, 62, 66-67

signature stage, 62, 68-69

technical meeting stage, 61, 63-66

sales-related questions, asking during interview, 136-144

commission structure, 137, 142-143

delivery, role in estimation process, 136, 141-142

lead generation, 137, 143-144

sales pipeline value, 136-140

sales process, 136, 141

sales track (career paths), 218-223

reasons to avoid, 222-223

reasons to pursue, 221-222

salespeople. *See* account executives

saving money as survival strategy, 175-178

scarce commodity (hiring criteria), 98, 112-114

scope creep, 93-94, 304. *See also* gold-plating code

Secrets of Consulting (Weinberg), 289

sector diversity, lack of, 5

security (on Maslow's hierarchy of needs), 184

selecting early technologies for specialization, 113

selection criteria (for getting hired), 98
    appearance, 98-101
    balanced life, 98, 123-124
    broad skill set, 98, 107-112
    enthusiasm, 98, 117-119
    interviewing skills, 98, 101-107
    network development, 98, 121-122
    scarce commodity, 98, 112-114
    team player, 98, 115-117
    technical community activity, 98, 114-115
    writing skills, 98, 119-121

self-actualization (on Maslow's hierarchy of needs), 182, 185-186

self-confidence, exercise and, 100

self-esteem (on Maslow's hierarchy of needs), 185-186

self-motivation, demonstrating during interviews, 105-106

selling products. See Push the SKU example

senior managers, 74, 87-89
    on management track career path, 209, 215-216

sense of ownership, 190

shelter (on Maslow's hierarchy of needs), 184

signature stage (sales process), 62, 68-69
    sales pipeline valuation, 139

single product focus, desire for, 269

skills, misrepresentation of, 94-95

sloth as career-limiting move, 243-248

small business operations, 227

smallball, defined, 338

Smelzer and Melzer Accounting example, 51-54
    dysfunction in, 29
    interviewing, 53-54
    prognosis, 54
    working conditions, 52

social business, 322

social networking sites, 4

software product developers, stereotypes of, 263

software product development
    asking about, 145-146
    desire for, 269
    risk in, 262

solution architects on management track career path, 209, 212-213

speaking engagements, asking about, 153-155

speaking skills in building your brand, 202-204

specialists, generalists versus, 113

specialization
    reasons for avoiding, 7-9
    selecting early technologies for, 113

staff augmentation, defined, 14, 329

standard of living. See living within your means

statements of work, 67-68

stereotypes of software developers, 263

Stockholm Syndrome, 36-37

subcontractors, asking about, 128, 132-133

success
    keys to, 305-306
    learning from failure, 273-274, 285, 291-292, 299-305
    skills needed for, 300-301
supervisors, leaders versus, 6
supply
    balancing with demand, 72
    Consultopia example, 312
support personnel, 74, 89-90. *See also* overhead
surfing the Internet on the job, 243-246
survival strategies. *See also* thriving in technology consulting
    client contract extensions, 174-175
    complementary skills, developing, 164-166
    fear avoidance, 157-160
    lead generation, 162-164
    living within your means, 175-178
    office politics, avoiding, 166-168
    overpayment, avoiding, 168-170
    "taking one for the team," 172-174
    value to client, providing, 160-162
    work ethic, demonstrating, 170-171
Sutton, Bob, 318
switching jobs as career-limiting move, 241-242

T

T&E (time and expenses), defined, 339
"taking one for the team," 172-174
target growth rate, asking about, 128, 133-134

target profit margin, asking about, 128, 131-132
teaching, importance of, 305
team in-fighting, 304-305
team leads on management track career path, 209-210
team player
    hiring criteria, 98, 115-117
    as survival strategy, 172-174
technical community activity (hiring criteria), 98, 114-115
technical interviews, 72, 80
technical meeting stage (sales process), 61, 63-66
    sales pipeline valuation, 139
technical sales specialists. *See* presales specialists
technical solution specialists. *See* presales specialists
technology
    business of, 339
    as human replacement, 10-11
technology consultants. *See* consultants
technology consulting. *See* consulting
technology focus areas for continuous learning, 196-197
technology trivia questions, answering during interviews, 104-105
TEDTalks, 290
thriving in technology consulting, 181-182. *See also* survival strategies
    building your brand, 202-206
        external branding, 204-206
        internal branding, 203-204

constant learning, 195-199
  business focus areas, 198-199
  process focus areas, 197-198
  technology focus areas, 196-197
enjoying your work, 186-191
  burnout, handling, 187-189
  fun, reintroducing, 189-190
  sense of ownership, 190
Maslow's hierarchy of needs, 182-186
meaningful work, 191-194
  as inventor, 193-194
  turning ordinary work into, 192-194
"win-win" thinking, 199-202
time and materials contracts, defined, 339
tracks. See career paths
training for maintaining skill set, 108-110
transparency
  defined, 339-340
  financial transparency, Consultopia
    example, 314-317
travel requirements, 267
  asking about, 145-148
trivia questions, answering during
    interviews, 104-105
trust, 3

U

unemployment, how to handle, 178-179
user groups
  attending, 114-115
  for maintaining skill set, 108-110
utilization
  defined, 13, 340
  explained, 21
utilization target, defined, 340

V

vacations to relieve burnout, 188
vampires, defined, 340-341
vendor management
  defined, 44, 341
  programs for, 46
verifying requirements, 309-310
vertical markets, 198
VP of sales. See senior managers

W–X

walking wounded, defined, 341-342
Waltzing with Bears (DeMarco & Lister),
    290
Waterfall development, 326. See also
    faith-driven development
  Agile development versus, 146
  defined, 331
whitepapers for maintaining skill set,
    108-109
"win-win" thinking, 199-202
work ethic, demonstrating as survival
    strategy, 170-171
work location, asking about, 145-147
work orders. See statements of work
working conditions
  Body Shop example, 41-43
  BOZO Consulting example, 31-32
  CHEAP Consulting example, 45-46
  FEAR Consulting example, 35-38
  Personality Cult Consulting example,
    48-49
  Push the SKU example, 55
  Smelzer and Melzer Accounting
    example, 52

wrath as career-limiting move, 248-250

writing skills

    in building your brand, 202-204

    hiring criteria, 98, 119-121

writing/speaking engagements, asking
    about, 153-155

Y–Z

yes man, defined, 342

Yunus, Muhammad, 322

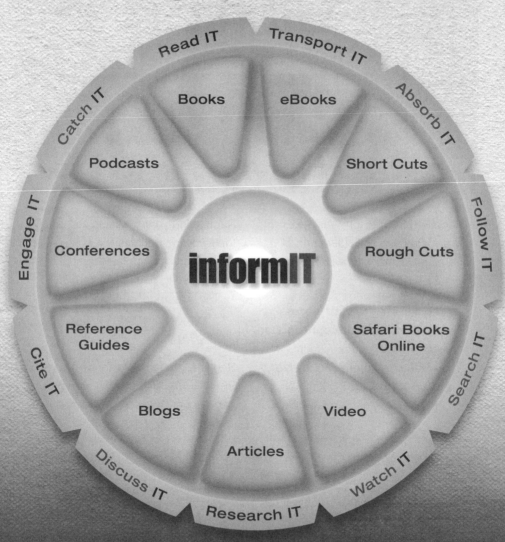

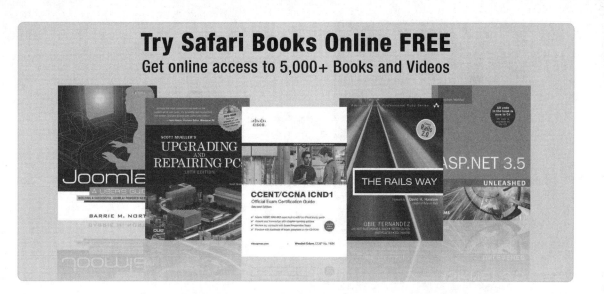

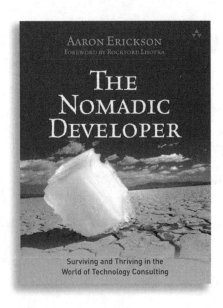

AARON ERICKSON
FOREWORD BY ROCKFORD LHOTKA

THE
NOMADIC
DEVELOPER

Surviving and Thriving in the
World of Technology Consulting

FREE Online Edition

Your purchase of **The Nomadic Developer** includes access to a free online edition for 45 days through the Safari Books Online subscription service. Nearly every Addison-Wesley book is available online through Safari Books Online, along with more than 5,000 other technical books and videos from publishers such as Cisco Press, Exam Cram, IBM Press, O'Reilly, Prentice Hall, Que, and Sams.

SAFARI BOOKS ONLINE allows you to search for a specific answer, cut and paste code, download chapters, and stay current with emerging technologies.

Activate your FREE Online Edition at
www.informit.com/safarifree

> **STEP 1:** Enter the coupon code: ECFHTZG.

> **STEP 2:** New Safari users, complete the brief registration form.
> Safari subscribers, just log in.

If you have difficulty registering on Safari or accessing the online edition,
please e-mail customer-service@safaribooksonline.com